Managing
Warehouse
and
Distribution
Operations

T. H. Allegri, P. E.

PRENTICE HALL
Englewood Cliffs, New Jersey 07632

Prentice-Hall International (UK) Limited, *London*
Prentice-Hall of Australia Pty. Limited, *Sydney*
Prentice-Hall Canada, Inc., *Toronto*
Prentice-Hall Hispanoamericana, S.A., *Mexico*
Prentice-Hall of India Private Limited, *New Delhi*
Prentice-Hall of Japan, Inc., *Tokyo*
Simon & Schuster Asia Pte. Ltd., *Singapore*
Editora Prentice-Hall do Brasil, Ltda., *Rio de Janeiro*

10 9 8 7 6 5 4 3 2 1

Library of Congress Cataloging-in-Publication Data

Allegri, Theodore H. (Theodore Henry)
   Managing warehouse and distribution operations / T. H. Allegri.
      p.   cm.
   Includes index.
   ISBN 0-13-564618-9
   1. Physical distribution of goods—Management. 2. Warehouse—
   Management. I. Title.
HF5415.7.A44   1993
658.7'85—dc20   93-17608
                                                                  CIP

ISBN 0-13-564618-9

PRENTICE HALL
Career and Personal Development
Englewood Cliffs, NJ 07632

Simon & Schuster, A Paramount Communications Company

Printed in the United States of America

About the Author

Theodore H. (Ted) Allegri is a Registered Professional Engineer in both Mechanical and Industrial Engineering. He has over 25 years' experience in materials handling having held successive positions as corporate Material Handling Manager and Manager of Distribution Planning for the Caterpillar Tractor Company in Peoria, Illinois.

He was president of the Go-Tract Systems, Ltd., in Montreal, Canada, a former subsidiary of the Rolls-Royce Group of Industries, and has owned and managed a fabrication and subcontracting plant for the International Harvester Company in Canton, Illinois. He worked, also for the General Services Administration as a Specifications Branch Chief and as a General Supply Officer with responsibility for over 19 million square feet of warehousing space in the ten regions of the United States.

His other experience includes consulting work with Werner-Dyer Associates in Washington, D.C., and materials handling consulting with the ESD Corp. of San Jose, California, for an assignment at the Avco-Lycoming Gas Turbine Engine manufacturing plant operated for the U.S. Army, as the sole source for the M-1 (Abrams) battle tank, in Stratford, Connecticut.

He was Executive Director of the International Materials Management Society, a charter member of the advisory group for *Factory Magazine,* and for four years was the editor of the Washington, D.C., Professional Engineering Newsletter. In addition, he has seven other texts in print including: *Principles and Practices of Materials Handling* (reprinted in Russia and India); *Handling and Management of Hazardous Materials and Waste;* and *Materials Management Handbook.*

He has a BA and MA from the George Washington University; has done graduate work at both Georgetown University and the Virginia Polytechnic Institute; and, has taught a short course in materials management at the junior college level.

65 Dynamic Practices for Improving Warehouse and Distribution Operations

This Book Shows You in Practical Detail the Proven Techniques for Managing Warehouse and Distribution Operations

One of the main objectives in this book is to provide, in layman's language, the state of the art in warehousing and distribution practice. It can help you develop a systems approach in order to integrate various functions within the plant, thus enabling you to attain **higher productivity** and the **least total cost** of operations.

The systems approach is the concept that views the whole operation in its entirety rather than regarding only one segment in particular. By observing how changes in this particular segment affect the operation as a whole, the **least total cost** may be obtained. As an example, improving the packaging of bin items received from vendors could add cost to the item; however, by doing so it will be possible to increase bin order picking inventory control, and packing line productivity. On the other hand, obtaining bin items in bulk from vendors, thus disregarding the systems concept, may decrease the cost of the item, but add much more to the cost of stocking the bins, inventory control, and packing.

The system approach, therefore, requires that you examine each facet of the entire gamut of operations in order to obtain the least total cost of the entire operation. What you do in one phase or department may affect the cost of operation in another area of the plant.

In using this book, you can get a firm grasp of the whole range of warehousing and distribution fundamentals—from manual methods to mechanized and computerized systems. By examining what other companies have done to solve warehousing and distribution problems and by actively selecting feedback from your employees, you can achieve the following objectives:

- Maximize Profits
- Utilize the Labor Force Effectively
- Encourage Productivity

In addition to the general objectives mentioned earlier, this book will provide answers to specific operating problems through proven techniques which may be adapted to your own plant requirements. The following list contains the main goals this book will help you to achieve:

65 DYNAMIC PRACTICES FOR IMPROVING WAREHOUSING AND DISTRIBUTION OPERATIONS

1. Make systems engineering work for you. Chapter 1.
2. Determine warehousing effectiveness. Chapter 1.
3. Improve production performance. Chapter 1.
4. Improve direct-to-indirect labor ratios. Chapter 1.
5. Maximize plant utilization. Chapter 1.
6. Reduce damage. Chapter 1.
7. Know where to obtain information on any aspect of warehousing and distribution. Chapter 1.
8. Achieve materials handling goals. Chapter 1.
9. Utilize manpower effectively. Chapter 1.
10. Use and maintain locator systems. Chapter 1.
11. Get the most out of material movement. Chapter 2.
12. Maximize plant layout effectiveness. Chapters 2, 16.
13. Use packaging more effectively. Chapters 2, 3, 13.
14. Utilize materials handling equipment effectively. Chapter 2.
15. Improve receiving handling. Chapter 2.
16. Improve shipping handling. Chapter 2.
17. Use the right containers. Chapter 2.
18. Unitize loads by means of the latest and best methods. Chapter 2.
19. Obtain carriers compatible with your shipping/receiving requirements. Chapter 3.
20. Design and/or change the physical plant to suit your needs. Chapter 3.
21. Integrate materials handling methods, equipment, and dock design. Chapter 3.
22. Properly identify incoming materials and merchandise. Chapter 3.
23. Handle backorders effectively. Chapter 3.
24. Mechanize receiving operations. Chapter 3.
25. Handle toxic materials in the workplace. Chapter 4.
26. Spot and unload carriers. Chapter 5.
27. Mechanize shipping operations. Chapter 5.
28. Minimize pilferage. Chapter 6.
29. Use computers effectively. Chapter 6, Appendix D.
30. Use barcoding effectively. Chapter 6.
31. Handle in-process materials. Chapter 6.

32. Computerize data and data collection systems. Chapters 6, 21.

33. Use manual systems for data collection. Chapter 6.

34. Know what kinds of storage equipment to use: where, when, and how much. Chapters 7, 8, 11.

35. Improve order picking at all levels: bin, bulk, and break bulk. Chapter 8.

36. Know what types of order picking methods and equipment to use. Chapter 8.

37. Minimize fire risk. Chapter 11.

38. Know the differences, advantages, and disadvantages between air-supported temporary structures and rigid frame buildings. Chapter 12.

39. Learn the best methods and materials for packaging in both receiving and shipping operations. Chapters 13, 14.

40. Understand packaging specifications and why they may be necessary. Chapter 14.

41. Know when to use preshipment testing for better packaging. Chapter 14.

42. Understand carrier responsibilities. Chapter 14.

43. Achieve container accountability. Chapter 14.

44. Understand corrosion inhibitors for packaging. Chapter 14.

45. Know the pros and cons of returnable and nonreturnable containers. Chapter 14.

46. Understand the ways in which to integrate manufacturing and warehousing in plant layout. Chapter 15.

47. Learn about facility and site planning. Chapter 15.

48. Optimize plant layout. Chapter 15.

49. Reduce the cost of materials handling. Chapter 15.

50. Apply materials handling principles to plant layout. Chapter 15.

51. Learn where, when, and how to use industrial robots. Chapter 16.

52. Plan robotic and human work stations. Chapter 16.

53. Prepare the climate for change in robotic and human work station arrangements. Chapter 16.

54. Get better work station layouts. Chapter 16.

55. Mechanize warehousing and distribution operations. Chapter 19.

56. Understand materials handling equipment and maintenance requirements. Chapters 18, 19.

57. Learn where, when, and how to use conveyors to improve efficiency. Chapter 10.

58. Learn how to provide quality safety training. Chapter 17.

59. Know what kinds of safety information and equipment are required by law. Chapter 17.

60. Justify equipment replacement. Chapter 20.

61. Learn rate of return, pay-back period, and present value concepts. Chapter 20.

62. Use computer simulation effectively. Appendix D.

63. Use work standards even when you can't measure. Chapter 21.

64. Use work measurement and performance standards. Chapter 21.

65. Obtain meaningful reports and statistics. Chapter 21.

The 65 dynamic practices for improving warehousing and distribution operations are real-world answers to questions that you are confronted with on an almost daily basis. It is the purpose of this book, therefore, to give you, the busy plant executive, practical solutions and information in as comprehensive a manner as possible in order to achieve greater productivity and greater return on investment in a practical rather than a theoretical fashion.

T. H. Allegri, P.E.

Table of Contents

List of Figures

1

Techniques for Improving Overall Warehousing and Distribution Effectiveness

HOW TO USE SYSTEMS ENGINEERING TO IMPROVE OPERATIONS AND CONTROL

It has been estimated that up to 25% of the cost of a product is added by storage requirements. This percentage varies from plant to plant and may be different for strictly warehousing and distribution facilities, in contrast to manufacturing companies that provide storage activities in support of production functions. Since warehousing and physical distribution have storage of items as a principal feature of each center with large amounts of capital tied up in inventory, the approach used in this book is to help the plant manager look at the operation as a whole with the express purpose of achieving the least total cost of the operation and thereby maximizing profitability. We know that while the merchandise is in storage we're not making any money on it, but simply paying for the cost of inventory. The systems concept makes it possible to increase stock turnover, and in addition, enables you to trim excess fat or noncontributing effort from any warehousing and distribution operation. How much you can trim depends on your answers to the following questions.

1. How large is your operation?
2. How many people are involved?
3. What kind of equipment is being used, not used properly, or not used enough?
4. How many of the operations that your personnel are performing are really necessary?
5. What kind of facilities are you using?
6. Are the facilities suitable for your operation?
7. What kinds of work standards are you using, if any?
8. Are you getting adequate reports?
9. What is the caliber of your workforce?
10. What is the caliber of your supervisory group?

1

The way in which you apply remedial action to these questions will determine the ultimate profitability of your operation.

In answering these questions you will recognize that many of the tasks being performed in your plant are interrelated. That is why we stress the necessity of taking a "systems approach" to warehouse and distribution operations. In this regard, the plant manager must provide guidance in order that subordinates think of operations in their departments as they affect not only their own activities but other plant functions as well. Interfering with this altruistic aim is the question of turf, which each manager or department head will guard zealously. As the plant manager you become the referee and have to make the judgment calls, and in the interest of obtaining the *least total cost* you may have to incur higher costs in one department that will result in larger cost savings down the line.

Since the most reliable yardstick of effectiveness in industrial enterprises is the cost and profitability of operations, you have to cut through the verbiage and data when examining statistical reports in order to focus your attention on the areas that are really causing problems.

As an example, when applying cost accounting terms, the labor force that transports the product in a distribution center is usually classified as "direct labor." As a busy executive you may see only accounts that read "direct labor," or "indirect labor," in the weekly or monthly report. The chart of accounts may reveal further descriptive text that indicates what is included in these categories. However, unless you thoroughly understand the philosophy behind the terminology some other person must be available to explain the variances that may occur from time to time—and this places you at a decided disadvantage in managing the enterprise. In this way you have to sift through the jargon and the semantic layer and direct the company's energies and resources to the relevant areas of

- Materials Handling; and
- Materials Management

This gives rise to the tunnel-vision syndrome, where your expertise in one or more areas of plant management sometimes obscures or overshadows the relevance of other aspects of operations. You should avoid being placed in this position if at all possible. That is why we are emphasizing the systems concept, and an analogy may be drawn between marshalling all of the company's resources and a shot for a space flight. In the latter event all systems are integrated to produce the ultimate objective and that is, a satisfactory launch.

You have to operate in a comparable way since you are responsible for integrating the activities of all the departments that compose your company. This integrated whole then produces the maximum profits over a period of time.

Whether you are concerned with short-term or long-range profitability is a complex question that many companies have to face at some point. As a plant manager, however, this is one problem that you will have to resolve early-on, because it will affect all of your planning and capital investment programs.

We shall discuss this element of your managerial decision making in Chapter 20 when the return-on-investment (ROI) concept is explored as it applies to warehousing and distribution. The ultimate objective is to achieve the least total cost of operations, thus maximizing profits.

HOW TO DETERMINE WAREHOUSE EFFECTIVENESS

Consistent with the systems approach to achieving the least total cost of plant operations is the need to know how effectively the functions of your organization are being performed. Keep the following points in mind:

- The least total cost may mean that one or two departments are incurring (or should incur) increased costs in order that other departments may achieve greater savings.
- Since each department in the plant is sacred turf to the department head, he or she isn't about to let the costs of the department rise, just to benefit another department.
- Since the summation of the various departments' costs influences company profits, you have to find out how well your warehousing and distribution operations are being carried out.
- The best way to find out how well you are doing is to order a meticulous industrial engineering study of operations.

Use Visual Inspection to Identify Workflow Problems

There is usually a direct relationship between the orderliness with which work is performed and the flow of work through the plant.

By visual inspection you can determine the following:

1. Whether aisles are uncluttered and will permit easy passage of materials handling equipment. If there are blocked aisles, you should obtain completely valid reasons from an operating standpoint.
2. Whether the aisles are clearly or adequately marked.
3. Whether safe practices for all materials handling equipment operations are being followed. (See Chapter 19.) If you find that forklift trucks and other mobile equipment are being driven too fast or recklessly, this will be an indication of problems in this department.
4. Whether there are fairly obvious mistakes in the arrangement of space. For example, there may be many intersecting aisles in your warehouse where materials handling equipment cannot pass without difficulty or where there are blind corners. Another obvious defect you might find is where walking traffic would interfere with the movement or passage of materials handling equipment.
5. Whether housekeeping practices are followed. Good housekeeping is another criterion for a smoothly functioning department.
6. Whether the floors in the following areas are in good condition:
   - working aisles
   - main aisle(s)
   - around any stationary machinery or equipment.

REMINDER: It is not only for the sake of appearances that you have to be concerned with the minimum aisle dimensions, safe in-plant vehicular speeds, and so forth. The Williams-Steiger Act of 1970 created the Occupational Safety and Health Administration

(OSHA), which established Federal and State regulations for these areas. For example, some aisles in the plant may be wide enough to accommodate vehicular traffic (i.e., the movement of powered materials handling equipment in both directions) but may not have the additional three feet for walking pedestrian traffic that is required by law.

In addition to this, aisles and pedestrian lanes must be marked clearly in order to minimize accidents. Floor conditions mentioned earlier are salient factors in plant safety. They are also important from the standpoint of materials movement.

WARNING: In a visual inspection of an area watch for:

- Oil spills.
- Leaking materials that are left where they lie.
- Spalling concrete.
- Loose blocks or missing blocks in a wood-block floor.
- Trash on the floor.

These conditions are almost always symptomatic of poor morale, low productivity, product damage, and lost-time accidents.

HOW TO IMPROVE DISTRIBUTION EFFICIENCY

Optimizing work flow is as important in warehousing and distribution as it is in manufacturing operations. The larger and more complex organizations require even more emphasis on the optimization of work flow than smaller companies, yet none can afford to neglect this factor. Warehousing and distribution centers, manufacturing plants, banks and brokerage houses, military departments, hospitals, and the like, all require the orderly flow of materials for the profitable conduct of their business.

The flow of materials in all of these enterprises, whether parts orders, bed pans, or steel stampings, must proceed from one point to another in a logical and methodical manner. As the volume of business increases, adding bodies to the operation may not solve the problem of increased demand for product. For these and related reasons, you may decide to promote the effectiveness of materials movement by mechanizing certain operations.

WARNING: Isolated efforts at mechanization may not always solve the problems of contending with growth: they must be integrated into the overall process using the *systems concept* as a basic consideration.

The fact that each department of the plant does not perform in a vacuum, and most entities within an organization are usually interrelated in innumerable ways, makes it extremely important that the warehousing and distribution operation be viewed as a systematic whole. Therefore, by looking at the total systems effect and assuring that there is an orderly flow of materials through the system, it is possible to avoid one of the more common errors of handling materials: the backhauling of products.

Avoid Backhauling

Backhauling or backtracking means that instead of being processed in a unidirectional manner, the material retraces its path(s) and is backhauled in the same direction from which it came, either in whole or in part. Because of the wasted time, labor, and even space caused by this undesirable practice, you must make certain that your shop foreman can minimize and control unnecessary backtracking. Since the difference between being profitable and marginally profitable depends upon how well your labor force is utilized, this is an area of concern that you should not overlook. In Figure 1-1 you will find an example of the costly and ineffective practice of backtracking where a forklift truck is being used as the means of transporting materials. In addition to wasting time, the forklift truck is adding unnecessary fuel, machine hours, and repair/maintenance costs to inflated labor hours.

Design Storage Racks to Meet Your Storage Needs

The design of storage racks may promote or impede distribution efficiency. You should determine that storage racks are properly designed to accommodate the pallet loads, containers, or packages that are received by your company. If the racks are too narrow or the spacing between shelf beams is too low, this becomes an inhibiting factor in putting materials away and in retrieving loads or packages for order-filling purposes. Also nonstandardized racks will cause problems and result in poor work performance, to say little of the effect on the morale of the work force.

WARNING: If the storage racks are higher than 12 feet, you must be aware of some rather stringent requirements imposed by federal regulations and (usually) local building codes. In some states, seismic considerations are a fact of life and must be dealt with; fortunately reputable rack suppliers are familiar with these regulations.

Use the Right Packaging

The kind of packaging materials used in products or items that are handled may promote or impede distribution efficiency.

If your company employs packaging engineers, it is their job to resolve packaging problems. Even small companies may be able to influence the manner in which suppliers package their products; therefore, whenever you think that the supplier's packaging is causing problems in your storage and warehousing operations someone in your company should contact the supplier and discuss alternative packaging methods. After all, what have you got to lose? And, sometimes what is right in the way of packaging for the giant companies, may make good sense with the smaller companies, too.

There are three levels of packaging that affect distribution effectiveness. Despite the fact that packaging often influences the *unit of issue* and *order quantities,* it is an often neglected aspect of distribution. For example, there are three levels of packaging that will have a considerable effect on profitability:

- the inner pack;
- the intermediate pack; and,
- the shipping container or overwrap.

Tailoring any one of them to your particular needs will add to the productivity of the distribution operation and will make order picking easier and better.

Assuming that the packaging of your product line(s) is capable of being improved, it would be feasible and worthwhile for you to assign a group of employees to study the

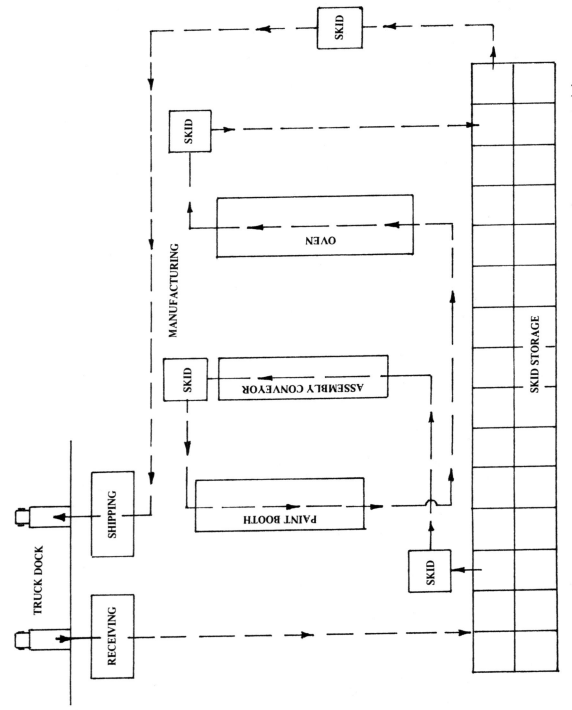

Fig. 1-1: An example of backtracking where a forklift truck is used to transport materials.

6

packaging of items being handled by your company. Several middle managers, the order-picking foreman, and even one of the order pickers should be on this committee. You should ask for a monthly report on items reviewed, action taken, and results to date.

The committee should review all items on a continuing basis. How many times a week, or a month, should be discretionary with the committee; the principal objective should be results that are achieved. When the committee is no longer productive it should be disbanded; however, if it does its job well and it is results-oriented, then some form of recognition or reward should be given to each of the members. The results of their work are newsworthy, and if there is a company newsletter a good deal of personal satisfaction can be granted to the committee members through this vehicle.

INTEGRATING MATERIALS HANDLING INTO YOUR SYSTEMS CONCEPT

By integrating materials handling into your **systems concept** you can maximize warehousing and distribution productivity. This concept is gaining in acceptability as more and more companies adopt this philosophy of operating their plants. A number of companies such as Caterpillar Tractor, John Deere, Allen-Bradley, and General Electric have joined the ranks of the automotive companies in integrating materials handling with equipment, packaging, storage, and order picking.

REMINDER: After adding the materials handling equipment required to transport product within the plant to your systems concept, the chain of related elements stretches out to include over-the-road carriers to your inplant and interplant transportation means.

A relationship in this chain of elements can be observed in the following concepts:

- The materials that are received from the supplier and other vendors must be capable, wherever possible, of entering the distribution channel, the warehousing and storage units, or production lines, *without repackaging.*

- The materials should be containerized, palletized, or otherwise unitized so that they may be unloaded from the carrier in the most effective way possible.

- The materials should be received in the proper lot sizes so that they are economically priced and in sufficient quantity.

- The materials must be unloaded with the most suitable materials handling equipment based upon the return-on-investment or benefits tradeoff.

- The materials must be unloaded in the shortest period of time with the least amount of labor input.

In analyzing the above remarks, you will find that there are many departments of the plant involved in the interrelated chain of elements. It is necessary to have the coordination of the following departments:

- Purchasing
- Inventory Control
- Production Control (or a comparable entity)
- Dispatching (traffic)

- Warehousing
- Receiving
- Equipment Maintenance

REMINDER: Your ultimate objective in the systems approach is to obtain the least total cost of operations; therefore, it is necessary to examine each of the various components comprising the system in order to obtain the degree of integration necessary to achieve this goal.

How to Improve Production Performance

Use Air Rights

When you make your periodic tours of the workplace, note how much of the plant's *air rights* are being utilized. Air rights are the cubic volumes of space within the area devoted to warehousing. A surprising amount of space may be wasted or underutilized by storing materials only one pallet load or one unit load in height. In other words, if you can look over the top of merchandise in any storage area, the chances are that the space is underutilized.

Standardize Pallet Storage Rack Openings

You should note whether pallet storage rack openings have been standardized so that the greatest number of pallets or containers may be stored in the racks without having to be repackaged or removed from one container and placed into another in order to fit into the existing pallet rack openings.

The height of pallet loads and containers is critical when purchasing storage racks. *Decide on the largest opening that is compatible with your container and/or pallet load sizes and with your budget.*

WARNING: Your company's purchasing agent should specify load sizes for incoming materials whenever it is practical or necessary to do so.

Maintain and Audit Your Locator System

Depending on the size of the warehouse, a locator system that is carefully maintained and audited periodically will improve productivity. The control of materials is more positive, there is less lost material, and less loss from pilferage. If the locator system is established in a logical manner, the order picker will be better able to locate material without backtracking. Also, a good locator system lends itself to the computerization of the whole function of order selection.

A well-planned and well-maintained locator system makes it possible for you to obtain greater flexibility with personnel since it is not necessary that the employee who is doing the order picking be familiar with the area and the merchandise in order to function satisfactorily.

Periodic Audits: Periodic audits of the locator systems where items are identified and the locations and quantities verified will help maintain the validity of the system. Randomly scheduled audits are extremely worthwhile and should be interspersed with the periodic audit.

WARNING: Although periodic audits may be performed by members of the same warehouse area, random audits should always be performed by members of another department.

Properly Maintain Materials Handling Equipment

You will improve productivity throughout the plant when you properly maintain materials handling equipment because downtime will be kept to a minimum.

Use Stretch-wrap

The use of *stretch-wrap* in consolidating, unitizing, and stabilizing loads will help you improve warehouse materials handling and outloading (shipping) practices.

Improving Indirect-to-direct Labor Ratios

There is both a necessity and a tendency in most plants to increase the number of indirect workers, service, and maintenance personnel, as more complex equipment is added to implement mechanization programs. Stacker crane retrieval systems (AS/RS), regardless of whether or not they are partially or fully automatic, require scheduled maintenance labor hours in contrast to simple bulk storage rack installations that require very little or no maintenance. In addition, all power-conveyor systems require maintenance, especially where sortation, palletizers, and any form of indexing or coding is being performed on any of the conveyor lines.

Problem Areas

Indirect labor may very well get out of hand when manual order picking operations are expanded in a rather rapid fashion to accommodate galloping growth in business volume. A happy problem to have you might say; however, when statistical data reveal that indirect labor is on the increase then you should put the following action program into effect:

- Initiate a systematic analysis of materials handling activity in order to minimize unnecessary labor effort.

- Make sure that the labor hours required to stock bins or put away merchandise do not exceed (or even approach) the number of labor hours required to select product.

- If labor unions are involved, the rationale for taking the above measures is to make the enterprise more profitable so that the job security of the total workforce is enhanced as the company's competitive position is improved relative to whatever competition there is in the industry.

- If the distribution center has a packaging department or a price marking operation, the same analytical approach and action program should be undertaken as in steps 1 and 2 above.

- Make certain that every department for which statistical data are available is able to maintain the proper indirect-to-direct labor ratio.

- If a department or operation within the company does not have adequate statistical data, make every effort to get the statistical coverage that you need in order to keep your finger on the pulse of the operation.

Planning Can Maximize Plant Utilization

The inevitable scarcity of land and the increases in labor and material costs, inflation, and so on, have made factory and warehouse space more costly as time goes by. This fact becomes even more apparent whenever a plant attempts to relocate or contemplates plant expansion. Since the cost of space and the dislocations, interruption in work flow, and all of the accompanying inconveniences have a negative effect on profitability, careful and thoughtful planning is very important. There are several different kinds of planning which we'll discuss briefly at this point and go further into in a later chapter:

- Layout Planning
- Financial Planning
- Utilization Planning

Layout Planning

Layout planning usually takes place when there is an actual facility, or may precede the construction phase of a plant. It concerns the placement of fixed equipment and machinery, work stations, and the like.

Financial Planning

Financial planning provides the funds and capital equipment that are needed by the company and usually involves the accounting department.

Utilization Planning

Since any major plant expansion requires a significant amount of labor hours from a number of different managerial components or disciplines together with a large amount of capital, it follows that before the company invests both time and money in enlarging the facility (or in a new facility), serious consideration be given to maximizing plant utilization. Take the same managerial team that would be gathered together for the purpose of staffing a relocation or expansion effort and give it the responsibility of determining if the present plant facilities are indeed being utilized to the fullest extent possible.

There are several practical reasons for taking this approach:

- Save money You will save the company's money if you can increase the capacity of the plant without resorting to the expense of either relocation or new plant construction. (In certain circumstances leasing space or "sale and lease-back" approaches have definite tax advantages and should be considered after undergoing the exercise of determining the extent of plant utilization that exists currently in your operation.)

- Determine space and equipment needs—Regardless of whether or not the decision is made to relocate, build, lease, or any combination of these, you would have to determine space needs for each department and the amount of equipment that is necessary at various levels of operation. The plant utilization study then can be considered a preliminary step that would have to be made in any event.

- Review equipment performance—Since the study of materials handling methods and equipment is a vital part of the process of maximizing space and plant utilization, periodic review of its performance has many benefits in terms of increasing plant productivity.

- Assess general operations—In addition, since there is an interdependency in the materials handling operation between production scheduling and inventory control, the plant utilization study will force you to look into these related departments that are sometimes neglected.

- Improve coordination among departments—Combining the previous ideas into an integrated whole makes it possible to maximize plant utilization by gaining larger insights into the way in which the plant is functioning. Therefore, you must take corrective action whenever and wherever it is required. In addition, by permitting and in some instances demanding, better coordination between such departments as purchasing and materials handling, or between production scheduling/inventory control and purchasing, a much better job of materials handling in utilizing warehouse and distribution center space may be accomplished.

How to Reduce Damage During Materials Handling

The forklift truck has been called "The Great American Destroyer." It is amazing how few people realize that even the smallest industrial truck (i.e., a forklift that is a riding-type, counterbalanced vehicle), weighs twice as much as the average automobile. The reason for this is that, in addition to the weight of the forks and fork body, there is a cast-iron counterweight to be considered; thus, a relatively small 2,000-pound capacity truck may have a counterweight that weighs one ton. As the forklift truck increases its lifting capacity, the size and weight of the chunk of cast iron in its rear end may be double, triple, or many times the amount of counterbalance found in the smaller industrial trucks. It is no wonder that this piece of equipment may cause so much damage in-plant.

Unfortunately, transportation equipment such as railway cars and over-the-road carriers may create damage problems prior to the materials' being received at the plant.

Here are some guidelines for controlling damage:

- Establish a good materials handling program backed up by sound packaging specifications.
- Make sure packaging specifications indicate the type of containers, packaging methods, identification of product, and so forth. (This subject is discussed in greater detail in Chapters 13 and 14, since it is essential to a successful materials handling program and the minimization of damage.)
- Maintain statistical control of product damage and other damage by type, severity, and frequency.
- Establish your own "damage limits," and whenever the trend starts to push into the unacceptable range, take swift action to correct the problem by assigning responsibilities to the department heads involved.
- Use training programs to curtail losses due to damage. Training in safety and materials handling should be at the top of the list.
- If your plant has a newsletter feature safety and materials handling periodically in various issues.
- Hold forklift truck rallies to focus on proper driving practices.

Improving Plant Safety

Over the past few decades safety, which was once relegated to a secondary position in most companies, has since taken a very primary place in plant operations, due largely to the establishment of OSHA regulations in 1970. Since the most important element of any safety program is the worker, concentrate on the individual to reduce the accident rate and the severity of injury. If this factor is disregarded, it makes no sense at all to be talking about the systems concept. Professional plant managers make safety their number one concern and instill the same recognition of this value from the top to the bottom of their staff. The expert practice of materials handling requires that each task involving the movement of materials become safer every time it is performed. Good materials handling practice attempts to eradicate all of the factors that contribute to accidents and an increase in the frequency of accidents. Insurance rates follow the upward trend of accidents as well as the severity of these incidents; this alone, without regard to humanitarian principles, should serve as a spur to plant management to improve the plant's accident record. Lost time accidents have a nasty habit of punishing all levels of plant management by the detailed paperwork that is required in reporting each and every occurrence.

Using the Just-in-Time (JIT) Manufacturing Concept to Improve Warehousing and Distribution Profits

JIT manufacturing may be compared rather favorably with MRPII, or Manufacturing Resource Planning, the successor to MRP (Materials Requirements Planning). One of the cornerstones of the JIT philosophy is to continually optimize the manufacturing system, and in this regard it is in reality a systems approach to manufacturing. In this process of integration and analysis, excess inventory is removed and the quality of the product is improved. Materials, parts, and components received from suppliers are the result of zero-defects programs and as such reduce the need for quality assurance inspection before being assembled at the receiving plant. In JIT the purchasing credo where parts are bought based upon price, delivery schedule, and quality, is changed so that quality is first, delivery is second, and price is third. Since quality is of prime importance the effect on warehousing and distribution in the manufacturing environment is significant. Space for storage and staging can be economically conserved. Only the parts that are required for particular assemblies are on hand. Lead times are shortened, and finished assemblies enter the distribution network as scheduled.

Getting It All Together

In this chapter we've touched upon a number of different subjects that serve as an introduction to the elements of the systems approach to warehousing and distribution. You have seen only the tip of the iceberg; what follows will form the basis of a systems philosophy that will bring it all together for increased productivity and profits.

10 AREAS FOR IMPROVEMENT THAT WILL INCREASE PLANT OUTPUT

The critical department or discipline presented here demonstrates how effectively the **systems concept** can work for your plant. Note that most of these areas are related in some way or another. They have been mentioned only in brief at this juncture, but each area will be developed in more detail later in the text.

Improve Packaging

Here are 12 ideas for how to improve packaging:

1. If your plant does not have a packaging engineer, give the responsibility for packaging to one individual and support him or her.

2. Make certain that the packaging engineer is communicating effectively with other plant packaging engineers. If your plant employs more than one packaging engineer, or other divisions, (i.e, distribution centers of your company) have their own packaging engineers, each packaging engineer should not work in a vacuum but should keep abreast of developments that are taking place in other areas of the company. If this is not done, confused signals will be sent to your suppliers.

3. Use the *unit load concept* within the materials handling operation to save a great deal of time and money. The unit load is designed so that it can be transported through the manufacturing, warehousing, and distribution cycle without being rehandled, i.e., without having to be transferred into different containers.

   The unit load is based on packing materials in *units-of-issue quantities*. A good example of this is in fasteners and fittings which can usually be delivered to assembly line or order picking stations in unit-of-issue quantities so that the necessity for counting parts or repackaging is eliminated completely.

4. Label unit loads correctly.

5. Establish plant packaging and shipping guidelines.

6. To obtain the maximum effectiveness of a plant-wide or company-wide packaging program, involve as many people as possible within the company. Because your company's suppliers are important to the success of the program they should be apprised of the company objectives in this area.

7. Make sure instructions and underlying principles of the plant's packaging program are spelled out with enough detail and specificity that the packaging process may be repeated, thus ensuring maximum effectiveness.

8. Ensure that your suppliers and other departments of your company are following the guidelines for packaging and unit load identification. You can do this by observing the way in which materials are received. Sometimes, just a walk through the receiving department and several of the plant departments is sufficient to obtain a good indication of the scope of the problem if there is one, or how well each of the departments is doing.

9. Get involved with the *ecology of packaging:* Wherever possible, recycle packaging materials rather than incinerating them or otherwise disposing of them. Corrugated board (cardboard) and most paper products can be recycled. Knock-down containers may be reused or recycled. Establish guidelines so that your department heads understand that when a container no longer is serviceable as a means of transporting materials, they should consider recycling the materials of which the container is composed. Anticipate the disposal method of the containers and packaging materials by specifying appropriate substances in your contracts with suppliers. As an example, unitized loads that are shrink- or stretch-wrapped with plastic (polyethylene)

film have reusable skids or pallet materials that may be recycled. Also, the poly-film may be collected and shredded or pelletized for reprocessing.

10. Make it a point to have your plant establish itself in the eyes of the citizenry as a good neighbor. Many communities have become incensed with the irresponsible way that some industrial materials and wastes are disposed.

11. Monitor packaging of outgoing shipments. You have better control, naturally, of outgoing shipments from your plant, since this type of packaging is done in-house. Although it is customary to have fewer problems in this area than in receivables, many companies have a tendency to overpack outgoing shipments. By maintaining good work habits, establishing packaging methods, and training packers properly, sometimes 50% of packaging material costs and many labor hours can be saved, not to mention UPS, freight, and handling charges.

12. Perform blocking and bracing of outgoing shipments effectively and economically. Assign responsibility for supervising this activity to one person.

Improve Materials Handling

Here are 18 suggestions for how to improve materials handling and maintain equipment.

1. Maintain an up-to-date *Materials Handling Equipment List.* For every piece of equipment you should have the following information:
   - An equipment number
   - Name of manufacturer, model, and capacity
   - Year it was purchased (date)
   - Area it is assigned to
   - Initial cost
   - Attachments it has such as: side-shifter, turnover clamp, prong, etc. (in the case of a forklift truck)

2. Establish a regularly *scheduled preventive maintenance program* at your facility.

3. Make sure all maintenance areas are adequately equipped to perform the types of services and repairs that are required.

4. Consider subcontracting for maintenance if your work force cannot handle this responsibility.
   WARNING: If the only maintenance being performed in your plant is *breakdown maintenance,* you are in trouble.

5. Maintain precise cost records for each piece of mobile equipment in the plant. The ultimate objective is to determine the *cost per hour* of operation for each vehicle.

6. Require each mobile equipment operator to perform a daily functions check prior to starting his or her work shift. The checklist should include the operator's name, shift and date, and the following information:
   - water level in batteries
   - fuel level

- oil level
- operative hour meter
- brakes, parking
- brakes, driving
- lights
- horn
- lifting (for forklift trucks)
- other items pertaining to the operation of the vehicle which may be critical such as tire pressure, and so on.

7. Establish an effective control system to maintain compliance with the start-of-shift checklist for all vehicle operators.

8. Determine through your staff that the proper materials handling equipment is used for performing every materials handling task in the plant.

9. Standardize materials handling equipment in the plant wherever possible. The cost and performance benefits are:
   - common parts and spares
   - common service
   - lower overall maintenance costs
   - better operator utilization
   - safer operation

10. Use hour meters on all mobile equipment. They are necessary for:
    - measuring the utilization of equipment
    - scheduling your maintenance program; e.g., oil changes, hydraulic fluids changes, and servicing of many other elements of internal combustion engines after so many hours of operation
    - scheduling replacement of critical parts
    - scheduling replacement of the entire vehicle or minor and major overhauls after so many hours of operation

11. Plan material movements so that forklift trucks travel less than 300 feet per carry.

12. Make sure there is standby equipment so that operators can obtain a "loaner" when their vehicles are out of service.

13. Color-code or otherwise identify your standby units so that they will be returned to the equipment pool when the repaired vehicle is returned to duty.

14. Make standby units available to each operating unit in order for the *preventive maintenance* to be successful.

15. Make sure all mobile materials handling equipment is assigned to operating units by a Materials Handling Engineer or other individual or group charged with this responsibility.

16. Assign materials handling equipment to an operating unit only after adequate study based upon a Return-On-Investment analysis. In this way neither too much nor too little equipment will have to be capitalized or leased.

17. Determine the costs and benefits of **ownership** of materials handling equipment versus **leasing**. This analysis should be done by the accounting department in cooperation with the plant's materials handling engineer or industrial engineer.

18. Forecast requirements for materials handling equipment sufficiently far in advance so they do not cause fiscal problems.

Maximize Materials Handling Staff Resources

Here are six tips for how to get the most from your materials handling staff:

1. Establish a *staffing table* for the facility that will include both direct and indirect labor.

2. Do a walk-through inspection of the plant to make sure:
   - *manual material handling* is being held to a bare-bones minimum.
   - employees are not walking excessively long distances for materials. The shorter the walking distances, the more productive the employee becomes.
   - mechanical manipulators or *put-and-take mechanisms* are being used for loading and unloading operations wherever possible
   - activities and work assignments are not being unnecessarily duplicated

3. Make certain that your supervisors have control over the work assignments in their areas of operation.

4. Measure the work load in each department to see whether the work force is distributed equitably. The rule of thumb should be that workers are placed where the work is. The ultimate goal is a balanced operation.

5. Inspect the truck and rail demurrage reports, which you should obtain on a weekly basis at the very least. If demurrage is not being used in lieu of leasing space, check to see how much of it is being caused by:
   - poor loading or unloading practices
   - lack of proper equipment
   - an understaffed operation or underutilized employees
   - poor supervision
   - equipment problems
   - poor or inadequate facilities
   - poor recordkeeping
   - shoddy over-the-road or rail equipment

6. Observe the relative work pace of the employees in your facility. Generally speaking, when morale is good the rate at which work is being performed will also be good. Good supervisors make good employees; therefore, you must give your supervisors the proper tools and time to create a good working environment.

Improve Materials Handling in the Shipping Department

Here are four productivity ideas for your shipping department:

1. Try to limit shipping locations within the plant; if this is not possible, improve control of materials and personnel. If shipping is performed from more than one central location in a facility, control of outgoing materials may sometimes get out of hand, leading to employee collusion with the carrier operator and increased pilferage and damage. (Bar coding and other security measures for both employees and merchandise will be discussed in Chapter 7.)

2. At the dock make sure space is adequate to handle materials without queuing problems or congestion. Have enough dock plates, truck spots, levelers, doors, and dock lights. Extendible dock lights are preferred so that the interior of carriers and other over-the-road vehicles may be safely loaded.

3. If you do any blocking or bracing of outgoing shipments, locate these materials conveniently and make them readily available to the blocking and bracing crew. Establish company standards for this activity if blocking and bracing are carried out on a regular basis. Excellent Department of Defense (DOD) manuals are available for these functions (see the Appendix).

    Sometimes your traffic dispatcher can get equipment that is equipped with load bars.

    Kraft-paper airbags for blocking are available from such companies as Stone Container Corp.

    Subcontracting for blocking and bracing may be more cost effective than using your own workers.

    Sheltered workshops can often be used to make blocking materials from lumber; however, since most blocking and bracing is made from green lumber with a high moisture content, a local source for this material should be obtained because once this lumber dries out it is virtually impossible to nail without splitting.

4. Make sure shipping activities are performed close to the last operation in the facility (which in most plants is the packaging operation).

Improve Materials Handling in the Receiving Department

Review the guidelines on improving materials handling in the shipping department: most of the caveats that pertain to Shipping materials handling apply also to Receiving. The following, however, are concerns particular to the receiving department:

1. Be aware that packing lists from certain suppliers may be extremely difficult to work with when checking incoming materials.

2. Tighten supervision of piece counting where necessary to ensure that the company is getting what it paid for.

3. Set up a procedure for reporting shortages or incorrect amounts.

4. Coordinate the functions of inspection and quality control in materials handling and the putting away of stock. When the outer wraps of containers are opened by quality

control for inspection purposes, make sure they are resealed and stamped or tagged by the inspector with a notation that the carton was opened by quality control.

5. Establish a proper methodology for holding materials that have not passed inspection or are awaiting laboratory reports on quality.

6. Properly identify material that must be put into stock before laboratory reports (or, in certain cases, resolutions of disputes with suppliers) have been obtained. For example, affix a "DO NOT ISSUE" label on all such materials.

Improve Plant Layout

The following tips can help you improve plant layout:

1. Plan carefully to derive the most benefits from plant layout. In general, plant layout is undertaken when new or expanded facilities are being considered. However, it is sometimes necessary to review the presently occupied facilities to determine if you can increase productivity by changing the physical and spatial relationships between departments.

2. Measure the effectiveness of each department before and after changes have been made.

3. Always plan for straight line flows of materials.

4. Always try to keep transportation distances between points as short as possible.

5. Avoid picking up and setting down containers or unit loads more than is necessary in order to process the contents.

6. Avoid back-hauling wherever possible.

   REMINDER: An important element of **space utilization** is the use of the cubic content of the facility. *Make every use possible of air rights!*

7. Include the plant materials handling engineer in the planning team for the new layout.

8. Make sure the materials handling engineer, the layout planner, and the processors in the group who have layout responsibilities are working as a team.

9. Do work measurement studies of the existing direct and indirect labor functions.

   REMINDER: Work measurement studies should be made before and after any changes are made in order that a comparison may be made to determine the cost benefits accruing to the changes. This serves two purposes: first, it is a measure of value received due to the changes; and second, it will serve to justify future expenditures of company funds for improvements.

10. Wherever possible consider including "fixed path" handling equipment in the new layout.

    NOTE: "Fixed path" handling equipment consists of conveyors, chutes, elevators, stacker cranes, and the like. Rigorous cost benefits analyses should be made whenever this type of equipment is being considered.

11. Make sure related operations are adjacent to each other.

12. Make sure aisles are adequate to accommodate the orderly transportation of materials and to provide for pedestrian passage wherever this is necessary.

13. Use areas outside the plant effectively for storage or for staging materials.

14. Store outside material close to the point of use.

15. Study the cost efficiency of installing additional doors to shorten the travel or transportation distance of materials that are stored outside.

16. Make sure outside storage material is adequately protected.

17. Consider whether shrink-wrapping can be used to better protect materials stored outside.

18. Consider using sheds to provide protection for outside storage materials.

19. Consider using rigid-frame plastic or air-supported plastic bubbles to add to the economy of outside storage.

20. Determine if rust and corrosion removal is a problem.

21. Monitor how much scrap, obsolescent materials, or spoiled inventory is being generated because of unrotated stock.

Arranging Equipment and Work Stations to Improve Efficiency

Here are eight ideas for work station configurations:

1. Improve plant productivity from the standpoint of layout by following these rules:
   - Arrange machines, equipment, and work stations for the easy delivery of materials, for maximum operator efficiency and convenience, and to ensure full use of machine capacities.
   - When conveyors are used, make sure they are at the proper height for the operator.

   WARNING: Sometimes conveyor installations are made that presuppose an operator of average height—usually male. The operator's work station should be adjustable for short, tall, and medium stature.

2. Wherever possible try to avoid having the operator bend into a tub or container for parts. Explore the possibilities of hoppers or tub tilters, scissors platforms, and the like, when organizing a work station.

3. Consider using special trays or racks to improve the productivity of a particular activity or a series of activities either in the present facility or in a receiving plant (when interplant shipments are concerned).

4. Arrange work stations to minimize the operator's walking.

5. For work stations that require the operator to remain in a constrained area such as in packaging, use rubber floor mats to minimize the operator's foot and leg fatigue.

6. Provide the work station with an adequate sit-down area for materials and make sure the materials are placed as closely to the operator as safety considerations will permit.

7. Position the supervisor's work station so he or she can see as large a portion of the working area of the crew as possible.

8. Remember that piece-counting precision is important in any order picking or inventory control function; therefore, make it possible to obtain accurate counts by using the following techniques:

   • bar coding wherever it will be cost effective. Most suppliers are now providing UPC (Uniform Product Code) codes or CODE 39 bar codes on all of their products. Counting can be done faster and more accurately using pen wand or laser scanners. In addition, stationary beam scanners may be used in automatic or semi-automatic modes to mechanize many counting and inventory control functions.

   • weigh-counting, especially for small parts like fasteners and fittings wherever it is economical to do so

   • prebagging of small parts by suppliers even if you have to supply the poly bags

   • setting up a bagging station in your packaging division (if the volume warrants). The bagging set-up could be comprised of a hopper, scale, weigh-counter, and a bagging, marking, and sealing operation.

Improve Planning

Keep in mind the following six planning suggestions:

1. Establish goals and priorities using project planning techniques.
2. Establish short-range and long-range goals based upon one-, two-, three-, or five-year and longer time periods based upon your business projections.
3. Integrate layout planning with your short- and long-range goals.
4. Make sure every department of the facility has targets based on the short- and long-range plans.
5. Keep in mind that your materials handling and capital equipment plans are especially important. You should have definite requirements based upon realistic additions and replacement of equipment.
6. Translate staffing plans and projections, training requirements, and the like into realistic, achievable goals. Some of the areas that should be covered are:

   • safety
   • materials handling
   • inspection and quality control
   • traffic
   • maintenance
   • plant engineering
   • packaging
   • hazardous materials handling
   • data processing
   • housekeeping
   • work measurement

- industrial engineering
- supervisory training

Improve Recordkeeping and Reporting

Here are five ideas to help you keep track of plant functions:

1. Institute a *cost reduction savings program* by empowering a committee composed of at least one member of each department and the accounting and financial area. The charter of the committee would be to monitor cost savings initiated within each department. "Employee suggestions" should be an ongoing part of the cost-reduction program. A system of rewards for savings that are achieved should be instituted, making the awards as quickly as possible after the suggestions are received. The suggestion program should be formalized with written procedures and forms. The company newsletter should encourage participation in the suggestion program.

2. Prepare a list and a layout of the plant that will delineate and record the total amount of space allocated to each function; for example, storage, maintenance, manufacturing, and so forth.

3. Obtain from your Maintenance and Plant Engineering departments monthly, quarterly, and yearly reports indicating the costs of maintaining and operating materials handling equipment and plant facilities.

4. Obtain demurrage reports on a weekly basis.

5. Keep a running tally on Receiving Department Due-ins. This reporting method will keep the Purchasing Department on their toes because it is their responsibility to see to it that suppliers are delivering their materials on time. Depending on the materials involved, if the supplier is the sole source of the material, the use of competitive sourcing becomes meaningless. Generally speaking, the effective purchasing department will spread the company's business equitably between two, three, or more suppliers based upon the dollar volume of the materials purchased.

Encourage Training

The use of training and orientation programs is important regardless of the size of the company. Training in materials handling will bring about considerable improvements in productivity, utilization of assets, morale, and the care with which most employees will handle materials.

2

Unit Loads, Containers, and Carrier Compatibility

HOW TO MAXIMIZE THE BENEFITS OF UNIT LOADS

The concept of the **unit load** has evolved with the development of the forklift truck as the cornerstone of industrial materials handling. Any plant, regardless of size, can make use of the unit-load concept, even if manually propelled pallet jacks are the sole means of intraplant transportation. A unit load is any quantity of materials designed to be lifted, transported, or stored in a single mass. In most cases the main logic of this concept is: The larger the mass that is moved, the lower the unit costs will become.

Three things that make a **unit load** effective are:

1. The uniformity of the individual items forming the load;
2. The ability of the items to be stacked or interlocked in a pallet pattern;
3. The ability of the items to support themselves when stacked without crushing or collapsing.

WARNING: Apply the unit load concept carefully, especially between successive work stations. Unless no other transportation means such as a conveyor or chute is available, the time and effort required to stack and unstack the unit load makes it impractical.

Two tests to apply when considering using the unit load concept are:

1. How much material (i.e., number of items) is to be moved
2. The interval of time between the operations at the successive work stations.

If you have relatively large quantities of materials to be moved between successive operations, consider conveyorizing the materials between work stations. If this cannot be done advantageously, consider rearranging the production elements or other equipment.

It is possible that the **product mix** may make it economically unfeasible to use conveyors; however, you should at least evaluate all of the possibilities before discarding this idea and reverting to the unit load concept or placing the materials into a container. Sometimes trays that fit on a skid or warehouse truck as well as on a conveyor may be the solution to the problem.

Whenever the time interval between successive operations requires that the materials be stored for a certain period of time, the unit load concept may be economically feasible.

REMINDER: Sometimes the production schedule may be rearranged to make successive operations follow continuously and in rapid succession. When this becomes a possibility work stations may be connected with:

- bridging conveyor
- a chute
- a storage silo
- a mechanical manipulator

NOTE: A mechanical manipulator is an industrial robot that is used to load and unload machines, to stack materials, and to perform highly repetitive and unskilled tasks. Some robots are programmable (i.e., they can be programmed to perform diverse tasks), others are not. A low-grade manipulator can be a put-and-take mechanism that can perform only the repetitive task that it was designed to accomplish.

Using Containers Effectively

A container may range in size from a small, manually handled box or tray used at a work station or stored in bins, to the large 8' × 8' × 40' seavan used in overseas shipping. One container is capable of holding only ounces, the other may hold a load of 20 tons. Again one container may be a unit load, or it may require many containers to make up a load that can be conveniently and economically handled in a unit.

REMINDER: The range of container sizes in a plant should depend on:

- the individual piece parts to be handled
- the volume (quantities) involved

Establish a Plant Container Program to Increase Profits

The design and/or purchase of containers should be accomplished only after a complete analysis of the company's short-range and long-range objectives. If container design and evaluation are done in haste, the company may make successive purchases of a type, size, and style of container that completely militates against standardization and effective materials handling. In other words, the container may not permit very much flexibility in in-plant handling or inter-plant transportation and may not be sized properly for today's major product lines.

Formulate a company policy to control any possible proliferation of container types, sizes, and materials. Appoint a chairperson to form a container committee with at least one representative from each of the operating departments. The chairperson should convene the committee to review any requests for new containers.

The point of this control is to avoid problems like the one experienced in one major Fortune 500 company where over 85 different container sizes and styles were being used. Through successive mergers and acquisitions the company had inherited large numbers of these different containers. Ultimately, because interplant shipments had become chaotic, a container standardization program was established which, at the present time, has managed to reduce the number of different container configurations to between 30 and 40. It has been a slow process because of the millions of dollars invested, but the company is determined to reduce even this number of containers to a more manageable quantity.

You can develop a *plant container program* that will save the company money and protect the product if you follow the simple rules below:

- Determine container sizes and configurations on the basis of the sizes and volume of parts to be handled.

- Limit the number of container sizes and configurations.

- Keep in mind the need for flexibility: container sizes and configurations should be reviewed plant-wide before adoption.

- Design the containers for maximum utilization.

- Properly identify your containers as company property. If the container itself cannot be numbered and identified, a metallic tag can be welded or fastened to it in a visible manner.

- Place tare weights on containers. This can be part of the ID-tag.

- Make sure each container has its own *purchase specification.*

- Inspect newly purchased containers for compliance as they come from the supplier if not 100% at least on a sampling basis.

- At least once a year count all containers by category. If captive containers (i.e., your own containers) are on an exchange program with suppliers ask the suppliers to give you a count at this time.

- Take pride in your container program and keep your containers cleaned and painted. In this way, employees will tend to treat the containers better, and container abuse will be minimized.

- In more sophisticated programs color-code containers by department or function.

- Make arrangements with suppliers and customers so that your containers (or the customer's containers) may be used for shipping. In this way some of the requirements for packaging may be eliminated or at least minimized.

- Analyze and examine the stacking features of rigid containers and the nesting characteristics of others. If collapsible containers are to be used, determine their longevity before investing company funds on any large quantity. Testing this feature through trials and demonstrations may be in order.

- Consider using wire-mesh containers that have certain advantageous features: they are self-cleaning and see-through. They are generally preferred over solid steel containers, especially where noise is a factor; depending on the type of wire-mesh container that is used, noise levels may be between 5 and 15 decibels lower when parts are dropped or tossed into the container, compared to solid steel containers. Wire-mesh containers may be used to wash parts without removing them from the container. Also parts placed in wire-mesh containers will dry and cool faster than like parts placed into steel containers. Both wire-mesh and solid steel containers are to be preferred over wood, plastic, and corrugated board containers from the standpoint of cleanliness, housekeeping, and fire safety.

Assessing Plant and Carrier Size to Determine the Design and Selection of Containers

If you want to achieve the greatest utilization of your container program you must apply a systems philosophy in which you examine the relationship of the plant facility and the carriers to the container size and configuration.

Plant Structure

Determine whether the building floors or the storage areas can support the loads which will be placed upon them. This applies to both indoor and outdoor storage areas. For example, concrete floor slabs placed on alluvial soil (i.e., formerly river bottom lands, that have very low shear value) will have a very poor load-bearing capacity. Check with the architect, builder, or landlord of the property in order to determine whether or not floor or storage areas will support the kinds of loading that you anticipate. In these times of product and related liability awareness, it would be well to get it in writing!

Size of the building bays is extremely important in determining the optimum size of containers to be purchased. Take measurements from inside to inside surfaces of columns in both directions. It helps also if you have the drawings of the building so you can mark the actual dimensions on them. Prepare a layout that will show how much clearance there is for forklift truck operation. Usually two to three inches between containers and columns will give sufficient clearance for handling equipment. (The same clearances apply when storage racks are used.)

Know the heights and widths of all entrances (i.e., door sizes) and note these dimensions on the building drawings. Determine the means of container transport. For example, it may make a difference in container configuration if industrial powered trucks, forklifts, or pallet jacks are the principal means of horizontal transportation. If elevators or reciprocating conveyors are to be used for vertical transportation, this may become a delimiting factor in container design.

Receiving or shipping dock ramps and ramps within the building may be another limiting element that must be considered in your container program. Container stacking heights will depend on container size, weight, and stacking characteristics. Ask the container manufacturer to supply his recommendation and documentation for safe stacking heights and container loads.

Carrier Size

There is a considerable range in the dimensions of both over-the-road carriers and railroad cars. There is also a wide range in the inside dimensions of overseas shipping containers whose lengths may vary from a 8' × 8' × 8' CONEX (military container type), TO 8' × 17', 8' × 20', 8' × 30', 8' × 35', and 8' × 40'. The doorway dimensions on all types of containers and carriers also vary as do the aircraft carriers' containers and pallets. See Figure 2-1 for an example of truck and railcar dimensional variations.

Ensuring Compatibility Among Containers, Unit Loads, and Carriers

Developing or adopting a container standard for your company requires careful analysis of the dimensional characteristics of your plant building and the means of transportation. In many instances unit loads and the means of transportation are increasing in size, and a

Truck van dimensions – May vary with manufacturer

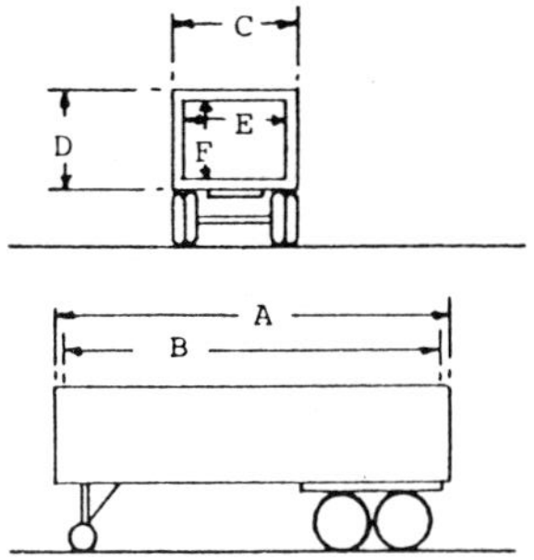

	DRY FREIGHT		REFRIGERATED FREIGHT	
	Approximate Range Available	Most Common Dimensions	Approximate Range Available	Most Common Dimensions
A Nominal Length	26' to 40'	40'	30'6" to 40'	40'
B Inside Length	25'7-5/8" to 39'6"	39'6"	29'8-1/4" to 39'2-1/4"	39'
C Inside Width	88" to 92-1/2"	92"	Up to 90"	90"
D Inside Height	76-3/4" to 106-3/4"	96"	71-7/8" to 101-7/8"	90"
E Door Width	88" to 91"	90"	Up to 90"	90"
F Door Height	71-7/16" to 101-7/16"	91"	67-5/16" to 97-5/16"	86"

Freight car dimensions – Based on cars presently being used, but may vary with age and builder.

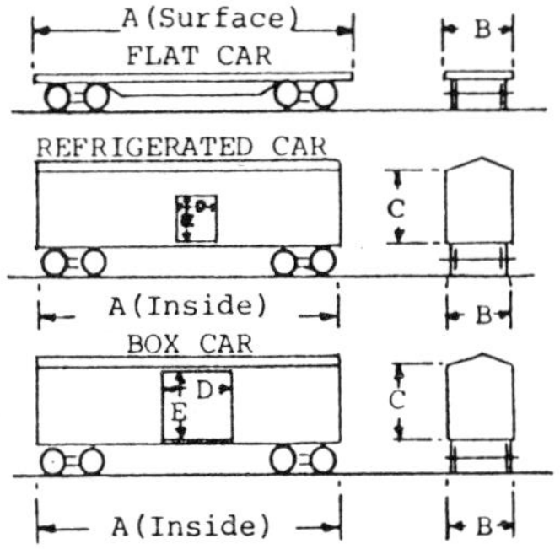

	TYPE OF CAR		
	Box Car	Flat Car	Refrigerated Car
A Inside Length	40'6" to 86'6"	36'0" to 89'0"	33'2-3/4" to 50'
B Inside Width	9'2" to 9'6"	8'4" to 10'6"	8'2-3/4" to 9'2"
C Inside Height	9'6" to 13'2"	–	6'8" to 9'0"
D Door Width	6'0" to 30'0"	–	4'0" to 10'1"
E Door Height	8'9" to 12'9"	–	6'0" to 9'4"

FLAT CAR

A (Surface)

B

REFRIGERATED CAR

A (Inside)

B

C

BOX CAR

A (Inside)

B

C

Fig. 2-1: Over-the-road truck trailers and railroad car dimensions.

company is stuck with smaller modules because of the already large investment made in these container sizes.

The objectives that you should adhere to center around these four principles:

- Whenever possible use the same standard container that comes from the supplier at the first point of use within the plant.

- Store in-process materials in the same standard container and transport materials intraplant without rehandling or discharging materials from them into a different container.

- Try to ship interplant or to customers in the same standard container.

- If it is not always possible to use the company's standard containers, consider substituting knocked-down (KD) containers so that it is possible to permit the user to return empty containers to your distribution center with a compaction ratio of at least 4 to 1.

NOTE: In lieu of steel or plastic containers you should not overlook the possibilities inherent in double-wall and triple-wall corrugated kraft containers and pallet boxes fabricated from corrugated board. Almost all of these materials are reusable and after their useful lives may be (largely) recycled.

HOW TO HANDLE UNIT LOADS FOR INCREASED PROFIT

In almost every warehousing and distribution center there is a requirement for unitizing pallet loads. We can divide the problem into the three main areas of receiving, shipping, and in-plant handling.

Unitizing Loads in Receiving

In the receiving department when loads are not unitized, your employees will have to manually stack materials on a pallet in order to facilitate further handling in your center. In instances such as these your receiving department should use 12-inch or 15-inch 70- or 80-gauge stretch wrap to bind the loads compactly for safe transport and storage. A quicker, safer, and more economical operation will result from the simple expedient of having *stretch wrap* on hand. Stretch wrap is a thin, transparent plastic film anywhere from 12 to 15 inches wide, supplied in 1500-ft rolls and is wrapped around palletized loads to increase their stability in transit and storage.

Unitizing Loads for Shipping

Establish the policy of unitizing outgoing pallet loads. Your customers will appreciate receiving loads that are unitized because it will save them time on the receiving end, and the merchandise will arrive at their site in much better condition.

Unitizing Loads for In-plant Handling

Regard in-plant handling of pallet loads in much the same manner that you look at your receiving and shipping departments. It is extremely wasteful in terms of labor time and damaging to product to haul unstable pallet loads. Sometimes the condition of floors or the distance traversed requires the most compact and stable loads that you can achieve.

Your periodic plant inspections will indicate if the in-plant handling is up to par. Good in-plant handling practices are safe ways to handle product and are contributing factors to the increased morale of your employees.

THE SIX MAIN METHODS OF UNITIZING LOADS

Your choice among the six main methods of unitizing pallet loads depends on your particular storage and shipping requirements:

- the stability of the load
- protection from elements and pilferage
- amount of labor and time required
- expense of unitizing

Method #1: Stretch Wrap

It isn't necessary to wrap the whole pallet load: A couple of turns of stretch wrap on the top tier of cartons is sufficient to keep the load intact even with fairly rough forktruck handling. A 1500-ft roll of 15"-wide stretch wrap costs approximately $9 per roll, so that about 40 feet of wrap (enough to make two turns of a 48" × 48" pallet load with a starting and ending tuck) will cost about 2.5 cents per load not including the labor time to wrap the load, usually about a minute out of the hour.

The advantages of using stretch wrap are as follows:

- it is cost effective
- it doesn't require energy
- no equipment cost is involved (unless automatic or semi-automatic stretch wrapping machines are employed)
- it doesn't require floor space when manually applied
- it can be used in refrigerated or heat restricted areas
- it doesn't require much inventory space
- it can be used with heat-sensitive merchandise
- if automatic or semi-automatic wrapping machines are used it doesn't require special wiring, i.e., existing electrical service may be used.

Method #2: Shrink-Wrap

The method for shrink-wrapping pallet loads is basically the same as that used for small consumer articles in retail stores. The difference is the mil-thickness (or gauge) of the plastic. You can handle a diverse array of products using this method:

- castings: use 4- to 6-mil
- forgings: use 4- to 6-mil

- fixtures: use 4- to 6-mil
- sheet metal parts: use 4-mil
- batteries (industrial, or automotive): use 4-mil
- bricks: use 6-mil
- grocery items: use 4-mil
- pharmaceuticals: use 4-mil
- soft goods: use 4-mil
- bagged materials: use 4- to 6-mil

Any material that can be palletized can be shrink-wrapped with the exception only of items that are relatively heat sensitive, because temperatures within the load may be increased to approximately 135°F for several minutes or longer.

One of the advantages of shrink-wrap is that the evidence of pilferage after the load leaves the plant is quite apparent. Because the load is so tightly encapsulated the only way to remove an item from the load is to cut through the plastic. Paradoxically, although the plastic has been pierced, the load will remain sufficiently intact that handling stability is usually not affected. That is one reason that shrink-wrapped loads may be used satisfactorily in break-bulk type of warehousing and distribution center operations.

Since most warehousing and distribution center operations depend upon forklift vehicles for transportation, pallet load stability is of primary importance in order to protect the product. Advantages of shrink wrap in this area are superlative for the following reasons:

- The plastic film firms and in shrinking compacts the load.
- The plastic film anchors the load to the pallet.
- The load can be tilted and even rotated in some instances without losing the integrity of the load.
- Since any material or product that can be placed upon a pallet can be shrink wrapped, it is the ideal material for unitizing pallet loads—this includes normally unstable pallet loads and loads with irregular contours or configurations.

Dust, Dirt, and Moisture Protection

Whenever it is necessary to protect merchandise from dust, dirt, and moisture, the use of shrink-wrap has no price competitive equal. This is true regardless of the degree of mechanization of the shrink-wrapping process. As an example, there are shrink tunnels, shrink rings, flow-through intermittent tunnels, or heat closets, which are relatively expensive; however, it is possible to shrink-wrap pallet loads with a shrink gun that looks like a sophisticated blow-torch, costing little more than $100.

Shrink-wrapped loads for severe weathering or relatively hostile environments should be placed on a plastic sheet which is first placed on the pallet. If the pallet is used or has loose deck boards, a sheet of corrugated board (or, 1/8" masonite) should be laid down before the plastic is draped on the pallet. The load is then placed on the pallet and shrink-wrapped by whatever means available. Shrink-wrapped loads can be placed out-of-doors for as long as two months and sometimes longer. The advantages of the plastic film wrapped load are, as follows:

- Moisture is not absorbed.
- The load covering (i.e., the plastic) will not lose its strength.
- Load contents are almost 100 percent dust and dirt free.
- Loads can be shipped in open trucks regardless of the weather.
- Loads can be stored outdoors for relatively long periods.

Method #3: Tie Ropes

Quick-tying ropes with special end hooks are sometimes used to tie the upper tier of cartoned materials, especially in distribution centers that have towlines or in-floor dragchain conveyors. These ropes are used mainly for in-plant handling because the ropes are reusable and cost of the ropes is a factor. One of the main disadvantages with these ropes is that because of their many uses they are attractive pilferable items. Another disadvantage is that with relatively unstable loads sometimes several ropes are required per pallet. Stretch wrap has largely replaced these devices.

Method #4: Rubber Bands

Large rubber bands as wide as four inches and as long as three to four feet can be used in much the same fashion as tie ropes with the same advantages and disadvantages.

Method #5: Filament Tape

Filament tape may be used to tie loads together for increased compactness; however, the same advantages and disadvantages noted for tie ropes and rubber bands apply, except that the one-side adhesive coated tape is a one-time only application.

Method #6: Glue

Wherever long hauls in motor trucks or railcars are required or where the loads are unitized on slip-sheets (see the section on Slip-Sheets in Chapter 4), you should consider using a high-shear, low-tensile adhesive such as H.B. Fuller Co. Type No. 133 Dextrin, or F4764 Resin. A slap-dab of adhesive on the top of each carton, and a few dabs on the slip-sheet are all that is required to ensure the integrity of the load throughout its journey. The cartons are readily removable, when required, because of the low-tensile strength of the adhesive. On the other hand, the high-shear characteristic of the glue keeps the load from shifting in transit.

3

Receiving Operations for Warehousing and Distribution

PHYSICAL ASPECTS OF RECEIVING

Every physical distribution system begins with the receipt of materials. From this point, material flow commences to fill the pipeline. The methods used in planning and operating a receiving department are the same for both manufacturing and distribution operations; therefore, no distinctions shall be made between the two departments in the information that follows.

NOTE: The length of time it takes for materials to be removed from the carrier, moved across the receiving platform and receiving area, and taken out of the receiving department is a measure of its efficiency. The shorter the time interval, the more efficient the operation.

The turn-around time can be measured in hours, days, weeks, or months, but if merchandise remains on the receiving floor longer than 24 hours, you have a problem. In a well-paced receiving operation incoming materials can be logged in, bar-coded or bar code counted, tagged, inspected, or inspection samples taken in a matter of minutes. Materials that are in short supply, back-ordered, or are needed to complete a shipment can be dispatched directly to shipping or to an order filling or packaging department. This presupposes, of course, that the individuals comprising the work force have been properly trained and have been provided the necessary equipment and methods to achieve a high degree of efficiency. To this end job descriptions will make training efforts more productive.

In some instances materials handling costs can amount to upwards of 35% of the cost of the product and in worst case scenarios the handling costs can rise to 80% and more. For this reason anything you can do to improve the receiving operation will pay big dividends for your company.

Designing Space Effectively

The difficulty of designing an efficient receiving department depends upon the product mix to be handled. Compounding this difficulty is the method of transportation used to bring materials to the distribution center; for example, railroad car, over-the-road carriers, city delivery trucks, United Parcel Service, U.S. Post Office vehicles, or a combination of these means.

The steps you must take to design an efficient receiving layout are, as follows:

- Determine the product mix of items to be handled, including a range of sizes, weights, and volumes.
- Decide upon the type of materials handling equipment required to handle the given volume of materials.

If you are designing a new plant layout it is much better for you to make the layout by determining what space is required, then placing walls around the space rather than to try to squeeze or stretch a function to make it conform to the available space. Since most receiving operations are planned for existing buildings, ingenuity and resourcefulness become the general rule of design in order to salvage a layout.

- Determine your ideal turn-around time.
- If you have an objective of turning the receiving floor over every four hours, calculate what effect this will have on crew size.
- Make sure you have provided space for anticipated growth and expansion.

WARNING: It is much better to have the receiving area pressed for space rather than having too much floor area. From the psychological viewpoint it is the tightness of space that places the pressure on keeping materials moving out of receiving into user departments.

- If material is to be inspected by quality control, provide a set-out space or a holding area (with necessary policy regarding who does what, and what happens to the material if accepted or rejected).

If a quality control laboratory is necessary, make sure one is included in the original plans. Afterthoughts in this regard are expensive, especially when chemical analysis is required and proper ventilation, lead-lined sinks and drains, hoods, and explosion-proof electrical receptacles and lights, oxygen and other gases are required, and so on.

Door Sizes

Common carriers, especially motor trucks, are becoming larger primarily in height. Therefore, if these trucks are to enter the building (i.e., into an enclosed truck dock), door opening heights should be at least 16 feet and as wide as 12 feet.

If the truck does not enter into an enclosed area but backs against a door opening in the building wall, the height of the opening should be based upon the largest forklift truck to be used to enter the truck. In other words you have to determine the lowered mast height of the forklift truck and then add a safety factor of at least one foot.

As an example:

- lowered mast height = 83 inches, say 7 feet;
- safety factor of 2 feet; thus,
- opening height of door should be 9 feet. (Normally, this type of truck door opening would be 10 feet high.)

The center-to-center (C to C) distances for truck doors should be at least 12 feet. By maintaining the C to C dimension, the truck driver will have 4 feet of clearance on either side of his 8-foot wide box (truck body). The necessary care that must be exercised by the driver in order to back into a crowded truck slot will more than compensate for the additional time spent, since this extra care will tend to minimize damage to adjacent trucks and the building. Not only have trucks and trailers tended to increase in size, but so have railroad cars. This is true for both refrigerated and unrefrigerated cars. Cars have been getting longer and doors have been getting wider; in addition, there are many specially designed cars traveling the rails. Depending on the nature of your business, you may be a recipient of one or more of these special cars on occasion. It is necessary at this stage of transportation development to provide railcar door spacing that will accommodate small railroad cars of 40-foot lengths and 6-foot-wide doors, up to cars that are 85 feet in length with proportionately wider doors (See Figure 2-1.)

Dock Heights and Other Dimensions

Truck bed heights (i.e., the decks) vary greatly; in addition, loaded and unloaded trucks vary in bed height. The bed of a fully loaded truck can be up to a foot lower than its unloaded height. The general trend in building dock heights is to make them lower than they were a few decades ago. Receiving platforms constructed thirty years ago were approximately 56 inches high, as a general rule. Today, a standard height of 48 inches has been almost universally adopted.

Reefer or refrigerated trucks have striated decks which permit cold air to circulate under the load. This raises the deck level several inches higher than normal, but a 48-inch high dock equipped with a dock plate, a leveler, can easily accommodate this load. (See Figure 3-1.)

Furniture warehouses and distribution centers are unique in that many of the trucks used to haul this type of merchandise are the drop-frame type, so that you should consider dock heights of 32 to 36 inches. If furniture is not the main business of your concern but you do receive a significant amount of furniture, make provision to have at least one truck dock with a height compatible with furniture-carrying vehicles. City delivery vehicles, vans, panel trucks and the like, require, at the most docks that are two feet high. In most instances ground level docks are sufficient for these smaller trucks. That brings up another point. If you intend to have a totally enclosed truck well, you can provide a dock for city delivery trucks by ramping up one end of the enclosed space. (See Figure 3-1.)

Dock Apron Design

You can make the receiving operation more profitable if you provide the necessary maneuvering space on the deck directly in front of the open door of the motor carrier. In addition to this, space for set out must also be provided. In a typical forklift truck receiving operation the minimum width of the receiving strip should be the turning radius of the lift truck used to unload the carrier, measured from the edge of the dockboard as the lift truck begins its backward turn, plus 3 feet.

As a practical example:

$$
\begin{array}{rl}
\text{lift truck turning radius} = & 7 \text{ feet} \\
\text{length of dockboard} = & 6 \text{ feet} \\
\text{add 3 feet} = & \underline{3 \text{ feet}} \\
\text{Total} = & 16 \text{ feet}
\end{array}
$$

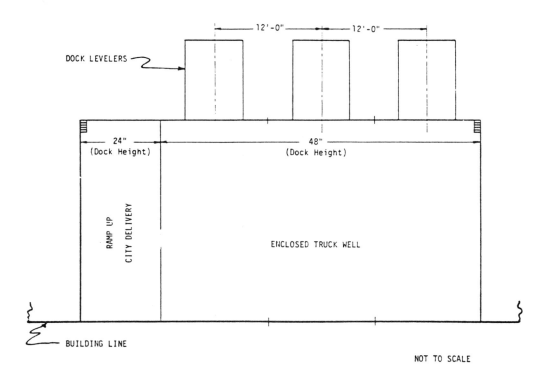

Fig. 3-1: Ramping up for city delivery trucks in an enclosed truck well.

The receiving docks of almost all of the newer warehouses have aprons of at least 20 feet, and a few have wider aprons.

The speed of an unloading operation will increase with the size of the apron since a forklift operator will be able to make his backward turn more rapidly given ample room to make this initial maneuver off the dockboard.

Dock Lights and Other Necessities

Good lighting is an important contribution to increased productivity and morale. Thus, after an incoming truck has backed into the dock slot with its rear doors open, there should be sufficient light on the dock for the truck driver and the receiving clerk to read bills of lading and receiving reports, and any other paperwork. This requires 30 to 50 lumens of light at a height of 30 inches above the dock floor which can be readily tested using a hand-held light meter.

Spot Light

In addition to adequate lighting, it is important to have a swiveling spot light mounted on a wall or column at the rear of the truck in order to flood the "working face" of the merchandise to be unloaded. This is necessary regardless of the time of day, but especially so when the day is bright and sunny, because the forklift operator's eyes cannot adjust quickly enough to the contrast in lighting between the bright exterior and the darker interior of the truck.

Advantages for truck interior lighting:

- It makes for a safer operation.
- It minimizes damage to the material being unloaded.
- It enables the forklift driver or the walkie-truck (pallet jack) operator to see the condition of the truck floor so that if there are any holes or deteriorated floor-boards, plywood decking, or the like, may be used to reinforce the floor temporarily.

A Stand-up Desk

Another convenience that helps to improve the effectiveness of the unloading operations is to have a small, stand-up desk or a stanchion with a flat writing surface in, or near the receiving dock area where the receiving clerk may review packing lists, check invoices, or examine the bills of lading.

Chocks and Stands

The OSHA regulations require that wheel jacks (trailer stabilizing jacks) be placed at the front end of a box when the tractor drops it off at a dock. It is also good practice to place wheel chocks under the rear wheels or to use a dock-installed trailer restraining hookup while the trailer is at the dock.

Air Lines

An air line on the truck dock will permit the air brakes on the trailer to be actuated after the tractor is removed.

Pay Telephone

A pay telephone should be installed somewhere on the receiving dock so that commercial truckers can make calls without disrupting the receiving office staff.

Specific Requirements in Receiving Freight by Railroad Car

In general most of the comments that have been made for unloading motor trucks can be applied to rail car handling. The major difference is the use of dockplates. As with carrier trucks, manually placed steel and/or magnesium dockplates (dockboards) are most commonly used for forklift truck entrance to rail cars. However, mechanical dockboards have been especially designed for rail sidings: They are safer to use than manual dockplates because there is no danger of their shifting out of place. Despite the fact that most commercially made manual dockboards have safety lips to prevent this from happening, sometimes the gap between the edge of the dock and the rail car is either too wide, or the difference in elevation between the dock floor and the car bed is too great to permit forklift trucks a safe passage, especially when backing out of the car doorway. Receiving freight by rail is less flexible than by motor truck.

Sometimes, when several cars are to be received on the same day, arrangements can be made with the rail freight office to have the cars spotted on your siding in a specified order. There are times when this service is very good, especially when the RR team tracks are not too far distant. (Team tracks are railroad yards where trains of cars are put together for various destinations.) Rail cars are usually spotted once a day by the railroad company; however, if your volume is sufficiently large, you may need twice daily service. You should inquire whether or not a service charge will be applied to this extra car spotting.

If you are receiving a high volume of freight by rail, your operation might need a small, captive donkey engine or a Tracmobile for spotting rail cars on track sidings. The benefit of the Tracmobile is that it has both railroad car wheels and truck wheels so it can negotiate both pavement and rails.

MONITORING DEMURRAGE CHARGES

Demurrage is the delay that occurs when a common carrier (i.e., a ship, freight car, or motor truck) is held beyond the time originally stipulated by the carrier for unloading or loading. In addition, it is the penalty or compensation that must be paid to the carrier for holding his equipment beyond the time ordinarily allowed. The charges vary with different locales.

NOTE: Keep current on what the latest charges are for demurrage. Also have your accounting department give you a weekly summary of all demurrage charges because this can become a significant dollar amount.

Demurrage is a distribution center problem that requires fine tuning—sometimes it is better to incur demurrage rather than incur the payroll expense of adding personnel or incurring large quantities of overtime. When the scheduling of incoming receivables becomes erratic, demurrage costs may get out of hand. As an example, at one distribution center a paper products company sent a whole year's supply amounting to 42 railroad cars in one shipment. There was nothing in the contract governing this transaction to prevent this catastrophe from occurring. Needless to say, the demurrage and overtime costs were enormous despite the fact that some of the cars were sent to other destinations within the distribution center network; however, this resulted in increased transportation charges.

NOTE: Make sure your contracts with suppliers spell out delivery times, frequencies, and the like; especially when buying quantities are large.

Small and medium-sized warehousing and distribution center operations that require temporary warehouse space may successfully use demurrage provisions (when these are nominal charges) to augment warehouse capacity. This is especially true when "specials" or "loss leaders" require a larger than normal supply of a particular item.

WARNING: Large and continuing demurrage charges are symptomatic of a poorly run receiving operation.

CONTROLLING THE IMPACT OF JUST-IN-TIME MANUFACTURING ON RECEIVING OPERATIONS

Where receiving operations are part of a manufacturing entity the ultimate end goal of the receiving function is to supply the manufacturing operation with a constant flow of the exact quantity of parts, raw material, semi-finished parts, and subcomponents such that there is an uninterrupted stream of materials into the manufacturing department enabling schedules to proceed according to plan. The Just-In-Time (JIT) manufacturing concept embodies all of these factors.

In order to benefit from the JIT concept you have to make a few concessions to the central control of materials. Good control requires that there be a centralized receiving location so that material can be checked in, counted, (sometimes weighed), inspected, and the like. In an oversimplification of the Just-In-Time manufacturing concept, when supplier contracts require that specific quantities of materials be brought to the point of use at specified times, it is often necessary to have supplier merchandise or parts brought to the factory door nearest to the point of use. As you can see, as several plant receiving points are added, the effectiveness of a centralized control function is diminished.

The advantage of JIT from the manufacturer's viewpoint is that it shifts, in large measure, the weighty factors of quality, piece count, inventory control, logistics support, and the like, to the supplier. You must oversee by random sampling at least that you are getting what you're paying for.

NOTE: It is obvious that quality parts will come only from a supplier who has established a reputation for integrity and reliability. These are considerations that may increase the cost of the components initially, but represent a savings when considered in the light of life-cycle, or overall costs.

Controlling the Size, Shape, and Quantity of Components Received via JIT

In JIT manufacturing—whether it be direct manufacturing or an assembly operation—the size and shape of the components dictate the quantity that can be stored in the allocated space. This quantity translates into the number of days' supply of the part on hand. There may be room for only one or two days' supply of the item, and a delivery schedule has to be worked out with the supplier accordingly.

Where large quantities of parts are concerned or where a number of different parts are to be supplied from one source, it may be necessary to have a resident inspector at the supplier's plant to ensure quality reliability. Of course, this type of resident inspection should be eliminated at the earliest practicable opportunity, because it tends to increase payroll costs and may be no more effective than the supplying plant's own quality control program.

Packaging

Packaging in the JIT program can be one of the most productive aspects of this concept of supplying a manufacturing production line. In keeping with ecological considerations, the less disposable dunnage that is used, the faster and cleaner the operation of line supply can be carried out. The ultimate objective for JIT is to eliminate packaging entirely. One way to do this is to develop trays or containers into which the parts may be placed. Stacking and nestable containers will save the most space, and if the nestable containers are contoured for the piece part, less damage is likely to occur in transit and in intraplant handling.

CONVEYORS AND OTHER METHODS OF UNLOADING CARS AND TRUCKS

Conveyors

When unpalletized or nonunitized merchandise is received at the distribution center or warehouse, it must be manually unloaded. If 25% or more of the carrier's contents must be removed, the most effective way of unloading small cartons is to employ powered telescoping conveyors or, next in order of effectiveness, gravity roller or skatewheel conveyors. In lieu of these methods, the palletizing of materials at the working face of the load, usually using a two-person crew, is a generally accepted method of unloading most loose-packed carriers, but it is not cost effective.

NOTE: You should specify in purchasing contracts how you want the merchandise to be sent to you. It is preferable and less costly overall to have the materials palletized and unitized using stretch wrap to consolidate the loads (as discussed in Chapter 2).

Alternate Methods of Unitizing Merchandise

Alternate methods for unitizing shipments that make unloading quicker and less costly are the use of either slip sheets or BOP sheets.

Slip Sheets

Slip Sheets are rectangular sections of single wall corrugated board (single wall signifies a cross section wherein fluted board is sandwiched between two plies of kraft paper) with a lip that can be grasped by a push-pull forklift attachment. Each forklift truck employed in this type of unloading must be equipped with a push-pull device, costing several thousands of dollars (approx. $9M to $20M).

When both shipper and receiver use push-pull attachments the following advantages may be derived:

- Slip sheets cost under one dollar each, versus pallet costs of about three dollars each for wood pallets of the expendable (one-way) type.
- Wood pallets have a tare weight (approx. 60 pounds each) and cube (at least 2.5 cubic feet each) that increase freight costs; slip sheets have a minimal tare and cube.
- When slip sheeted loads are stacked in a warehouse, approximately 2.5 cubic feet are saved for each unitized load.

BOP Sheets

The average weight of a BOP sheet is approximately 8 pounds, and like the slip sheet it is composed primarily of a sheet of single wall corrugated board. The difference is that the BOP sheet has two fiberboard bellows on its bottom side that permit forklift truck fork entry. A small rectangular section of polyethylene at the opening of each bellows guides the forklift truck's chisels (tines) into the bellow-slot, permitting the entire load that has been placed upon the corrugated sheet, to be transported.

The advantages of the BOP sheet are similar to the slip sheet; however, the BOP sheet does not require the use of special forklift truck attachments for either loading or unloading. (A further discussion and evaluation of BOP sheets has been included as Appendix A, since this relatively new development has a great deal of potential for warehousing and distribution operations.)[1]

Slug Loading and Unloading

Powered telescoping conveyors and gravity conveyors are relatively effective ways for unloading or loading carriers. The unitized load, however, makes the above methods look painfully slow and ineffective in comparison since large blocks of merchandise can be removed by a forklift truck at one time.

---

[1]A recent development, by BOP Sheet marketers, has combined the advantages of the slip sheet with those of the BOP sheet by adding a lip that combines both slip sheet and BOP sheet features.

Some fast-paced receiving and shipping operations are designed to benefit from both conveyors and unit loads. Conveyors placed in the bed of the motor truck allow unitized loads or containers to be moved into the truck singly or in complete truck load quantities. One method is to place gravity roller conveyors on the floor of the truck body; a further step in the direction of mechanizing this operation is to use a motorized chain-driven roller conveyor to load or unload the "slug," where all of the contents are emptied in seconds. This method requires that the receiving or shipping dock be equipped with conveyors to receive or set out the unitized loads in truck load quantities. Another slug loading (or unloading) operation makes use of a shuttle-bed, or walking beam arrangement that enables the entire motor truck to be unloaded (loaded) in minutes.

The above methods for improving unloading and loading operations are not new by any stretch of the imagination, since most of these concepts have been with us for almost four decades. The major problem with all of these methods is that they must be sold up and down the line so that the personnel who have to live with these handling improvements are convinced of their efficacy, provided that there is sufficient volume to justify their use. In addition, it requires constant supervision to see that the principles of operation are not violated, that the equipment is properly maintained, and that it is not abused by warehouse labor.

OUTDOOR STORAGE

Yard storage of receivables is a relatively inexpensive way of holding certain types of materials that can be stored in the weather, for example:

- lumber
- steel
- castings
- forgings
- export packed materials

While it is obvious that the above materials are suited to outdoor storage, many materials that are normally stored inside can be kept outdoors with adequate protection. The three main methods of providing protection from the elements are:

1. Wax-impregnated corrugated containers. The most notable example of this type of container, which will hold up even under several months of tropical rains, is the triple-wall corrugated container often used by exporters and the military establishment.

2. Plastic (usually polyethylene) drapes, sleeves, or tubes. Clear plastic leaves the load exposed to ultraviolet light which may affect chemically unstable materials; however, black plastic may be used to screen out the sun's rays effectively.

3. Shrink-wrap (described in Chapter 2). Shrink-wrap (not to be confused with stretch wrap which is mechanically wound around the load and gives no outdoor protection) is an exceptionally fine way of maintaining the integrity of the load.

While the principles of yard storage are in direct contrast to JIT manufacturing techniques, there are times when yard storage makes a good deal of sense. As an example, the use of quantity buying as a strike hedge where you feel that an important supplier may be shut down for a considerable period of time; or, where quantity purchasing of distress sale materials gives you an important competitive edge, and the like.

At the present time, there is no economical method for providing outdoor storage for most grocery items, soft goods, stationery, and so forth. These materials cannot be stored outdoors in their own shipping containers or packages.

Yard storage space is your company's most visible sign of effective management and, therefore, should be handled efficiently and neatly. Disorderly piles leave lasting negative impressions on customers, visitors, and your neighbors. While it is difficult to stack and contain some materials, you should make every effort to present the best view possible to the outside world. The old adage that if it looks good it must be good holds true here.

If the material to be stored out of doors is regular in configuration, or if it is stored in containers, steel tubs, and so forth, any of the six following arrangements patterned after indoor storage configurations can make your storage yards look good.

Block Storage

The highest density storage is obtained using the block storage method (see Figure 3-2).

Advantages

- Best utilization of space
- Lowest storage costs
- Best cube utilization of outdoor space

Disadvantages

- Added material handling cost, since if FIFO method is employed, there is the added materials cost of moving containers in order to obtain the "first-in" units.
- When storing dissimilar parts in the block, getting at the correct part numbers may involve considerable forklift truck and driver time since a number of containers may have to be moved and shifted.
- When all of the stored products are similar it is very difficult to control the turnover of stock.

Back-to-back Storage

Inasmuch as back-to-back storage requires more space dedicated to aisles, it is much less economical in terms of space utilization than block storage; however, it provides a much faster operation (see Figure 3-3).

Advantages

- Each container is readily accessible from the aisle.
- Controlling inventory is easy.
- The storage and retrieval operation is fast and economical in terms of forklift truck and operator time.

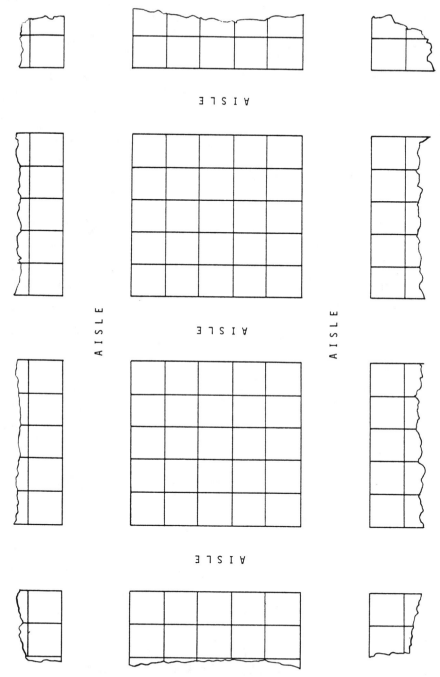

Fig. 3-2: Layout showing block storage method.

Disadvantages

- If containers are stacked more than one high or if FIFO storage requires that one of the lower containers be selected, it means that the forklift operator has to destack and pick out the desired container.

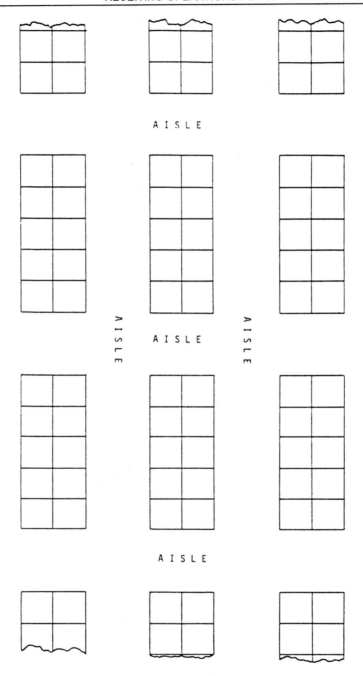

Fig. 3-3: An example of a back-to-back layout plan.

- A large amount of space is wasted in main aisle and cross aisle areas.
- Aisle widths are in direct relationship to the turning radius of the largest forklift truck to be used in the operation.

NOTE: If the aisles have been sized for a sideloading industrial truck, then it would be impossible to use a counterbalanced forklift truck in the same narrow aisles, since the forklift truck would require a much wider aisle in which to function. While there are several manufacturers of right-angle stacking forklift trucks on the market, the largest commercially available unit has a lifting capacity of only 6,000 pounds, which might be a limiting factor in the type of yard storage plan to be adopted. There are, however, sideloading trucks which may be obtained in 4,000- 6,000-, and 10,000-pound and larger capacities.

WARNING: In purchasing specialized equipment for yard storage, it may be necessary to buy at least two of each model especially since one of them should be used as a backup vehicle for repairs, maintenance, and the like.

Sawtooth Storage

Sawtooth storage is rarely used either indoors or outdoors; however, it saves aisle space and, therefore, there are occasions where its use may be justified. The main advantage to be gained with this storage pattern is that a counterbalanced forklift truck may enter the face of the stack and get to every container from an aisle that is only slightly wider than the width of the forklift truck and load.

The major disadvantage of this storage pattern, because there is no turnaround space, is that the lift truck operator must do a good deal of his driving in reverse. This tends to slow down transportation time, because the forklift truck driver has to go slower and exercise greater care in backing through the aisle. (See Figure 3-4.)

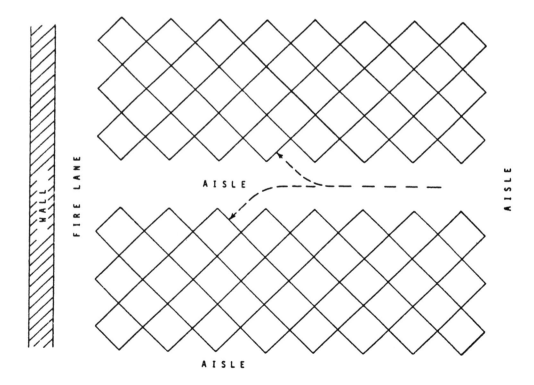

Fig. 3-4: The sawtooth storage arrangement results in narrower aisles, as shown in this illustration.

Tiering Racks

Tiering racks are used in order to stack loads on top of one another. The tiering rack provides the platform upon which to place the next load. Tiering racks can be either rigid, knock-down, folding, or can be composed of stacking irons that are fastened to each corner of a wood pallet.

Advantages

- Crushable items, or items that do not stack well of themselves, can be safely stored in the racks to heights of three or more tiers.
- the unitized load may be transported directly to the point of use without having to be removed from the pallet. (See Figure 3-5.)

Cantilevered Storage Racks

The cantilevered storage rack comes in several different configurations. It can be a single-sided unit where all of the cantilevered arms are on one side. This type of unit is usually lagged to a wall or floor for stability, although some heavy duty units do not require lagging. If the unit has arms on both sides of the central upright member (a double sided unit) then it is self-standing and doesn't require lagging.

Cantilevered racks can be used either indoors as in furniture warehousing, or outdoors for steel, bar stock, tubing or lumber storage. In some instances, cantilevered racks have been modified to the extent that decking has been placed on the supporting arms. When decking is added the usually high loading capacity of the cantilevered rack may be used to support heavy loads. The absence of outboard (or paired) uprights makes this modified cantilevered rack extremely suitable for long, awkward loads that normally could not be placed into conventional storage racks.

An A-frame cantilevered rack does not require lagging to the floor, but due to the isosceles configuration of the uprights is limited in size and height. The standard shape of the cantilevered rack, on the other hand, is limited solely by the type of handling equipment used to load and offload the frames (See Figure 3-6.)

Storage Racks

Storage racks are probably the most widely used method for storing materials in warehousing and distribution operations. In most distribution centers they are used indoors; however, they are often used to good advantage in outdoor applications, especially where space is limited and there is the added necessity for having every container or unit load of material instantly accessible. Because of the amount of company funds usually invested in storage racks, it is extremely important that you become familiar with the various features and characteristics of storage racks as explained in Chapter 11.

At this point you need to be aware of the following general factors affecting the use of storage racks:

- Pallet storage racks may be used back-to-back as free-standing units either indoors or outdoors.

Photo courtesy Tier-Rack Corporation, St. Louis, MO

Fig. 3-5: Knock-down tiering racks used for storing materials several tiers high.

- Where pallet storage racks are used back-to-back they must be tied together using approved fastening means.
- If single rack units are used they must be lagged to the wall or floor, depending upon the application.
- In most back-to-back installations, stops must be placed between the units so that a forklift truck operator cannot push loads on the adjoining storage rack into the next aisle.
- For most outdoor applications the quality of paint (enamel) to be used should be specified by the purchaser; this includes the surface preparation as well.

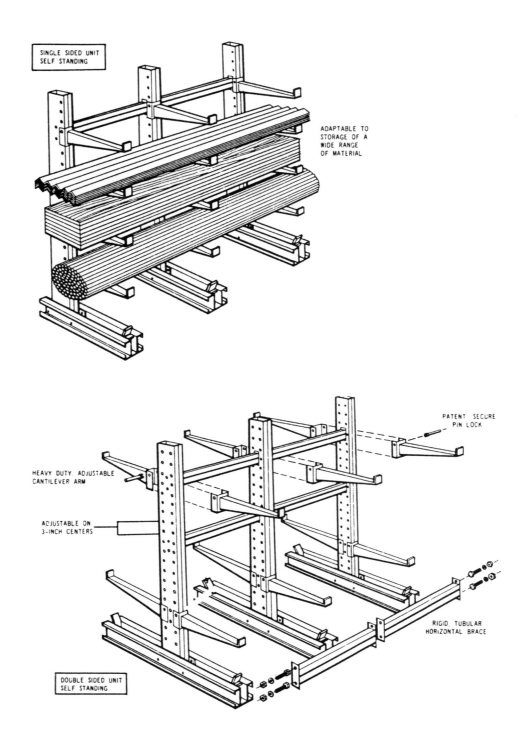

Fig. 3-6: Examples of cantilevered racks used in both indoor and outdoor storage.

ORGANIZING RECORDKEEPING IN RECEIVING OPERATIONS

In order to have a smooth-running receiving operation, one that will make money for the company instead of wasting it, you have to organize all of the physical and mechanical operations and integrate them with a no-nonsense streamlining of paperwork. It cannot be overemphasized that systematic control requires that you know *where the merchandise is at all times!*

In order to accomplish this basic concept, all of the receiving areas (including outdoor storage areas) should be clearly marked with floor locations. After this has been done using floor markings and overhead signs wherever possible, choose one of these two methods to record incoming material locations:

- Use Kardex, Access, or a similar card file system if locating materials is to be done manually.

- Use computer terminal data entry if such equipment is available. (As computers have become more affordable, even small companies can benefit from their speed and precision.)

When materials stored outdoors pass from the jurisdiction of the receiving department to the materials control department, as they may in some instances, an enormous amount of double handling can be avoided if the receiving department knows where to send each incoming truckload of material.

NOTE: By keeping the lines of communication open between the receiving department and the materials control (or materials management) department, labor hours will be minimized.

CONTROLLING PAPERWORK

The three primary objectives of the receiving department are as follows:

- Identify incoming materials
- Verify (by means of piece count, stock number, quality control, etc.) incoming material
- Move incoming material as rapidly as possible to its assigned storage area, or point of use within the plant.

These objectives require a certain number of paperwork transactions and other clerical functions in order to properly control all incoming materials.

Documenting Truck and Rail Receipts

As soon as the incoming truck has been spotted at the proper (or convenient) truck dock location, you must record the following information:

- Truck's time of arrival
- Date
- Driver's name

- Trucking company
- Bill(s) of lading numbers

The above documentation is necessary in order to provide an audit trail for the purpose of tracing material. When the truck has been unloaded, the time the unloading was finished must be entered into the log. This information is useful when demurrage charges must be verified. The same but separate documentation should be maintained for railroad freight cars.

Identifying Materials

In order to receive and store materials expeditiously all incoming merchandise must be clearly and rapidly identified. In your periodic plant inspection tours you should verify that all incoming materials are tagged or labeled with *legible information* despite the fact that the data are stenciled, handwritten, or barcoded.

NOTE: Without violating the chain of command, the receiving department must communicate the requirement for legible and complete information for all incoming materials with the purchasing department, since it is this department that negotiates specification requirements with your company's suppliers.

As part of the purchasing specification the following information is mandatory:

- Purchase order number
- Complete part number
- Number of pieces in each package or the unit of measure
- Date the material was packed (month, day, year)
- Gross weight of the package in pounds and metric
- Designation of latest model or engineering change number
- Supplier's name, address, supplier code number, and code indicating what supplier plant produced the material

Verifying Packing Lists and Due-ins

In addition to the identification and labeling requirements of the purchasing specification, the supplier must include a packing list with every shipment. The packing list indicates what should be received and the total quantity. This list is absolutely essential in order for the receiving clerk, or checker, to accept the shipment. It may take several forms:

- computer printout
- typed list
- barcoded list
- optical character list
- tape

After the receiving clerk logs in the shipment, the due-in board can be adjusted and the accounts payable office can be notified. The due-in board is a graphic display for a limited number of due-ins. This manual device serves to expedite delinquent shipments in small operations. Where the number of due-ins is fairly heavy this type of information can be stored internally in a computer. The computer can summarize receiving activity and periodic printouts can alert both the purchasing expediter and the receiving clerk of the necessity for prodding the supplier. In Just-In-Time manufacturing and in certain warehousing and distribution centers that have adopted the JIT methodology the graphic display and the computer follow-up may not be necessary.

USING COMPUTERS IN RECEIVING FOR CASH PAYBACKS

A dedicated computer, a PC, or a computer terminal in the receiving office will enable the receiving clerk to enter the packing list information directly into an on-line receiving system. When this happens the computer printer will automatically produce a ticket that can accompany the load. Even barcoded information can be produced to make data entry and processing of the due-ins faster and more precise, eliminating all of the manual transcription errors that can occur. As many tickets as there are loads can be produced automatically by the printer after the packing list information has been entered into the computer. The computer program should produce a stock ticket that will indicate where to store the load, or to what point within the plant the material should be directed.

Once this information from the packing list has been entered into the computer, the following events occur:

- Accounting department is apprised of the receipt of the material.
- Purchasing department is given a periodic printed report.
- Both accounting and purchasing may check on status of the materials by using their own respective terminals.

There are a number of off-the-shelf computer programs for receiving. The receiving functions described above can be adapted or spliced into any number of these programs, and the following deviations can also be included as "exception routines":

- partial incoming receivable—only a partial shipment is received
- hold for inspection
- defective shipment—identifies a shipment that will be returned to the supplier
- hold for price adjustment—indicates a defective shipment that will be accepted after a price adjustment is negotiated with the supplier
- damaged-in-transit—indicates a shipment that must be held for further disposition (a carrier or supplier packaging problem).

While there are a number of exception routines to contend with in any computer program, it is possible to find any number of effective programs for performing the larger part of the receiving clerical operation without reinventing the wheel.

PROCESSING BACK ORDERS EFFECTIVELY

If your receiving department is handling back orders effectively it is another good sign that your organization is working well. Since the major objective of the receiving group is to move incoming materials as quickly as possible to the point of use (or storage), back orders must be detected quickly as they are received. The back order must be flagged immediately upon arrival so that your receiving clerk does not inadvertently send it to storage rather than sending it directly to an assembly or production line, to an order picking line, or into the shipping department where it may be urgently needed to complete an order, and so forth.

In general, back orders are sent directly to shipping if an order is awaiting completion before shipment; however, it is sometimes better to send a customer a partial shipment rather than hold merchandise for back-ordered material.

When this lapse occurs, the customer should be warned beforehand that a partial order will be sent, in effect, obtaining the customer's permission to give him a short shipment. A weekly report on partial shipments with customer names, and so on, should be required from the shipping department so that you can monitor the frequency of these slips in service.

As standard operating procedure, your receiving department should have established the mechanics for flagging each due-in that contains back orders so that they may be handled expeditiously. In a computerized receiving operation the receiving system should scan the list of due-ins so that a move ticket will be produced indicating the urgency of each back order as it is received.

4

Receiving and Shipping Hazardous Materials

WHAT CONSTITUTES HAZARDOUS MATERIALS

By definition, a hazardous material is any toxic, corrosive, radioactive, flammable, or explosive substance. A substance is also considered hazardous if it is packaged in a container considered to be dangerous, for instance a pressurized can. According to law each supplier must comply with all local, state, and federal laws and regulations that apply to the labeling, shipping, storage, and handling of hazardous materials.

WARNING: Pressurized cans are considered hazardous materials, regardless of the contents; therefore, if any of your incoming or outgoing materials consist of these types of containers, by law, you are responsible for training your employees in the proper methods for handling, storing, labeling, and shipping these materials.

Title 49 of the Code of Federal Regulations (CFR) contains requirements for the training of personnel in the handling and shipping of hazardous materials. The regulations of 49CFR require that severe monetary penalties be exacted for failure to train personnel in the proper preparation of hazardous materials for shipment.

BASIC METHODS OF HANDLING HAZARDOUS MATERIALS

Determining the correct marking, labeling, packaging, and preparing shipping documents for hazardous materials is not simple. In fact, a logical, programmed sequence must be followed, and if the technician bypasses any phase of the program, it is highly likely that the results (requirements) obtained will be incorrect.

The following illustrates the proper procedure for deriving the necessary regulatory information:

First, the technician reviews 49CFR, "Subpart B"Tables of Hazardous Material, Their Description, Proper Shipping Name, Class, Label, Packaging and Other Requirements, Section 172.100," in which the purpose and use of the hazardous materials tables are described in detail. A copy of CFR Title 49 can be obtained by writing or calling the Government Printing Office, Washington D.C.

Then the technician locates the DOT (U.S. Department of Transportation) shipping name in 49CFR, Sec. 172.100 and 172.101. The first three columns give:

- the common name of the hazardous material
- the proper DOT shipping name
- the DOT hazard classification.

In some instances a hazardous material may not be listed under its common name. In this circumstance, the proper shipping name may be found by using the generic name based on the hazardous material's chemical family, its end use, or its hazard class. For example:

Column (1)	Column (2)	Column (3)
Common Name	Proper DOT *Shipping Name*	DOT Hazard *Classification*
Pitch Oil	Creosote, Coal Tar	Combustible Liquid

WARNING: If the material appears to meet more than one DOT class definition, the highest one on the list in Section 173.2(a) of 49CFR is the one to be assigned unless the exceptions in Sec. 173.2(b) apply. When a material is classified using the highest classification definition, the other classifications cannot be disregarded: it must comply with the regulations as specified in Sec. 172.402, "Additional Labeling Requirements."

The classification definitions are located in 49CFR, Sec. 173.0, as shown in Table 4-1.

Table 4-1. Hazardous materials classifications and definition references.

Classification	Definition
Combustible Liquid	173.115(b)
Compressed Gas	173.300(a)
Corrosive Material	173.240
Etiologic Agent*	173.386
Explosives	173.58, 88, 100
Flammable Compressed Gas	173.300(b)
Irritating Materials	173.381
Nonflammable Gas	173.300
Organic Peroxide	173.151(a)
ORM—A, B, C, D**	173.500, 1200
Oxidizer	173.151
Poison A	173.389

Flammable Liquid	173.115(a)
Poison B	173.343
Radioactive Material	173.389

---

*Etiologic agent is defined as a viable microorganism, or its toxin, which causes or may cause human disease and is limited to those agents listed in 42CFR 72.25(c) of the regulations of the Department of Human Resources.

**ORM means Other Regulated Materials that do not meet the Department of Transportation definition for the other hazardous materials classes, but do possess enough hazardous characteristics to require some regulation.

Labeling Hazardous Materials

Labeling instructions are covered in Subpart E of 49CFR Sec. 172.400. The required label information may be found under column (4) of the Hazardous Materials Table of Sec. 172.101, 49CFR.

When a material that is corrosive is not listed in the Hazardous Materials Table but meets the definition of Poison B, the material must be labeled "Corrosive Material," and "Poison B," as explained in Sec. 172.402 of 49CFR.

Exceptions to the Hazardous Materials Labeling Requirements

Column 5(a) of the Hazardous Materials Table mentioned above contains specific references to sections of the CFR for "exceptions." These exceptions usually apply to limited quantities of the substance in question. Table 4-2 indicates general types of exceptions based upon the volume of product to be shipped and the type of packaging that is used. This packaging is DOT-approved and differs only from DOT specification packages or containers simply because they are not fully specified in Part 178 of 49CFR. When packaging materials in accordance with these exceptions relief is given from labeling *except for air shipments,* and from using a DOT specification package.

Table 4-2.

Hazard Classification	**Exceptions**
Flammable Liquids	173.118
Flammable Solids, oxidizing materials, and organic peroxide	173.153
Corrosive Materials	173.244
Compressed Gases: flammable gas and nonflammable gas	173.306
Poison B Liquids	173.345
Poison B Solids	173.364

Many limited-quantity exceptions include reference to an ORM-D (consumer commodity) class that allows further exceptions if the commodity meets the criteria for reclassification in Sec. 173.500 and 173.1200. Commodity reclassification paragraphs are shown in Table 4-3.

Table 4-3.

Hazard Classification	ORM-D Reference
Flammable Liquids	173.118(d)
Corrosive Liquids	173.244(b)
Corrosive Solids	173.244(b)
Flammable Solids	173.153(c)
Oxidizers	173.153(c)
Organic Peroxides	173.153(c)
Poison B Liquids	173.345(b)
Poison B Solids	173.364(b)
Compressed Gases	173.306(a)

Unless one of the specific ORM-D exceptions in Table 4-3 applies, then no further exceptions are allowed for reclassification. The ORM-D category has a gross weight (maximum) limitation of 65 pounds per package.

Packaging Hazardous Materials

If the material quantities or type of packaging do not qualify for the exceptions, it is necessary to follow the instructions for the specific type of packaging required. The references leading to the packaging directions may be found in column (5)(b) of the Hazardous Materials Table, quoted above. The sections listed in column (5)(b) specify the approved methods for packaging and packing materials (packaging is the interior wrap, and packing refers to the exterior wrap). The sections in question do not give any relief from marking, labeling, or from providing the correct shipping papers unless there are provisions for a specific exception.

Packing of Containers

There are weight limitations for DOT containers, as follows:

Specified DOT containers must be embossed on the head with raised marks, or by embossing or die stamping on the footing of drums. In addition, printed symbols must be placed in rectangular borders for fiberboard boxes, in the following manner:

DOT-37B*** or, DOT-12B***. Asterisks are to be replaced by the authorized gross weight at which the container type was tested, as an example: DOT-37B450, or DOT-12B40, and so forth. A DOT container should not be filled with regulated material to a weight greater than the design load limit.

ESTABLISHING EMERGENCY RESPONSE (ER) PROCEDURES FOR HAZARDOUS MATERIALS ACCIDENTS

If your plant is receiving or shipping hazardous materials there is a definite need for your personnel to know how to respond in the event of a hazardous materials incident. As an example, if a truck carrying hazardous materials is spotted at one of your receiving docks and suddenly begins smoking, or fire can be clearly seen in its cargo, what can you or should you and your personnel be expected to do? If the truck manifest is not readily available, what can you do to identify the contents of the truck? Surely your personnel cannot be expected to know the properties and hazards of every material that may be involved in an incident.

Establishing an Emergency Response Team

Establish your own company ER Team in order that the response to emergency situations occurs very much as a conditioned reflex. Backup members should be appointed to fill in if someone is missing.

WARNING: The ER team at your company is not (normally) trained or equipped to handle hazardous materials incidents directly. Your local fire department will perform the physical (i.e., hands-on) effort.

It is your responsibility to train your in-house ER team to carry out the following steps of your Emergency Response plan without hesitation:

- Immediately notify the fire department.
- Clear the area.
- Close the loading dock door.
- Have the trucker move the truck away from the loading dock, if possible.
- Determine what hazardous chemicals are present.
- Call the Chemical Transportation Emergency Center (CHEMTREC) as soon as possible and provide the names of the hazardous substance and shipper.

NOTE: CHEMTREC should be called for help in all chemical emergencies involving spills, leaks, fire, or exposure. *Call toll-free 800-424-9300 day or night.* (In Washington, D.C. the number is 483-7616; outside the U.S. call (202) 483-7616.) CHEMTREC will place its response network into action at once. It can provide emergency information on the hazardous substance, notify the chemical manufacturer to send trained assistance, work with the fire department, provide the hospital with first-aid information if exposure to individuals has occurred, and serve as the command center for follow-up action and clean up.

CHEMTREC is a public service of the Chemical Manufacturers' Association (CMA), which is a trade organization composed of chemical producers. Available 24 hours a day, it is the single most comprehensive repository of all of the technical information known regarding commercially obtainable chemical substances. The agency was established in 1971 with the main objective of assisting ER personnel in responding to emergencies by promptly providing information on the best ways to control hazardous chemical incidents and chemical substances that are unknown or unfamiliar to emergency response personnel.

Your ER team can find out what hazardous materials are in the truck from the shipping papers that the trucker is required by law to carry in the cab of the tractor. If for any reason these are not available, several ways to narrow down the specific identification may be found in the following places:

- Package markings
- Placards
- Four-digit identification numbers
- Types of shipping containers

When the above means for identifying a hazardous material(s) are unsuccessful, take the following steps:

- Try to obtain information from the trucker or your warehouse personnel.
- Call the shipper or manufacturer with the vehicle name and number.

To summarize, in order to reduce the harm of a potentially dangerous incident there are three factors that must be taken into account; these are:

- The name or names of the specific substance or substances must be known.
- The hazardous characteristics of the substance(s) must be understood.
- The necessary control actions must be taken. Linking whatever information the in-house ER team has obtained with the information and know-how of the fire department's ER team, and combining it with the technical assistance of CHEMTREC is extremely important in any emergency situation.

Refer to the DOT's Emergency Response Guidebook

Another excellent source of information that should be made available to your in-house ER team captain is the "Hazardous Materials, Emergency Response Guidebook," DOT P5800.3. The manual was developed for use by fire fighters, police, and other emergency services personnel as a guide for initial actions to be taken to protect themselves and the public when they are called upon to handle incidents involving hazardous materials. This booklet should not be construed as a guide for action for your in-house ER team (it is the fire department that will deal hands-on with the incident): it should only be read to focus attention on the hazardous nature of some chemical substances and to enhance the care with which hazardous chemicals are handled within the warehouse and distribution center.

The guidebook is composed of five sections:

- Sec. 1: a numerical index of hazardous materials (yellow pages) that lists the chemical substances by their 4-digit identification number. This is followed by the corresponding "Guide No." The "Guide Nos." are contained in a separate section of the guidebook (Sec. 3).

- Sec. 2: this section is cross-referenced to the first section since all of the chemical substances are arranged alphabetically by "Name of Material." The chemical name is followed on the same line by the "Guide No." and the "I.D. No."

- Sec. 3: this section is composed of a series of response guides organized according to single or multiple hazards. They describe the potential hazards of the substance, in abbreviated form, and they prescribe the initial, emergency action to be taken by the response team.

- Sec. 4: this section is a combined table of the minimum isolation and safe evacuation distances for removing unprotected people from the hazardous areas.

- Sec. 5: this section illustrates some of the most commonly used placards and provides a Guide Number (sec. 3 above) below each placard to indicate what hazard is present and what responsive action is immediately required.

Copies of this manual may be obtained from:

International Association of Fire Chiefs
Attention: ERG, 1329 18th St., N.W.
Washington, D.C. 20036

For further information on the subject of hazardous materials that would be of value to a plant manager in a warehousing or distribution center environment, see *Handling and Management of Hazardous Materials and Waste,* by T. H. Allegri, P.E., Chapman and Hall, New York, London, 1986.

5

Shipping Operations for Warehousing and Distribution

PHYSICAL ASPECTS OF SHIPPING

The essence of good management lies in the ability of the plant manager to achieve a high degree of productivity by maintaining employee morale at a superior level and instilling a spirit of team work throughout the organization. There are a number of ways you can attempt to do this. Encouraging a friendly rivalry between the shipping and receiving departments can serve a useful purpose in increasing productivity and in boosting morale.

Production scoreboards in both departments can be used to good advantage by letting employees know where they stand in relation to some of the targets and objectives defined by plant management. For example, "tons shipped," or "line items shipped," and the like, have a significant effect on managing the shipping department. (The receiving department should have targets that are appropriate to that department, viz: tonnage, line items, dollar volume of receivables, number of trucks unloaded, and so forth.)

WARNING: The shipping department is the single functional area of the plant that is most susceptible to collusion involving theft. For this reason, the physical characteristics of the shipping department and the necessary paperwork and control have to be integrated to maintain the greatest degree of accountability for every piece of material that passes across the shipping dock.

Designing Shipping Space Effectively

Warehouse and distribution center shipping areas tend to be larger in square feet of floor space than receiving areas. There are several reasons for this since loads are set-out awaiting carriers, or partial loads are assembled, sometimes at a relatively slow rate. Bearing this in mind, the product mix of materials that must be handled by the shipping department is a determining factor in deciding how to arrange this area. It may be necessary to provide pallet storage racks or bin shelves, if a significantly large number of smaller containers or packages are to be combined with bigger unit loads. If you are considering this, the placement of the racks and bins must be handled judiciously so as not to interfere with good material flow.

Also, if a portion of the shipping function is to be devoted to boxing or crating, then you must provide space for this ordinarily dusty operation in some relatively remote, well-ventilated but contiguous area. The same objectives can be applied to paint booths and protective-coating activities such as cosmoline and grease (oil) dipping. Ideally, it is much more cost effective to plan areas such as these at the end of the production line, rather than have them spill over into the shipping department. It makes more sense to package a product, paint it, or give it a protective coating as the last operation at the end of a fabrication line, rather than to place it into a temporary container prior to packaging it and then have to remove it from the temporary container. This double handling is a wasteful practice that could be eliminated by better planning of the production facilities in the initial stages of plant layout.

Integrating Materials Handling with Dock Design

In Chapter 3, on Designing Space Effectively, all of the elements and caveats that pertain to receiving can be applied to shipping:

- Door sizes
- Dock height levels
- Overhead lighting
- Dock lights
- Desk stanchions
- Enclosed docks
- Chocks and stands

Similarly, dockboards, both mechanical (manual) and electro-mechanical, are good to have, not only because they are safer than the old-fashioned dockplate but they permit a more efficient use of labor and labor hours.

In addition to the elements of hardware discussed above, the shipping area should be designed so that it will be easily accessible from all parts of the plant. Thus, as loads are built up on the shipping floor they can flow directly into the carrier as expeditiously as possible.

If, in the early stages of development, shipping mechanization has been sidelined for one reason or another, make every effort to ensure that future plans include some type of conveyorization or mechanical handling. With this in mind, advise your planning staff to guard against boxing themselves in so that future mechanization may be virtually impossible to accomplish. As an example, columns or other structural elements could obstruct the routing of a future conveyor system. Future planning may also require projections of volumes to be handled with particular attention being given to whether or not tractor-trains, driverless tractors, in-floor dragchain conveyors and the like may be feasible in the space allocated for these systems.

Spotting Carriers

You will remember that we noted the importance in receiving operations of being able to spot carriers at a particular truck or rail dock. It is just as important in shipping to have a specific carrier right at or near the outgoing shipment. Since most carriers are outloaded by forklift truck, it cuts down on travel distance and time. In addition, it tends to eliminate any possible cross-traffic that would occur if this rule were not strictly followed. The outgoing shipment should also be set out in one assigned location insofar as it is possible to do so, and the scheduling of incoming carriers should be accomplished with clocklike regularity.

NOTE: Check to see how your shipping supervisor performs his carrier scheduling:

- Shipping supervisors should maintain a log of carrier call-ups versus response time. If they don't they can't rate carrier performance properly.

- Carriers should be notified and warned when they do not respond quickly to a call for a vehicle or tractor.

Loading Carriers

The work of loading a tractor trailer when pallet loads are uniform in size is not too difficult a task for an experienced forklift operator. On the other hand if the freight to be placed onboard the trailer varies in size, weight, and configuration, loading becomes an art. Most motor truck drivers have sufficient skill in placing heavy loads in their trailers; however, some drivers do not possess adequate skill nor have they been properly trained in load placement. Weight distribution in over-the-road carriers is extremely critical, and truck loading of certain products requires skilled supervision if there is much difference in the weight (density) of materials being outloaded. An amateur has no business in such loading since it would be a mistake of serious consequences if for example the heaviest items were placed in the tail end of the trailer. It is often possible to obtain assistance from the trucking agent and you should not hesitate to explain this to your shipping supervisor. Also, if you have sufficient volume to justify the requirement, the shipping department could very well support a trucking agent in residence at no extra cost to you as a shipper.

Proper Dock Equipment

Lighting levels on the shipping floor and at the dock should be at least as high as required on the receiving dock. (Please review Chapter 3 since the functions of shipping and receiving have much in common in terms of equipment and methods.)

THE USE OF MECHANIZATION IN SHIPPING OPERATIONS

Mechanizing shipping operations has proceeded with inexorable certainty over the past several decades, and a number of attempts have been made to improve the effectiveness of outloading in all types of physical distribution and manufacturing companies. A two-pronged approach has been used in attempting to increase the productivity of the shipping function:

- The use of conventional, off-the shelf or commercially available equipment

- The use of computer driven equipment in conjunction with high-tech customized equipment or other forms of mechanization and automatic identification data entry (primarily bar coding)

Conveyors

The goal of the shipping department in any distribution center is that when the carrier arrives at the dock all of the material may be outloaded without the necessity of performing a *second* order-picking operation. In other words, all of the material for a specific shipment should have a prescribed space. The moment that order selection has to take place on the shipping floor, it spells the beginning of wasteful and time consuming chaos. To avoid this dilemma most nonmechanized shipping departments store materials only one tier high over most of the available floor space and in the process waste a great deal of the air-rights or cubic content of the facility.

As an alternative to the "prescribed space plan" where locations for materials are assigned and the "one-tiered spread" in which orders are placed on the shipping room floor in only one layer or pallet-load high, some shipping departments have used in-floor and on-the-floor conveyors, skate-wheel conveyors, and both gravity-type and powered roller conveyors. The in-floor conveyors are powered; however, the roller conveyors may be the gravity-type or powered, depending on the volume of output desired. The powered conveyors are usually controlled by a push-button station at the front or off-loading end of the conveyor line. Skate-wheel conveyors are always used with relatively light loads and are nonpowered, gravity flow types.

The conveyor lines in the above systems usually use one or more dedicated lines for each carrier, more often than not with a specific destination.

NOTE: When installing any type of conveyor system in shipping, consider the following factors:

- When preparing the layout take care to avoid obstructing the traffic flow.
- Wherever possible use the company's present industrial powered equipment unless the tradeoffs of scrapping obsolete equipment are carefully planned.
- Storing materials in a random sequence on conveyor lines requires that every item (or pallet load) be instantly retrievable by the power trucker; that is, the forklift operator must be able to get at the load and remove it from the conveyor in order to place it into the carrier. If material is scheduled on the conveyor line in the trucker's first-in, last-out sequence then it has to be scheduled onto the conveyor line in that order. The trucker and shipping dispatcher need a means for accomplishing this task when mixed destinations are involved.

NOTE: When the shipping floor is nonmechanized (i.e., the *prescribed space plan* has not been established for one reason or another) and the *one-tiered spread* is how the shipping department chooses to operate, then a *locator system* should be used to locate materials that are placed in the shipping set-out area. Of course, the floor has to be partitioned off and numbered or lettered by set-out, bay area.

When conveyors are used in the set-out area a locator system can be very elementary; for example, a pigeon-holed cupboard with each cubicle representing a conveyor line. When bar coding or radio frequency tags are used as the shipping labels for each load, finding the correct materials is simplified.

Tractor Trains

Warehouse tractors can be powered by gas, liquid propane internal combustion engines or electric battery. They usually haul several trailers at a time and are fairly versatile pieces of industrial equipment. Gas and LP gas powered vehicles are widely used where materials must be hauled a relatively long distance or where these vehicles serve as the connecting link among several buildings. LP gas and battery powered vehicles are preferred where a considerable amount of tractor-trailer time must be spent inside the confines of one building because of the noxious fumes emitted by straight gas tractors.

When tractor-trailer trains are used to support the shipping function, consider the following factors:

- If palletized material is to be held on the trailers until offloading into a carrier a large amount of shipping floor space is wasted.

- A better use of the tractor-train is to use it to transport materials into the shipping department from other areas within the plant and to off-load the trailers immediately into their set-out areas.

- Since tractor-trains require a large amount of space to turn around, only straight-line runs into the shipping department should be contemplated.

- Right angle turns with a tractor-train consume less floor space than a U-turn, but remember that *tracking* occurs so that the corner of a turn will be cut increasingly as the number of trailers pulled increases.

Automatic Guided Vehicles (AGVs)

AGVs or driverless tractors have been used in warehouses and factories since the 1940s. Initially they were rather slow in establishing themselves as a reliable and cost effective means for transportation. At the beginning their guidance systems were marginal; some of the earlier manufacturers even used war surplus guidance mechanisms in an attempt to lower their high purchase prices. Fortunately, over the intervening decades reliability has improved considerably. Some of the advantages and disadvantages are the following:

- The conditions of the floors have to be fairly good and uniform in surface treatment. Bumps, potholes, large cracks, railroad tracks and the like present special, although not insurmountable problems. In other words, fix them!

- AGVs can be readily sabotaged or damaged by disgruntled employees.

- They are relatively high priced and require regular maintenance attention.

- The savings in labor hours can sometimes justify their use.

- They are especially effective when integrated into a larger, mechanized system.

- Some AGVs are capable of being used as warehouse tractors, and can be taken off their guidance lines for manual use.

Towconveyors

Large tonnages can be handled easily using in-floor dragchain conveyors that are commonly called *towconveyors*, primarily because their carts are towed around on a fixed path by an in-floor dragchain. They are used extensively in large warehouses and distribution centers as well as in manufacturing where vast tonnages must be handled daily. Towconveyor carts are comprised of a four-wheeled, warehouse trailer with a drop-pin on the front end that engages with a pusher dog element of the drop-forged chain conveyor operating in a track in the warehouse floor. The towconveyor is essentially driverless since once the front end pin has been dropped into the track slot its operation is automatic, even to the point of being pulled to and through various spurs, by means of an indexing mechanism mounted on the front end. In addition to the drop-pin, the front end is equipped with a bumper mechanism that will release the pin from the pusher dog in the track, thus setting the cart brakes automatically and making it possible to stop the cart in a queue. When the preceding cart moves ahead, the drop-pin will again engage the pusher dog and be pulled to its prescribed (indexed) location. Towconveyor travel speeds are set fairly low, usually at human walking speeds not exceeding three miles per hour, in order to avoid pedestrian and vehicular accidents.

Advantages and disadvantages may be apparent from the following:

- Where tonnages are significant it is possible to justify the ROI (return on investment).

- There are thousands of successful towconveyor installations worldwide.

- A towconveyor installation comprising motor drives, controllers, sensing units, panel boxes, wiring, and so forth may be less than the cost of the several hundred drop-pin carts required to complete the system, since the carts themselves are expensive.

- The main disadvantage is that mistakes in laying out and installing the track are difficult and costly to remedy, since the track is laid in concrete in a metal trough. (See a further discussion of tow conveyors and plant layout in Chapter 15.)

Overhead Dragchain Conveyors

Overhead conveyors, monorail conveyors, overhead dragchain conveyors are essentially the same; and warehouse carts are pulled by center poles, or carriers are pulled by dogs on the conveyor chain. The degree of sophistication of overhead conveyors is comparable to that of AGVs or in-floor towconveyor systems with switching on spur lines or dumping contents at designated destinations, and the like.

A review of advantages and disadvantages follows:

- Rerouting this type of conveyor system is not as expensive as changing the layout of an in-floor towconveyor.

- Neither changing the overhead conveyor or the in-floor conveyor should be taken lightly; such changes involve considerable expense.

- The necessary overhead structure of the building, overhead trusses, or steel frames placed along the path of the conveyor, limit the application (installation) of this type of conveyor.

- While there are numerous installations of in-floor dragchain conveyors, there are probably more overhead conveyor installations because the overhead type can be scaled down to smaller applications with a satisfactory ROI.

Summary of Mechanization Systems

For the purposes of this summary we shall omit the mechanized and nonmechanized conveyors laid out on the shipping floor, but concern ourselves with the tractor-trains, AGVs, towconveyors, and the overhead conveyors used as transportation means to shipping, as follows:

- Towconveyors—used on large volume movements only.
- Driverless tractors (AGVs)—used on small to large volumes.
- Tractor-trains—used on both small and large movements.
- Overhead conveyors—used on small to large movements.

6

Optimizing the Use of Computers in Shipping Operations and Handling In-process Materials

ELECTRONIC DATA INTERCHANGE (EDI)

In the past few decades high technology concepts developed in other fields have been successfully adopted to help move merchandise across the shipping floor and to eliminate the bane of every warehouse and distribution center—excessive paperwork. Thus, by eliminating as much of the manual clerical details as possible, we can contribute to increased productivity and thereby increase profitability.

One of the ways to decrease paperwork and, paradoxically, simultaneously increase the communications effectiveness among carriers, suppliers, and the distribution center and its branches has been the technology of Electronic Data Interchange, or EDI as it is commonly named. Although carriers have been slower to adopt this new methodology, important air and motor freight companies are jumping on the bandwagon. Three such companies are Burlington Air Express, Delta Airlines, and Consolidated Freightways.

Garment manufacturers and major clothing retailers have also banded together to enhance communications, minimize errors, and shorten response times between the manufacturing entity and the retail clothing outlet via transportation channels. As a result of this cooperative effort, the clothing industry promoted standards for automatic identification and data communication by means of their Voluntary Interindustry Communication Standards Committee (VICS). One of the problems the carriers are faced with, of course, is antitrust legal action; however, this hasn't deterred Consolidated Freightways and for the time being it is enjoying the competitive position as part of the communications link in the garment and other industries.

Advantages of the EDI concept are significant:

- electronic purchase orders
- barcoded carton tags

- electronic invoicing
- real-time status reports
- tracking shipments
- automatic data collection
- advanced shipping notices which contain: contents, value, colors, mode of transport, receiving branch, and so on.

In addition to the above advantages, EDI makes it possible to ship smaller quantities more often directly to retailers with a greater degree of precision. The precision with which shipments are made is important because if a carrier loses one of these smaller shipments to a retailer, it is more disastrous than if the carrier misdelivers (or loses) one carton of a larger order for a distribution center. When a carrier implements the EDI methodology, a parcel can be tracked through the system by means of automatic data collection (automatic identification—mainly barcoding) and the information can be relayed via computer much more efficiently than by other means.

An advantage to the carrier that makes a good selling point in promoting EDI is that by obtaining advance shipping notices the carrier can consolidate more loads, thereby saving money in the bargain.

VICS is using the UCC-128 Serial Shipping Container Code as a standard means of data entry. The nine-digit, barcoded number is placed directly on the shipping container by each manufacturer. The digits are not significant unto themselves, they merely identify the contents of the container so that when the manufacturer electronically scans that number at the shipping dock an EDI message is sent to the recipient retailer in the form of an advanced shipping notice; thus the recipient knows instantaneously what is being shipped: the entire contents of the shipment and other information such as value, sizes, models, colors, method of shipment, and the like.

Another benefit of EDI is that each time a retailer sells an item, the barcoded tag (which is attached) is scanned by the salesperson using a barcode scanner. This data is transmitted via computer directly to the manufacturer for stock replenishment. By this method inventories can be kept to a minimum with a subsequent reduction in cost.

According to the Bekins Specialty Distribution Service, a major trucking company, EDI allows manufacturers and retailers the opportunity to have their computers "talk" directly to the Bekins computers using software developed by the Transportation Data Coordinating Committee (TDCC), or Bekins' own communications network (BECOM). Simply put, there isn't a faster or more accurate way to place, change, track, or invoice a customer's order. The minute the data is entered in the shipping company's computer, the Bekins truck is ready to pick up the order. A completed bill of lading will be prepared by Bekins and arrive with their truck.

The EDI program transmits shipment data to the shipper's computer around the clock. To obtain the status of a shipment, the company's mainframe computer is accessed using the appropriate assigned company reference number. Inasmuch as the Bekins computer reads each individual contract, price rating is accurate and automatic, which has the added benefit of permitting electronic invoicing that eliminates paperwork and constant auditing.

EDI and Automatic Identification (Auto ID)

Automatic identification has grown mightily with a large part of its emphasis on supermarket checkout. That is really only the tip of the iceberg, however, since Auto ID has penetrated deeply into almost every facet of the transportation and distribution industries. When EDI is integrated with Auto ID it forms the basis of what has come to be known as a Quick Response program (QR). The results of this phenomenon are:

- Portable data collection in warehousing
- Use of remote terminals at collection points in all parts of the warehouse
- Use of radio frequency terminals provides real-time communication.
- Auto ID can be used by carriers to track and report freight movement throughout the various points of transit.
- Each time a piece of merchandise is moved the event is noted and this information can be used to update status reports.
- Inventory data can be automatically relayed back to suppliers to initiate reorders.
- The tracking of sales can be recorded as they occur.
- Retailers and wholesalers can obtain up-to-the-minute sales information.
- Inventory status becomes a matter of real-time information.

LOCATOR SYSTEMS

When the product mix of materials to be shipped is fairly low or when materials are not held for excessive lengths of time on the shipping floor (as they can be sometimes in accumulating orders for an overseas consignment), then a shipping locator system may not be required. The simplest types of designation of locations on a shipping floor are:

- Overhead signs
- Warehouse bay markers
- Any combination of signs and floor location markers

There are many shipping departments, however, where the use of simple visual locator systems does not work, such as when orders consist of many small and large packages and when smaller merchandise has to be combined with pallet-loads of materials, and the like. Also, sometimes shipping documentation for various orders requires special handling and cannot be processed in the usual routine procedure and must be kept in an up-to-date and current fashion.

NOTE: You should inspect shipping department operations periodically and check shipping documents with materials that are set out on the shipping floor. You can usually tell after only a cursory examination what the history of these materials is. For example, the length of time materials remain on the floor, on the average, should be determined by a random sampling of materials. If this review is not satisfactory, that is, if time on the floor can be measured in two, three, or more days, you may have to establish a limitation such as a 24-hour or 48-hour turnaround criterion.

Once you have established this objective for your shipping department you can use your computerized locator system for reporting status. (See Chapter 3 where we delineated receiving floor criteria.) If your shipping department manager cannot adhere to this strict regimen, you have little choice but to reorganize this department.

Barcoding and Other ID Methods

Depending on the industry segment in which your warehousing and distribution operation finds itself, the barcode labeling of merchandise may comprise Code 39, Interleaved 2 of 5, or the Uniform Product Code (UPC) which is used throughout the food and supermarket industry.

NOTE: If you find that you are receiving different merchandise with more than one of the standard barcodes imprinted thereon, you may be advised to adopt a data entry system that can automatically convert each barcode type through its own programming system without having to use separate equipment to read the different codes. Many bar-code scanners on the market can now do this readily.

By having barcode labels, RF tags (radio frequency) or OCR labels (optical character recognition) on materials entering the shipping department, a satisfactory means for locating and tracking this merchandise is available. For example, as merchandise is received into the shipping department, a clerk can scan the labels of the shipping containers and note the floor location into a hand-held data entry device. Every time the merchandise has to be moved the new location is coded into the shipping terminal either in real time or in a batch unloading method, where periodically during the day the hand-held device is downloaded.

Packing Lists

A packing list can be generated as the outgoing materials are loaded into the carrier or prior to loading-out by means of scanning each barcode label in the shipment. If the packing list is prepared prior to loading-out, then as the material is loaded into the carrier it is barcode scanned to ascertain that all of the materials on the packing list are, indeed, in the shipment.

Auto ID labels placed on every separate piece of outgoing material will help prevent collusion between the trucker and the shipping department personnel, because each bill of lading has to be certified as having been received by the trucker and at the receiving end by the recipient.

NOTE: Where a captive fleet of motor trucks is maintained, and where full truck loads of materials are shipped, truck seals may be used in order to prevent over-the-road stopovers and outright theft.

Dispatching

The use of Auto ID and EDI has simplified status reporting so that the term Quick Response, or QR, will soon become second nature to both receiving and shipping departments. The advance notice of shipments is a boon to recipients, but both shippers and receivers are constantly in need of having to know where their shipments are and when they will arrive—sometimes to the very hour of arrival time.

Satellite electronic communication provides an accurate method for obtaining timely location reporting, and most carriers can provide excellent status information. Some carriers even permit shippers direct access to their information systems.

Computerized Routing Systems

Another methodology that has gained increasing favor among private fleet operators and common carriers which has the capability of benefiting shippers is the use of computerized routing systems. Using Operations Research (OR) techniques (a form of mathematical linear programming science) it is possible to dispatch customers' orders in the best and most economical delivery sequence within each truck route. With this methodology it is possible to maximize the use of vehicle capacity and minimize the truck miles traveled by examining each recipient's geographic location and order size. A great deal of backtracking and backhauling can be eliminated using OR techniques in this fashion. The benefits from this technique are obvious:

- Improved customer service through faster delivery
- Fewer miles traveled, better cost containment

Another name for this dispatching method is Dynamic Routing. The method permits changes:

- in daily routing
- in order patterns
- it can ensure that the same driver gets the same route and delivers to a particular destination.

Highly developed geographic coding systems allow shippers to pinpoint customer locations for routing purposes. The systems indicate geographic coordinates for the customer addresses and permit the operator to point to a location on a computerized map when the computer doesn't recognize the address.

NOTE: In the near future it will be possible to link routing systems with satellite location systems so that users will be able to plot current (up-to-the-minute) location with vehicle routes and schedules.

HANDLING IN-PROCESS MATERIALS

In order to obtain the maximum output from the various inputs that are made to your enterprise (i.e., from invested capital by the entrepreneurs, the owners, or shareholders), you have to completely and intelligently integrate all of the activities that make up the complex. In order to do this you have to visualize the systems approach concept and instill this type of thinking in all echelons of management from the top to the bottom of your company.

You are well aware by this time that change starts from the top! And your managers should be encouraged to develop this rationale. How well your managers develop and adopt this philosophy depends in large measure on how well they handle the various inputs at their disposal, for example:

- **Labor**—Labor inputs comprise the available labor hours from all of the employees in the group—factory workers, clerical assistance, supervisory, maintenance, and the like.

- **Skills**—Skills are probably the single most important ingredient (after money) of all of the factors involved in the systems approach directed towards evolving the objective of the enterprise that is, profit. Managers who uses all of the skills (the combined intelligence of their staff) at their disposal is in the best position to achieve this objective.

NOTE: You cannot adopt the systems approach to in-process handling unless you are constantly aware of all of the input ingredients involved.

- **Raw Materials**—These can be purchased finished, semi-finished, or raw (raw materials of a distribution center would be finished and packaged; raw materials in a manufacturing-production plant might be steel plate, bar stock, dress goods, or latex).

- **Services**—These are the inputs provided by lawyers, tax accountants, medical staff, consultants, and so forth.

- **Utilities**—Include gas, electricity, oil, water, steam and anything that powers the enterprise.

- **Equipment**—Encompasses all of the tools of production, including materials handling equipment and computers.

Controlling In-process Materials

First let's start with a definition of in-process materials handling:

> In-process handling is the movement of materials from point-to-point as they move within the production or order-selection (order-picking) cycle.

In manufacturing and production, sporadic movement of materials as well as storage and retrieval elements occur. There are similarities in processing materials in both the warehousing of a manufacturing plant and in the warehousing that occurs in a distribution center. As an example of elements in manufacturing entities, raw or purchased finished materials are received and then transported to one of four destinations, as follows:

- All of the material may be held in temporary storage awaiting inspection, pricing, and so forth.

- Some of the material may be placed in short-, or long-term storage until it is required.

- Some or all of the material may be transported directly to assembly lines to become part of a complete product or a subcomponent part.

- Raw material can be transported to a production line where it may be machined, and the like.

Approximately 95% of the time that material is in a manufacturing plant it is usually in the storage mode, being transported or being otherwise handled. Only about 5% of the time is it actually undergoing some form of machining, or processing (the value-added phase of its life).

NOTE: Since most of the time that material is in a manufacturing plant it is either being warehoused or handled, this is where the most money is to be made by examining in-process control.

The control of in-process materials is one of the key elements in the systems approach to materials handling for warehousing and distribution operations. Keeping this in mind regard the following as essential factors:

- Know how much material is on hand at all times. In other words, your inventory records should be accurate. Check this periodically with your inventory control personnel. Obtain monthly statements of inventory precision from cyclic inventory tallies.

- Know where your material is at all times. This means that the locator system should be as close to the 100% accuracy mark as possible. Since warehousing is your game, you should make random checks to determine how precise your locator system really is!

Manual and Computerized Systems for Data Collection

In some very small plants manual systems for data collection may still be used effectively; however, where there are 10 or more employees, the use of PC computer terminals that permit data entry by a barcode or the employee's payroll number has become standard procedure. Collect the following data:

- Quantity produced
  —how many pieces fabricated
  —how many line items picked
  —how many packages wrapped
- The amount of time required
- An indication that the last job has been completed and a new job is to be started.

Since there is a wide range in data collection devices and methods there is hardly any problem in customizing or achieving off-the-shelf hardware and systems to suit almost every budget. Although data collection for in-process materials status reporting, production information, and the like does not require very much in the way of materials handling equipment to accomplish this task, it is possible to combine information with materials handling equipment to achieve worthwhile results, especially when high volumes of transactions are concerned. Thus, another method for controlling in-process parts and obtaining production information, viz., in terms of line items shipped or processed, is to place the material in a high-rise high-density stacker-crane retrieval installation and use either a punch (Hollerith) card or tape-controlling means, or electrically interconnect the hardware of the stacker-crane with a process-control computer.

7

Order Picking in Physical Distribution Operations

TYPES OF ORDER PICKING OPERATIONS

The direct labor functions in physical distribution facilities are found in four specific areas:

- Receiving
- Shipping
- Order selection (order picking)
- Packing

NOTE: There is a certain similarity between these functions and in-process handling in the manufacturing activity.

For the convenience of discussing the various facets of order picking the following explanations serve to differentiate the three types of order picking operations that take place in a typical warehouse:

- **Bulk**—loads go in and out of storage in the same container, unitized pallet load, or skid.
- **Break-bulk**—the large unit load is broken down, and large portions, individual packages, or pieces are weighed or counted from the original unit load. Depending on the size of the unit load, this break-up of the original load may occur several more times until there is nothing left of the original load, or the remaining pieces are moved into bin storage.
- **Bin**—bulk merchandise is broken down into its component parts, individual cartons, or pieces, and usually hand-counted or weight-counted as a means for filling a customer order.

CHOOSING BIN SHELVING

Since almost any small shop equipped with a press brake can make bin shelving there are many different makes of bin shelving on the market, and the pricing is fairly reasonable because of the competition among suppliers. Most bin shelving can be categorized into four different load classes, as follows:

Class		Shelf Load
Class 1 (light)	unreinforced	up to 200#
Class 1-A (moderate)	front reinforcement	up to 450#
Class 2 (medium)	front and rear reinforcement	up to 600#
Class 3 (heavy duty)	front, rear, and center reinforcement	over 600#

(See Figure 7-1 for an illustration showing cross-sectional views of bin shelving and the use of reinforcements to increase the load capacity of shelving materials.)

Bin shelving is sometimes (less satisfactorily) classified by the type of upright post that is used to support the shelves. The upright is important because it is the main load carrying component of the unit. Uprights are classified into four principal categories, and since there are many suppliers there are many variations of these basic styles as follows:

- Tubular
- Structural iron or T-section
- Angle
- Beaded

(See Figure 7-2 which depicts the four basic styles of bin shelving upright posts.)

Shelf load capacities also may vary, based on the design of the upright posts, gauge of the upright post steel, and the type of clips used to hold each shelf in position on the upright post.

Your selection of upright posts will be influenced by the type of merchandise to be stored in these units. For example, if you are storing textiles, bins with structural steel T-section posts are not desirable because of the possibility of snagging materials on the somewhat rougher edges of the posts. In this instance, tubular posts (see Figure 7-2) would be more appropriate.

NOTE: While the industry standard for the upright posts is 7'-3", higher or lower sections are also available. Therefore, when comparing quotations from different manufacturers, the upright post height should be taken into consideration.

Most bin shelving is made of 18-gauge steel, which after degreasing is given a coat of gray shop enamel. However, if color coding or decor requires it, most suppliers will provide custom colors at an added cost. Other standards involve shelf size, either 24 or 36 inches wide, and depths range from 12 inches to 18, 24, and 36 inches. Depths of 48 inches or deeper are rarely used except in commercial paper or art companies. The usual bin section is 87 inches high although higher units may be obtained.

The sheet steel from which bin shelving is fabricated is usually (light) 18-gauge and it usually pays in the long run to have a front reinforcement usually made of 12-gauge steel (see Figure 7-1) inserted in the leading edge of the shelving, especially on the two bottom shelves of each bin section. There are two advantages in installing reinforcements:

- increase the load capacity of the shelf; and
- decrease the chance that the shelf will bend in the middle, because invariably stock pickers will stand on these two shelves to reach higher shelves in the bin section.

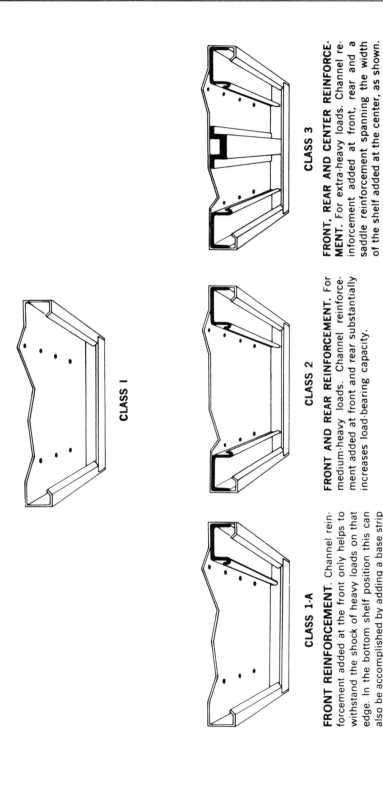

CLASS I

CLASS 1-A

FRONT REINFORCEMENT. Channel reinforcement added at the front only helps to withstand the shock of heavy loads on that edge. In the bottom shelf position this can also be accomplished by adding a base strip under a Class I shelf.

CLASS 2

FRONT AND REAR REINFORCEMENT. For medium-heavy loads. Channel reinforcement added at front and rear substantially increases load-bearing capacity.

CLASS 3

FRONT, REAR AND CENTER REINFORCE-MENT. For extra-heavy loads. Channel reinforcement added at front, rear and a saddle reinforcement spanning the width of the shelf added at the center, as shown. A pair of shelf side supports is also used.

Fig. 7-1: Cross-sectional views of bin shelving, showing an unreinforced shelf, and the methods used to increase load capacity.

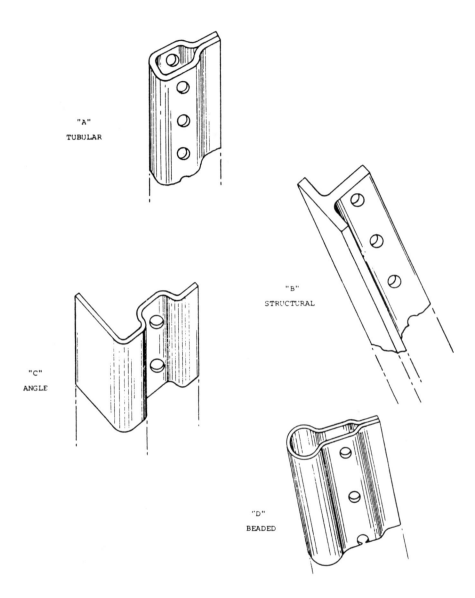

Fig. 7-2: Cross-sections of four basic types of bin shelving upright posts.

NOTE: If your bin sections are taller than 87" you might want to consider using front reinforcements on the three bottom tiers of your bin shelving. Despite the fact that your bin pickers ordinarily have to use rolling ladders to reach the top shelf levels, when a ladder isn't at hand they will stand on the first three bin shelves to reach the higher tiers.

WARNING: When comparing bids be alert to the fact that 12-gauge steel is the normal thickness of shelving reinforcements. When you buy new shelving with shelf reinforcements, it pays to make a random check of the completed installation to determine if all (on a sampling basis) of the reinforcements have been installed.

It will save you money if you can segregate your bin items by weight. By estimating the total load on a shelf for each item, you can put all of the light weight items (by volume) into light duty shelving and heavier materials can be placed into more strongly reinforced bin sections. If the total number of heavier materials is relatively low, say 10 to 15 percent or fewer of the total number of bin items, the bottom shelf of each bin section can be reserved for these items.

Choosing Bin Hardware—Clips and Label Holders

When you have the task of purchasing new bin shelving it is particularly imporant that you examine the clips that hold the shelves to the upright posts. They are of two types—relatively easy to assemble, and difficult to assemble. There is no better way to get your new bin group off to a wrong start than to purchase equipment on the basis of price alone. Therefore, you should satisfy yourself that the type of clip supplied with the shelf will be easy to assemble.

Some relatively inexpensive bin shelving is of the "open" type and the upright posts are cross-braced with steel straps on sides and back. There is nothing wrong with this type of shelving, but items may tend to collect a little more dust than with "closed" shelving, i.e., shelving with side panels and backs.

All shelving manufacturers punch the front faces of their shelves with holes for the installation of bin label holders. Many bin installations simply slap a pressure-sensitive label on the leading edge of the shelf. Ultimately this practice begins to look like the cheap operation it started out to be, and productivity suffers as a result. Be advised that some label holders are difficult to snap into place and are easily dislodged, especially on the bottom three tiers of the bin unit where the order pickers often step to reach the higher shelves.

The bin label should be printed in your office or by a printer on good quality white card stock with black waterproof ink. The type face of the labels should be as large as the label holder will allow so that the print will be clearly visible with the light provided in the order picking aisles.

Designing Bin Lighting

In many bin picking operations lighting and light levels appear to be an afterthought rather than something that must be designed into your order selection operation. As a general rule there are many bin operations where you are lucky to obtain 30 to 50 lumens measured at 30 inches above ground level. Managers should realize that they can improve productivity as a direct result of increasing light levels in bin picking operations. In stopwatch time studies conducted by the writer, increasing light levels above 50 lumens improved bin picking rates from 10 to 50 percent, and when light levels reached 100 lumens (at 30 inches above ground level) productivity soared to record levels, almost doubling picking rates. Good lighting levels also decrease fatigue, and where barcoding is not employed, order picking errors.

Fluorescent lighting fixtures should be supported by laying steel T-sections across the tops of the bins and fastening the fixtures to them. Egg-crate fluorescent covers should be a part of each fixture to shield order pickers or bin stockers from glare. Poor performance and poor morale are results of ignoring the proper arrangement of bin lighting.

Advantageous Bin Features

Continuous and Discontinuous Bin Units

Many shelving manufacturers can supply you with bin dividers or partitions if you desire to keep part numbers (items) separated. Also when ordering bin shelving you can start out with a section called a "starter unit," and add subsequent pairs of uprights to the starter unit. Each additional pair of uprights adds another bin section in a continuous sequence.

Unfortunately, if at some later date you wish to move the units, you must unload the shelves and disassemble the units—truly a time- and labor-consuming effort. Instead of using the "continuous" sections, use "discontinuous" sections (i.e., freestanding units with four corner uprights), so that you can move or rearrange bins without unloading the shelves and stripping or knocking down the bin sections. In general, even a fully stocked discontinuous type of bin section can be moved by a forklift truck by chiseling the forks under two back-to-back units of 36-inch wide bin sections, or four 24-inch wide bin sections.

Modifying Shelf Sizes

Examine the manufacturer's specifications to determine how the shelf sizes you have selected may be modified with quarter or half dividers, drawers, and bin boxes, and the like. Furthermore, if you intend to store a number of small items like fasteners or fittings it would probably be much better to introduce a rotary stand or two adjacent to your packing line to provide for a small number of incidental items. However, if you have a relatively large number of small parts, especially parts of large dollar value, you should use modular drawer cabinets. These cabinets come in various widths and depths, usually of counter height, three and four feet wide, two to three feet deep and with drawers that are from one-and-a-half inches in height to several inches. These cabinets may stand alone or be stacked as high as your ceiling. There are even specially designed trucks and ladders to order pick from these units.

THE INFLUENCE OF METHODS, EQUIPMENT, AND ATTITUDES ON PRODUCTIVITY

Materials handling equipment and methods of order picking greatly influence the productivity of bin operations. For this reason, the best possible equipment should be used in this functional area, based on a satisfactory rate of return on the capital used to acquire the equipment.

Another consideration in this area is that instead of purchasing materials handling equipment—

- leased equipment may provide a better ROI (return on investment); or
- a lease-purchase agreement may be negotiated with most industrial equipment suppliers. (Materials handling equipment and order picking methods are discussed extensively in Chapter 8.)

It is paradoxical that, in the main, a combination of method and equipment that works well in one region of the country may not produce equally good results in another. The quality of the labor force depends in large measure on the competitive arena in which the company is located. Smaller companies in proximity to larger entities usually cannot compete with wage scales and fringe benefits that are sometimes vastly superior and tend to skim off the cream of the work force. When this circumstance prevails, work attitudes tend to suffer and morale becomes a significant factor in decreased productivity and abuse of materials handling equipment.

In order to resolve regional differences in employee attitudes which may affect productivity, and as a general rule for operating the warehouse and distribution center:

- Keep employees informed of contemplated changes in methods or equipment, and any other changes that may affect them (viz., changes in hospitalization, work hours, shift changes, supervisory and management, organization and other company policy).

- Inform the department supervisor of contemplated changes involving his or her functional responsibility before any of his or her employees are notified.

- If the facility is a union shop, inform the various officials and stewards of the labor organization of contemplated changes. (If the plant management's plans do not involve proprietary information, it might be advisable in some instances to involve the union management in the early phases of planning for change.) A significant amount of labor unrest is created unnecessarily by a short-sighted management that cannot bridge the communication gap that sometimes exists between the labor force and the company.

8

Layout, Methods, and Equipment for Profitable Order Picking

INDUSTRIES DEPENDENT ON ORDER PICKING

There are many industries in the United States and throughout the world that are, strictly speaking, order picking industries. As an example of these industries we have the following:

- Pharmaceutical supply houses that distribute thousands of products of many different manufacturers in bulk (when promotions call for large quantities of an item), in break-bulk, or binnable quantities from units of one to thousands, even to quantities as small as one bar of a special soap, and so forth.
- Wholesale frozen food distributors.
- Automotive parts suppliers who generally sell wholesale, but are not averse to delivering one unit of an item, much in the way that pharmaceutical supply houses do.
- Wholesale grocers who cater to the independent supermarkets and to a few of the "Mom and Pop" stores that somehow persist.
- Rack jobbers that distribute novelties to supermarkets and other businesses.
- Vending machine merchandise distributors.

When you add your company to this impressive gamut of industries and compound this with all the order picking that is performed by commercial and industrial concerns to satisfy their assembly and production lines, dealers, and distributors, there is a vast number of companies worldwide with needs and requirements similar to your own.

TRADITIONAL ORDER PICKING LAYOUT, METHODS, AND EQUIPMENT

In traditional order picking, bin shelving of relatively low overall height, 7'3", is arranged in a rectangular configuration, as shown in Figure 8-1.

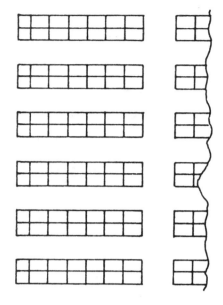

Photo courtesy Lyon Metal Products, Inc., Aurora, IL

Fig. 8-1: Typical bin section layout.

Backup stock is usually stored on top of the bin sections, adding another tier to the bin section at no additional cost other than the slovenly appearance it gives to the bin area (which should be avoided if the distribution center is required to look like a showplace).

Order picking carts used in the traditional layout usually are 24 inches wide by 36 to 48 inches long and approximately 32 inches high with two molded rubber (70-durometer) front wheels that swivel and two stationary rear wheels, 5 inches in diameter. The aisles in our conventional layout are 36 inches wide, with cross-aisles that are slightly wider, usually 4 feet in width.

The bin area is not very large, perhaps 10,000 to 30,000 square feet in overall coverage, and with the picking cart that is used, two bin carts cannot pass each other in these aisles. Stocking is performed either by the picker or by a stockperson who works on a swing-shift. If the order picker does the stocking, he or she will usually do this at a prearranged time, usually the first hour or two of the start of his or her shift. We have provided 100 lumens of light (measured at 30" above the ground) and have arranged our stock by zones so that the fastest movers are the last items to be picked and are located closest to the packing line.

The order picker receives his picking assignment on punched cards (Hollerith cards) arranged in a picking sequence so that the order picker will follow a prescribed path through the bin area.

NOTE: In the picking zones described above, the fastest-moving items, in addition to being located closest to the packing line, should always be located on the middle bin shelves. This places the high volume items in the best and most convenient location for the order picker.

In most order picking operations, merchandise is sent to the bin area in bulk quantities, i.e., in palletized unit loads, skid loads, or large bulk containers, and so forth. One of the critical factors in bin operations is the location of backup stock. Customarily, the backup stock that supplies the bin operation is located in close proximity to the bin area. The back-up stock is most conveniently placed in pallet storage racks surrounding the bin area, as shown in Figure 8-1. As a substitute or in addition to storage racks, bulk merchandise may be stored on the floor in blocks, on tops of bins, or in any combination of these methods.

NOTE: If there is any seasonality to the product line, such as antifreeze in an automotive supply house, or special "deals," such as in grocery or pharmaceutical houses, space should be allocated in the layout to take care of these added volumes.

Sometimes there is a "break-bulk" requirement that must precede the order picking operation and should be integrated into the planning for the sake of maintaining a balanced and systematic flow of work. Not infrequently a customer may require a half a case or more of a particular item. This is not a full pallet or unit load and may be more than contained in the bin quantity. It becomes a break-bulk item which indicates that

- Some of the unit load must be placed with the customer's order;
- Some of the unit load may be placed in the bin shelving; and,
- Some of the unit load may have to remain in the bulk storage area.

In the event that you have to employ two shifts in your order picking department, you must counterbalance the productivity advantages by

- the additional supervision required; and,
- increases in other overhead costs.

Despite the drawbacks, the fact remains that shelf stocking time, which is approximately 75% of the *total* order picking time, must be phased into packing and delivery schedules that are the objectives of this department.

If the bin selected items have to be packed, each order picker can place a number of wire baskets on his or her cart, ideally keeping each customer's order in a separate basket then placing his picking tickets in the basket, it would all go to the packer together. To avoid this type of double handling some companies require that the order picker pick and pack directly into a corrugated carton. There are some advantages and disadvantages in this method. Although most experienced bin pickers are pretty good at sizing the cartons to be used for their orders, some companies maintain that this method increases carton costs because the bin picker usually selects a larger carton than necessary in order to save time and eliminate the possibility of selecting a carton that is not large enough, and the lower productivity of the picker does not justify the pick and pack method.

However, some soft goods companies use wire locking-top bin baskets that stack one on top of the other in the transportation vehicle; and, since each customer store in the system has been allocated a specific number of baskets per delivery, this appears to be a satisfactory method.

Conventional Bin Layout

The main purpose of the conventional bin layout is to achieve a proper flow of materials from backup stock to bins and flow racks, and to provide the best possible pick to pack routing that space will permit. As an example of a conventional bin layout, see Figure 8-2.

The salient points to be observed in conventional bin layout are as follows:

- Pallet storage racks provide spaces for backup stock.

- An area has been reserved for "specials," the seasonal or promotional type of merchandise, loss-leaders, and so forth. This area has been placed close to the picking and packing conveyor line.

- Part of the "set-out" area may be used for "short" items that come directly from the receiving department.

- Part of the "set-out" area may be used for stocking purposes where pallet loads of merchandise may be placed to restock the bins. This material comes from other parts of the warehouse and distribution center.

- The bin sections are arranged in the conventional rectangular mode with their aisles at right angles to the picking conveyor in order to shorten the walking distance.

- The rectangular bin layout has been split down the middle to accommodate the picking conveyor, thus decreasing walking distances.

- When the picking conveyor is placed in the middle of the bin section, the bin orders have to be married (i.e., combined) since half the stock numbers (or line items) are on one side of the conveyor, and the other half are on the other side. In order to have one stock picker complete the entire order the split bin section has been modified, as shown in Figure 8-3. Note that there are no flow racks in this arrangement.

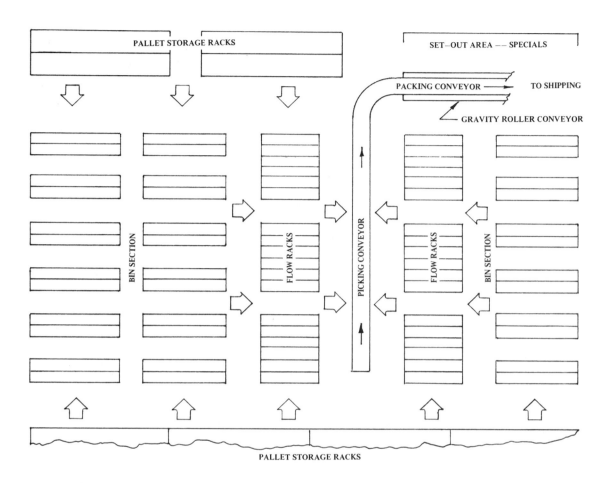

Fig. 8-2: A conventional bin layout showing the flow path from selection to packaging.

- When placing flow racks adjacent to the picking conveyor, as in Figure 8-2, the conventional wisdom is to place all of the fast-moving items in these racks. This requires that fast-moving items be combined with slow movers to complete the order.

The combining of separate parts of the order for the purposes of packing, or assembly for shipment to the customer, is a time-consuming effort that has many adherents despite its drawbacks. There are still a number of companies that use only one picker for the entire order. The decision to combine several parts of an order (i.e., combining the efforts of more than one picker for each order) or having only one picker for the entire order depends on factors such as type of items, layout of the bin section and/or equipment arrangement. When the method of combining orders is used the picking conveyor has to be modified with the addition of gravity conveyors (either skatewheel, or roller), usually on both sides of the conveyor. The placement of the gravity conveyors alongside the powered conveyor enables the packer to consolidate orders from several pickers in the bin section.

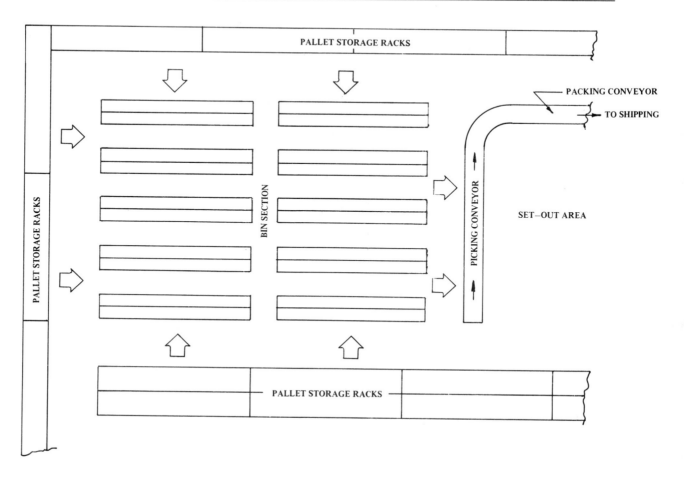

Fig. 8-3: A conventional bin layout with all of the order picking performed on one side of the picking conveyor.

Flow Racks

Since "walking" and "examining documents" comprise a large part of the bin picker's work effort (as determined by stop watch time study), the more that can be done to minimize these facets of the order picker's job, the higher his productivity. The use of flow racks (see Figure 8-4) decreases walking time significantly.

Ordinarily bin-picking productivity varies from approximately 20 to 35 items selected per hour. With flow racks, alone, picking productivity jumps to approximately 45 picks per hour. Many pharmaceutical supply houses, for example, use flow racks because the front picking face permits a large number of items to be available to the order picker, thus reducing walking time. A bin layout devoted entirely to flow racks and pallet storage racks makes a great deal of sense, especially if the frequency of issue of items is relatively high.

Figure 8-4 indicates the reasons why flow racks are superbly adapted for high volume order picking operations. They have several advantages over bin shelving as follows:

Fig. 8-4: Examples of flow racks.

- They can be restocked while order picking is being performed on the front face or picking face.
- The widths of the service lanes (i.e., the troughs down which the items travel to the picking face) may be varied to accommodate each individual item.
- Either individual items or case goods may be selected in these units.
- First in–first out (FIFO) control of inventory is assured.
- Walking on the part of the stock picker is held to a bare minimum.
- While really fast movers can be placed on the middle, easier to reach shelves, no shelf is really too high to reach by a person of average height.
- In order to have a dependable flow of cartoned materials in the flow lanes to the working face, you can adjust the angle of flow and the type of lanes used. For example, with certain products you can use ordinary inexpensive masonite board for the chutes and the products will slide well enough to get from the back of the rack to the front working face. With other products you may have to use the relatively more expensive plastic roller wheels or plastic-covered runways.

- Damage to the bottom shelves is eliminated because the stock picker doesn't have to stand on them to reach for material over his head.
- Most important, the number of line items for the front, picking face can be dramatically higher than for the customary 3- to 4-ft width of the common bin shelf. This is the main reason that walking time for the order picker is kept to a bare minimum.

Figure 8-5 illustrates a typical flow rack installation: rows of pallet storage racks supply the flow racks and the flow of materials is continuous and in one direction only. There are periodic breaks in the rows of flow racks in order to provide a means of communication between stockers and order pickers.

Determine Your Fast Movers

In order to determine how fast your fast movers are really moving, you should require that a "Frequency of Issue" listing be obtained from your computer department (assuming that you have one) or from accounting. By tabulating customer orders by stock numbers on a monthly basis it is possible to learn a great deal about your distribution center.

Fig. 8-5: Example of a flow rack installation.

- How fast are the fast movers moving?
- How many stock turns are you having?
- What items are the fast movers?
- What is the seasonality, if any, of your items?
- Is there a seasonality factor for fast movers?
- Do fast movers move once daily? more than once?
- What items are the slow movers?
- How many units of issue do the slow movers represent?

The answers to the above questions can make it possible to relocate items in the bin area profitably and to rid yourself of the "dog" items. Periodically, dog items may be retained based upon the requirement of one or two good customers, and it is a service feature that comes under the heading of goodwill.

NOTE: Before discontinuing an item it might be advisable (and another gesture of good public relations) to sound out your customer prior to actually eliminating the item(s).

IMPROVING ORDER PICKING RATES WITH A RADIAL BIN LAYOUT

One of the disadvantages of the conventional rectangular bin picking layout illustrated in Figure 8-1, is that the order picker must frequently retrace his or her steps in order to proceed from a stock number in one row to another in a different row. In an attempt to eliminate as much of this backtracking as possible, the writer initiated a new concept in bin layout which changed the layout from a rectangular configuration to one that is radial, i.e., like the spokes of a wheel. (See Figure 8-6.)

At the hub of this operation is the supervisor's work station, which is another advantage of the radial system because it permits him or her to have a better view of the entire bin arrangement. In addition, the bin pickers do not have as far to walk in obtaining picking tickets or instructions.

As you can see from the layout illustrated in Figure 8-6, the walking distances for both order picking and bin restocking have been vastly decreased, thus increasing the effectiveness of both operations. The actual mechanics of layout is quite simple, because once the four corners of the bin area have been designated, chalk lines are struck, then aisles are set off two feet on each side of the diagonal chalk line, giving 4-feet wide diagonal aisle widths. Using conventional bin shelving, order picking rates of 45 to 50 picks an hour can be readily sustained, making this method fairly competitive with flow racks since walking time between picks is reduced considerably. Computer sequencing of customer order picks based on stock number location increases productivity even further.

CREATE MEZZANINES TO BENEFIT FROM AIR RIGHTS

Whenever you have 14- to 18-foot ceilings and you're utilizing only 7 to 9 feet of this height (standard bin heights), you should remind yourself of real estate and utility expense. The cubic content of a distribution center should be as important to you as square footage

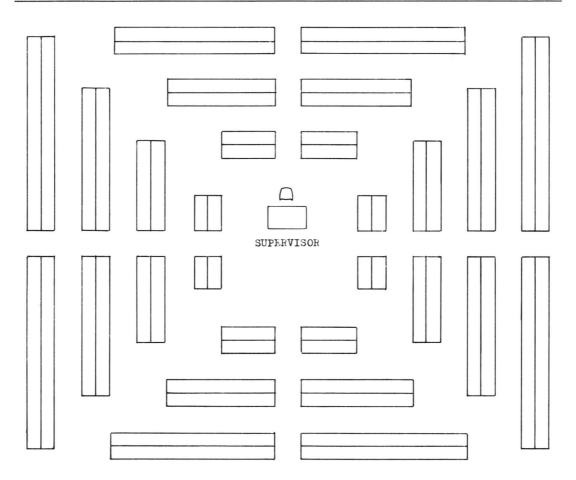

Fig. 8-6: Radial method of bin layout that saves walking time and improves bin picking efficiency 50%.

area. The bin picking operation is an area where it is possible to utilize air rights and recapture some of the valuable space that you are paying for.

Most bin sections can be layered with another bin section simply by topping them with open grating or 1⅛-inch tongue and groove plywood and providing a stairway at one end of this newly erected mezzanine. If tongue and groove plywood is to be used, your fire underwriters will probably require that the underside of the plywood have a steel laminate as additional fire protection. Also fire extinguishers should be placed in conspicuous locations on this upper tier.

If you are constructing your own mezzanine in-house, using slotted angle or structural tees and angles, it is advisable to reinforce corners of bin sections using structural steel angles to help support the load. It is of utmost importance that there be no sway in the structure when an order picker traverses the floor with a loaded cart. None of this type of construction should be attempted without expert, professional advice.

There are a number of suppliers of mezzanine structures, and all of their products may be placed over and around existing bin areas without having to move any bin sections. In other words, the entire mezzanine may be purchased as a package with stairways, and the like, that are prefabricated to your dimensions and shipped knock-down, then erected on the site with minimum interference to current operations. Another provision should be a set-out area where forklift trucks can place pallet loads of materials on the upper level and remove loads, if that is the only means for transporting picked materials to the packing line. In lieu of this, a chute or powered conveyor may be used to connect the mezzanine level with the packing line. Another advantage of having a powered conveyor connecting the mezzanine with the ground level is that instead of or in addition to using the guardrail set-out area, the powered conveyor can be reversed to send stock from below to the mezzanine level.

WARNING: If a set-out area is provided on the mezzanine, then provision should be made for a safety gate enclosure, or chain device to protect workers from accidentally falling off the platform.

When converting the Hingham, Massachusetts Industrial Shipyard building into a distribution center the writer was fortunate in having virtually unlimited overhead space. The building was composed of three bays that were 100 feet wide and almost 1000 feet long. The center bay had headroom of 70 feet, and it was in this area that the writer located a double decked bin area. In addition to the conventional bin arrangement the upper tier had a flow rack area. Transportation of picked items was achieved by placing a powered conveyor that reached from the mezzanine level to the packing area below. The entire bin area was surrounded by pallet storage racks where the bulk materials were on the same level as the bin section, thus readily available to the bin stockers from the interior of the bin section and serviced by forklift truck from outside the bin area.

NOTE: You should be aware of the OSHA requirements for mezzanines, and your mezzanine supplier should be prepared to furnish you with a certificate that the mezzanine installation meets all OSHA, local, and state ordinances and building codes.

- All exposed edges of the mezzanine must have a railing.
- The railing must be 3½ feet high.
- The bottom of the exposed edge (the portion under the railing) must have at least a 4-inch high kickplate.
- Every interrupted section of the guardrail (where the guardrail has been removed) must be equipped with chains or other satisfactory means of protecting the workers on the mezzanine.

High-stacking and High-density Bin Operations

In warehouses that are part of manufacturing plants, bin order picking installations may be as high as 40 feet. This height is a limitation imposed by forklift trucks in which the operator travels upwards to the bin opening in the truck cab. These bin-picking installations are not the ordinary type of high line item volume operations, but are usually captive to the manufacturing plant where large numbers of relatively slow-moving items are stored. Some parts may move out at the rate of one piece per month or less, yet because of company policy, or because of manufacturing lead times they must be on hand and available.

This type of high-stacking and high-density bin installation may be further mechanized and picking-productivity enhanced by giving the truck a guidance system very similar to a driverless tractor and having it follow a wire imbedded in the warehouse floor. The wire emits an RF (radio frequency) signal that guides the truck and will obey the commands of the operator in the cab of the vehicle. In addition to the semi-automatic guidance system, a CRT visual display terminal in the cab will indicate the next stop of the cab at the command of the operator; thus, a whole sequence of order picking stops may be carried out by the order picker following the instructions on his or her computer console.

NOTE: Employees should be selected very carefully for these high-stacking and high-density bin operations. Not everyone is psychologically and physically prepared for the isolation and working heights that these tasks require.

Using Automatic Storage and Retrieval Systems (AS/RS)

It wasn't too long ago that warehouses and physical distribution centers such as the large mail order houses could keep pace with increases in order-filling volume only by hiring more employees. Fortunately, the pace of mechanization has kept pace with demand, and the larger companies have been able to employ sortation systems and computer-controlled stacker-crane retrieval systems to enhance their capabilities for order filling. It has been found, also, that using stacker-crane systems that are computer-operated permits tighter control of merchandise moving into and out of storage: when used in conjunction with bar coding these systems can virtually eliminate pilferage.

Associated with the stacker-crane concept is high-density storage that so far has been limited to a little over 100 feet in height and only the aisle width needed for a stacker-crane to operate. Since it is possible to reach ceiling levels with storage racks it was a natural outcome of this development for buildings to be entirely rack-supported. The West Germans during their tremendous economic surge in the late 1960s built the first rack-supported structure. This building was also equipped with an automatic stacker-crane AS/RS system. Not to be outdone, the Ford Motor Company in its Degenham, England plant built a rack-supported building in which the storage racks were 110 feet high. The building was equipped with Dexion racks and was also serviced by a computer-controlled AS/RS system.

The rack-supported building was by no means an entirely new concept, although high racks as used in Europe were not attempted here, primarily because insurance underwriters and building codes militated against using the high-rise principle. In this country buildings with 30-foot ceilings placed them within the operating range of the industrial forklift truck of about 30 feet of mast height. These operations, however, are slow and the order picking productivity is relatively low. Ford Motor has constructed at least two high-rise warehouses, one on the West Coast approximately 65 feet high, and one in Buffalo, New York at 90 feet. American Cyanimid broke with tradition and in Bound Brook, New Jersey it erected the first stacker-crane retrieval system in a rack-supported building.

NOTE: If the underwriter's insurance considerations can be surmounted, the economics of labor, materials, maintenance, land value, and tax structures will often militate against the erection of a rack-supported, high-rise, high-density AS/RS building system. This type of installation may have a rather lengthy payback period, say from four to five or more years, which may not be within the usual ROI period for your company's capital investments. As a matter of fact, almost all AS/RS installations show a rather poor ROI; therefore, the justification for these installations usually rests on the premise that better control of the stored materials will be realized.

Buildings over 70 feet high are still very rarely built in the U.S.: they have enjoyed greater popularity abroad due to the higher land costs there. Industrial forklift trucks can be used in installations that permit stacking up to 30 feet in height. There are a few order picking trucks that will go as high as 40 feet; however, at these heights picking speeds are much slower and unit costs go up. The high-mast forktrucks and stock-picking trucks are very expensive, and maintenance costs are high. Thus, if high-rack, high-density storage is desired and justifiable, it is much better to consider the use of fixed-path, stacker-cranes. (See Figure 8-7).

Nevertheless the advantage in using mobile rather than fixed path equipment is that mobile units can travel in and out of storage rack aisles to a work station, assembly line, shipping area and the like, whereas most stacker cranes are confined to the aisle they work in unless a transfer device is available. If a transfer car system is used, one stacker-crane may be used to serve more than one aisle at a considerable savings in system costs.

AS/RS systems are usually so expensive that they are not within the economic means of the small plant since systems such as these may range in price from $500,000 to over $20 million and more. In addition, there is usually a significant amount of engineering that goes into every system despite some claims that these systems are off-the-shelf. Each installation's criteria are somewhat different; for example, storage rack opening width, height, depth and capacity, number of rack openings to suit the number of containers stored therein, building column spacing, and the like, require software programming that is unique to each system. Therefore, when a system is relatively extensive and includes complete computer control, far from being off-the-shelf, the system design, installation, and testing may require anywhere from two to three years from start to finish, sometimes longer.

One of the main justifications for the installation of an AS/RS system is that it provides control, primarily because the area in which the AS/RS operates is off limits to everyone but the machine. Even when a stacker crane (a machine with a cab and manual controls) is used, this justification is certain to be employed.

From an electromechanical viewpoint all AS/RS systems are composed of five distinct parts as follows:

- A storage and container rack system
- A conveyor system on the front end at right angles to the storage rack aisles
- The stacker cranes that operate in each aisle
- The computer that controls and drives the entire system
- The software package used in computer control.

Usually, in the extensive systems of most AS/RS projects, the storage racks can be the largest single item of expense. In addition, if special containers are used, these may also bear a considerable part of the overall budget for the installation. As a rule of thumb, about one-third of the cost of an AS/RS system is spent on storage racks, one-fourth on conveyors, one-fourth on the stacker-cranes, and the remainder is spent on computer hardware and software.

In the main, storage rack systems may store combinations of containers as well as unitized or palletized loads. The only limiting factors for the stacker-crane built-in load handling device would be the size, weight, and configuration of the loads to be stored or retrieved.

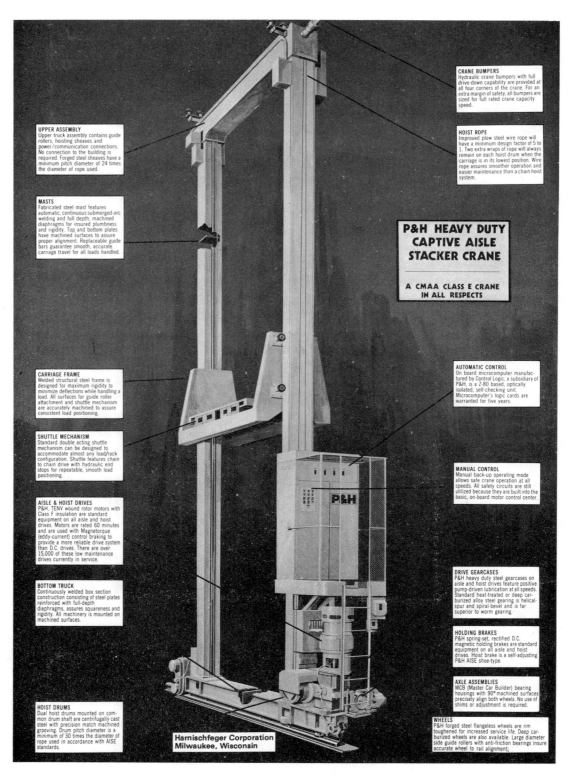

Fig. 8-7: A fixed-path stacker crane.

Advantages of Using AS/RS Systems

Greater Space Utilization

It is possible to obtain greater utilization of both floor space and air rights (i.e., cube utilization) since the storage racks can be much higher than in ordinary industrial truck operations. Also, aisle widths can be made only as wide as the stacker-crane mechanism requires, thus eliminating the wider aisles required by mobile materials handling equipment.

Faster Order-picking Operation Cycles

Since stacker-cranes can travel in unobstructed aisles that are isolated from pedestrian and vehicular traffic, they can travel at maximum operating vertical and horizontal motion so that both directions may be combined to obtain an almost straight line vector to each storage rack opening. Thus, the cycle times for both bulk (unit load) selection which may be accomplished without an operator aboard, or in bin order picking where an operator will have a work station in the cab of the stacker and pick from containers in the storage racks, are usually superior to conventional order picking where an operator drives or accompanies mobile materials handling equipment (either industrial forklift or order-picking trucks).

More Stable Stacking Heights

In stacker-cranes, the additional stability at great heights provided by this equipment permits faster cycle times with greater operator confidence. Of course, in unmanned, completely computerized systems, operator confidence is not a factor in cyclic rates of order selection.

More Flexible Work Loads and Work Areas

Using stacker-cranes it is possible to have load platforms of any desirable size without the restrictions that would inhibit platform size in mobile materials handling equipment where the overturning moment limits size and load parameters.

Fewer Operator Accidents

In a stacker-crane the operator travels with the load and can index the load platform accurately for either placement or retrieval; stops and limit switches can be built into the system. In a completely automatic (i.e., unmanned) stacker-crane this loading and unloading feature is done, also, automatically. In contrast to this, the operator fatigue and the parallax (or visual distortion) involved in viewing a load 30 feet above the ground surface from the cab of the vehicle becomes a stress factor that leads to accidents.

Even in stock-picking trucks, working above ground in a very unstable cab is another factor in the cause of accidents. Suffice to say, the stacker-crane has a better safety record than industrial forklift or stock-picking trucks.

Less Equipment Maintence Required

Since the major power source for the stacker crane is the electric feedrail or the festoon cable, there is never any requirement for recharging batteries or obtaining another tank of gas. Thus, there is no time wasted in obtaining fuel or in changing batteries. There is, however, a necessity for maintenance which may be accomplished in off-shift hours, but in any event this compares favorably with mobile materials handling equipment maintenance requirements.

Greater Mechanization for Improved Efficiency

The stacker-crane system is a step closer to the completely automated warehouse, since it requires fewer employees to operate and service. The AS/RS is a proven system, also, since a large number of these installations have been made in the past two decades. Complete computer control of the storage rack area is both possible and practical up to the front end of the system where human intervention is still necessary. Nevertheless, the use of AS/RS systems does free up personnel that may be used in other parts of the enterprise, or may be displaced by normal labor turnover and attrition.

Disadvantages of Using AS/RS Systems

More Skills Required

Since a computer-controlled device such as an AS/RS is much more complicated electrically than manually operated mobile materials handling equipment, it will be necessary to upgrade or hire the skills required to maintain and service the equipment.

Warehouse Floors Must Be Absolutely Level

AS/RS loading devices require fairly high precision in locating and indexing their mechanisms to the storage rack opening in order to avoid interference of the mechanism with the structure. Thus, in pouring a warehouse floor prior to the installation of an AS/RS system, tolerances of ±.50 inch may be required in order to avoid the necessity for excessive shimming of the storage rack uprights to achieve uniform levels. Also, periodic adjustment of the loading mechanism and shimming of the rack structure may be required if there is any settling of the warehouse floor over a period of time.

CAUTION: Preloading the soil prior to the erection of a warehouse in which an AS/RS system is to be installed is an absolute requirement.

Stricter Sizing Requirements for Containers and Unit Loads

Since the loading and unloading of AS/RS systems is accomplished using either unitized loads or containers, other requirements must be considered. First, the size of the container or the unitized load must be fairly uniform unless it is a container that is captive to the AS/RS system; in other words, it must conform to the size of the opening of the storage rack in which it is to be placed. In some systems which do not use captive containers or slave pallets, special openings may be reserved for oversized loads, and the AS/RS computer will have the capability of recognizing this requirement through a photoelectric sizing unit at the front end of the system where incoming loads are screened for height, width, and length at a photo-electric work station.

Second, the weight of the load must be within the tolerances established for the system; thus, the front end screening device must have a load cell station where all incoming loads are examined by weight and overloads are rejected.

Greater Need for Increased Fire Protection

A considerable investment in a sprinkler system is required in AS/RS systems, because not only are overhead sprinklers required, but in some high-rise systems intermediate level sprinklers may be required, thus adding to the cost of fire protection.

Mini-Retrievers

Mini-retrieval systems are a spinoff of the AS/RS in which pallet loads of materials may be stored in pallet racks that may be 100 or more feet high and are selected by a stacker crane operating in its own lane putting pallet loads away and retrieving them to a work station at the head of each lane. Some of the more sophisticated AS/RS systems can off-load the pallet to a conveyor system where it can be dispatched and indexed for a number of different locations.

The mini-retriever is similar in many respects to the AS/RS except in load sizes, where the upper limit is usually in the neighborhood of 400 pounds per bin opening or tier. Figure 8-8 illustrates a popular type of mini-retriever system.

Some units can perform a "store" command on the way into the system and retrieve materials on the way home. The operator at the working face of the retriever may have a conveyor upon which incoming and outgoing materials may be placed. Depending on the size of the installation one operator can be placed between two system consoles and operate two mini-retriever systems alternately. Because of spinoffs from the AS/RS industry, the reliability of the mini-retriever has been excellent, and its productivity has been exceptional. Some mini-retriever operators may, also, package materials that they order-select; but again, this depends on the size, quantity, quality of packing and so forth.

NOTE: The security of materials stored in mini-retrievers is very good, also, since the whole structure may be secured against pilferage.

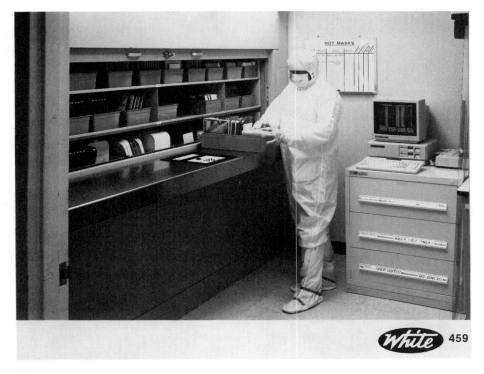

Fig. 8-8: The coming of age of the mini-retriever, a breakthrough in order picking productivity.

9

How to Select a Sortation System That Assures Least Total Cost in Materials Handling

TYPES OF SORTATION SYSTEMS

Once you decide that mechanization is necessary to keep pace with increased volumes and labor costs in sorting packages and other products, you need to make additional decisions: what equipment to purchase, how much is necessary, what will it cost, and is the payback sufficiently attractive to make the installation feasible. This chapter will answer these questions.

In the past few decades, the art of sortation has advanced very rapidly. Several manufacturers have sortation systems that can sort from 6,000 to 12,000 pieces per hour. The cyclic rates maintained for these sorting systems can reach astonishing speeds of 100 to 200 pieces per minute.

Because of the high productivity obtainable with these types of high-speed sortation systems, you can get a return on your capital investment for this equipment in a little over a year in some applications. Of course, the larger systems will take slightly longer to amortize. Sorting systems that are now available make it practical to convey anything from fruits and vegetables to stereos at a safe and measured pace.

Tilt-tray Systems

In some tilt-tray conveying systems, packages speed along the conveyor on individual trays. The control devices used to track the material and the tilting (which permits merchandise to slide into any number of sorting positions) are usually controlled by a minicomputer. In addition to considerable increases in sorting productivity, tilt-tray conveying systems also use as much as 50% less floor space than other systems.

Coded Belt Conveyors

Another high-speed sortation system is composed of a belt conveyor which has particles of ferrous metal embedded in its substrate. These particles can be energized to contain a binary coded charge. In other words, an indexing head underneath the conveyor imparts or energizes that particular section of the conveyor over which the package rests. And, as the package travels down the conveyor it will be diverted according to the code which has been imparted in the belt at that particular point; thus, the package will be diverted into a sortation lane. This type of sorting also reaches fairly high speeds; however, since an operator has to impart the code at a particular station along the conveyor, the number of cartons sorted will depend upon the ability of the operator to rapidly code the destination of each package so that the indexing head under the conveyor will properly code the material of the substrate.

Conveyor Systems with Bar Code Scanners

In other sorting conveyor systems the packages or materials can be bar coded and then the bar codes read by scanners alongside the conveyor which will actuate diverters to divert the package into its proper sorting lane.

Ongoing Innovations in Sortation Technology

We have come a long way from the earlier means for indexing conveyors, which were purely mechanical. Some of the earlier indexing means had rotary wheels with pins on the perimeter. Each pin was analogous to a section of the conveyor, and the rotating motion of the wheel corresponded to the speed of the conveyor in the preset ratio. This indicates how far we have come in the sortation technology since relatively few of these old, mechanical systems exist today, and for the most part many of our indexing means are accomplished electronically.

Innovations in this area of sortation are being accomplished fairly rapidly. For example, it is even possible to apply solid-state memory controls for modernizing existing tilt-tray sorters or belt diverter installations. In these systems, the memory control accepts the commodity and destination information from a keyboard, processes the information, then tracks the merchandise to its destination, and actuates the tilting trays or the diverters to accomplish the sortation. The memory-controlled unit just described is adaptable to either low- or high-speed sorting. It can also be used in automatic or manual loading systems, and it can be interfaced with many computers for code translation or to generate statistics for management information.

In addition to such sortation systems, there are other conveyor memory controls. Some have photoelectric scanners that read retro-reflective tape stuck to each package. The error rate in reading in the sortation systems of this type is fairly low and certainly exceeds 98% effectiveness.

PLANNING FOR MECHANIZATION

In overseeing a large-scale mechanization project of your sortation system, make certain that your project engineer and task force understand and are committed to the systems approach to materials handling. They should define the problems pertaining to the sortation project, then go backward in the chain of handling events in order to obtain the greatest value for the company's materials handling dollar by assuring that the *least total cost* for materials handling is obtained.

In the systems approach to the problem, the project leader and the task group should consult with the purchasing and inventory control departments, because purchase quantity, delivery schedules, and the way the material is packaged have a direct effect on the productivity of the ensuing materials handling, and thus affect the cost. Additionally, inventory policies affect the number of times the material is handled and the how and where of storage.

In many instances, the type of packaging used determines the type of handling equipment to be employed, as well as the time required to unload the carrier and place the material into the storage area, or transport it to the first point of use within the plant. Two matters should be decided early in the planning: whether the package can be handled by conveyor, and, how much standardization of packaging can be obtained from the suppliers. You can also avoid many double handlings of materials if the skid heights of vendor packs (i.e., the expendable pallets or skids used by many suppliers) are compatible with the materials handling equipment to be used; that is, the thickness of forklift truck pallet forks or the thickness of pallet-jack forks.

Make the Project Objectives Clear

The project leader and the task group should organize and define the problem so that the objectives of the sortation system design are clearly stated. This helps the members of the task group to understand the scope of the problem and, in addition, it can suggest other possibilities that will make the final design specifications more substantive and realistic.

After the objectives have been outlined and finalized, a schedule of events should be prepared in order to draw up a PERT or Gantt chart of the many steps involved in the systems approach to sortation.

Obtaining Data for the Sortation System Design

Data must be collected prior to the formulation of specifications for any mechanization system. What data is to be collected depends, of course, on the nature of the project. Since this system concerns package sorting you have to know what incoming and outgoing workloads are now, and have been over a period of time, so that trends may be detected and volumes extrapolated into the future. Usually, there is a periodicity in volumes handled that will sometimes depend on the time of day, the day of the week, and often the time of the month and year. For instance, holiday seasons impart a seasonality to certain businesses and products.

In order to accurately review the design specifications for the sortation system, the task force requires basic data. For example, in studying the receiving platform operations as part of the integrated systems plan, some of the data required pertain to truck arrival and departure times. This information can be obtained from the truck registers or the logs that are kept in the receiving department. To clearly define the problem involved in the receiving department, which has a bearing on the overall concept, the task force will need data on the weights of materials, pieces per hour, total number of units, and the like. A very important component of systems design consists of measurement, for the following reasons:

- If the operation or function is sufficiently complex (as the sortation problem will be in most cases), the data obtained can provide important areas for cost reduction.

- The data obtained by the task force can be developed into work standards or elemental time standards, which are often required to indicate what is being accomplished in the several departments with the existing resources of personnel and equipment.

- If data is obtained prior to the actual system installation, then it will be possible to compare the results after the installation of the mechanization with the costs incurred. Therefore, you have a frame of reference to verify that your decision to proceed with the mechanization was worthwhile, or not.

During the data collection and measurement phase, the various problems (which have been defined as objectives) will become apparent. In the actual process of developing the data, the relationships of the various departments and departmental functions should, also, become apparent. A secondary benefit of the data collection and measurement phase is that flowcharts can be made showing the actual paths that parts and materials take. These flowcharts can be used to analyze plant operations.

Optimization for Least Total Cost

One of the principle objectives of the task force is to find the throughput cost of the sortation system in order to compare this with the present costs, and then to keep refining the system, if at all possible, to obtain the least total cost for the project. Inevitably, there will be some compromising and tradeoffs will be made to keep costs within bounds. Nevertheless, it is this "compromising" that will effect, in the final analysis, the least total cost of handling for the system.

The task force could use systems simulation techniques to study a wide range of data in order to determine what could happen under various parameters of operation. (Appendix D discusses how to use computer simulation in warehousing and physical distribution.)

The Systems Approach Requires Good Interdepartmental Communications

You must establish communication with all departments that will be affected by the new developments in your plant. As soon as you have decided to go ahead with the new sortation system, you should ask all departments involved to send representatives to a general meeting at which the broad objectives of the new development will be outlined. At this time you should introduce your project leader to the group. In the interest of the total systems approach, it is absolutely essential to get the cooperation of all involved departments and to keep in close touch with them as the project progresses. The project leader must have the personality and charisma to get along with these departments and to keep their cooperation throughout the project. In other words, your project leader should be able to promote the sortation system project.

Installing the Sortation System

The first step in the installation of the sortation system is to prepare bid specifications and to obtain a suitable number of quotations, at least three or four, if capital equipment is involved.

NOTE: Some companies don't realize how much time and expense are involved in preparing a qualified bid on any major project: the cost to submit a bid may involve thousands of dollars. Your task group should review the companies in the field who can handle the type of installation that you are proposing, and select three or four to bid on the project. To facilitate the decision-making process the team should prepare a bid matrix in which the various characteristics of the specifications are outlined against a numerical rating for each company. Then they can assign an arbitrary point value to these characteristics so that the best-qualified companies will have the highest scores in your evaluation.

Your task group should establish the criteria for the project early on. With help from the purchasing department, the proposal can be priced out, arbitrarily, so that you have a budgetary figure for the ROI computation and a management decision.

When the bids are received from the suppliers, the task force can evaluate them against the matrix to determine which company is the successful bidder. The bid specifications should have a section on testing and debugging. The successful vendor should also be required to warranty its work. In addition, after installation the equipment must pass the company's acceptance tests, and a debugging period should be permitted according to the specifications so that the warranty period will begin after acceptance, and not before.

Evaluating Results of the Sortation System Installation

After the installation has been completed and it has been successfully debugged and accepted, there should be a relatively short shakedown period in which the operating personnel become familiar with the operations. At this stage, data collection begins on the performance of the new sortation system by using work standards or throughput measurement, or even work sampling to determine the success of the project. (See Chapter 21 for guidelines on how to use work sampling.) These new measurements will indicate how well the targeted objectives have been accomplished and if the new sortation system projected will deliver the ROI.

10

Effective Use of Conveyors for Warehousing

WHERE YOU SHOULD USE CONVEYORS TO BEST ADVANTAGE

There are many types of conveyors, and they are found in many types of industries with the possible exception of the oil and chemical companies. In many companies, especially the industrial production operations, conveyors are used to pace the operation, i.e., the speed at which the conveyor is driven determines, to a certain extent, the speed of whatever production takes place on the conveyor line. In the physical distribution industry and warehousing in general, the relative speed of the conveyor can also be used to pace certain types of operations. This is not to say that we have "speedup" conditions, however. If you have work standards for your operation, your technicians will know exactly how fast or how slow to run each particular conveyor.

It is best to use conveyors where the flow of work is more or less continuous and can be directed along a fixed path. In contrast to this we have *batch processing,* which can be accomplished by means of forktrucks and palletized loads where the product is only required sporadically; also, batch processing can use the pallet system where delays in delivery are not particularly upsetting to any schedule. Nevertheless, if a steady and sufficient stream of material is required, some type of conveyor should be used because of its efficient delivery system.

A large degree of versatility may be built into the conveyor design: it is possible to start and stop conveyors and to interrupt the flow of materials to suit various conditions in the plant. Conveyors can transport virtually any quantity of packaged goods or other materials to suit a large diversity of processing or physical distribution requirements.

There are many types of conveyors that are available at the present time, including both portable and fixed units. A certain disadvantage exists when installing a fixed or in-floor conveyor system in that once it has been put into place it is fairly inflexible concerning alterations in its location should capacity or the type of materials to be handled change. There are other advantages, however, that heavily outweigh this drawback; for example, conveyors can carry material along fairly direct routes and at extremely high rates of capacity. They can be placed at virtually any level from floor level, at personnel workstation heights, or they may be carried and elevated above the heads of the workers and above processing operations.

One of the major advantages of placing conveyors overhead is that they don't necessarily have to occupy valuable floor space and can utilize the air rights above storage racks or picking bins to good advantage. When elevating conveyors your technician has to determine how much of a load the overhead structure of the plant can carry. It might be necessary to strengthen the overhead structure to support the load imposed upon it by the conveyor and the materials that the conveyor will carry.

Conveyors that are properly designed and installed are usually very reliable in operation requiring only a minimum amount of down-time for routine preventive maintenance servicing. In this regard they are particularly desirable for distribution center operations, especially for routine and continuous processing.

NOTE: Make sure your technicians put every conveyor in your plant on the scheduled preventive maintenance (PM) program. If the PM is done regularly and according to schedule, you should have a minimum of down-time in conveyor operations.

The importance of preventive maintenance scheduling cannot be overemphasized. If a package conveyor breaks down in the middle of a work shift, for example, in a mail-order house or warehouse, it causes innumerable delays throughout the system as well as making a large number of employees idle and a large number of customers unhappy.

THE TYPES OF MATERIALS THAT CONVEYORS HANDLE PROFITABLY

There are three broad classifications of materials that can be handled by conveyors:

- packages
- loose materials
- hazardous materials

We will exclude from the three basic categories "bulk materials" since physical distribution centers do not generally handle such things as granular materials, crushed rock, flour, sand, cement, slurries, or liquids.

Packages

Packages can be corrugated cartons, wood boxes, drums, and bagged materials. Package specifications which indicate the shape, dimensions, and weight of the package as well as the contents may have an important significance on the type of conveyor to be used. Therefore, any special characteristics of the conveyor should be spelled out: whether the contents will be affected by temperature or humidity changes, whether the contents are flammable or nonflammable, what sorts of exterior packaging materials are to be encountered. These specifications have an important bearing on the characteristics of the conveyor surface itself. As you can see in Figure 10-1, conveyors can take many different shapes.

Loose Materials

Your physical distribution operation may have very little requirement for a belt conveyor that can be used with loose materials, but such capabilities are possible.

Photos courtesy Interlake Material Handling Div., Lisle, IL

Fig. 10-1: Different types of conveyors.

In specifying a conveyor for loose materials the conveyor manufacturer should be advised of the type of materials to be conveyed, including the weight per foot of conveyor space (or per linear foot) and the dimensions and composition. There may be special characteristics of the materials, such as temperature, fragility, or the question of hygiene, such as in the handling of pharmaceuticals or food, fruit, or bakery products.

Hazardous Materials

Hazardous materials refer not only to chemical substances that may be toxic or difficult and dangerous to handle, but also to a somewhat neglected area which is just beginning to be understood fully. Dust from a wide variety of materials that in themselves are not volatile but when airborne can form exceedingly explosive mixtures. An extreme case, grain elevators and other large, reinforced concrete structures have been literally blown apart by dust explosions.

It is just such potential hazards that would require that the conveyor manufacturer be given as much information as possible in the specifications for the conveyor.

While there are still sporadic instances of explosions that are caused by dust accumulations in the air, explosion suppressant systems are now available that can be used to prevent the occurrence of these sometimes fatal and disastrous accidents. Systems employing liquid Halon (a fire-suppressant) under pressure, with extremely sensitive and quick acting sensors, are being employed so that within milliseconds of the buildup of the ion composition of the explosive mixture, the valves of the Halon tanks are themselves exploded by a cartridge and the liquid Halon traveling at bullet-like velocities gasifies and combines with the explosive mixture, thus dampening the reactive substances to a harmless mixture.

TYPES OF CONVEYORS

Gravity Conveyors

There are two types of gravity conveyors in widespread use; the steel roller conveyor and the skate-wheel conveyor which is a lightweight conveyor and made of aluminum. Steel roller conveyors are relatively inexpensive, they are readily assembled and installed, easily adjusted, and can be used for a wide variety of different types of packaged materials and any other goods that can roll on a conveyor. Nonpowered, gravity roller conveyors can be used either horizontally or with a downward slope wherein the gravity is relied upon to move the load. Although roller conveyors are usually made of steel tubing, aluminum roller conveyors are also available, but they are a good deal more expensive, although they are easier to handle manually than the heavier steel roller conveyors, which usually require several persons to handle, or one operator with a forklift truck. Roller and skatewheel conveyors can both be used to support functions like the bin-picking operation or packaging operation when they are placed in the horizontal position, and the packages are moved along simply by pushing them as the chore is completed. The skatewheel conveyor with its extremely light weight is easily portable and can be used to unload materials from trucks and other conveyances. Figure 10-2 shows a gravity skatewheel conveyor being used to unload a truck. You will note that while stands are available for the conveyors, the temporary use of a barrel or a drum and a carton is an impromptu type of fix that will substitute for a stand as shown in this illustration.

Fig. 10-2: An illustration of a skatewheel conveyor used for truck unloading.

Steel roller conveyors of the nonpowered type are portable although they are considerably heavier and usually they are moved by means of a forklift truck. Where there is considerable abuse the steel roller conveyor is to be preferred because it will stand up to fairly rigorous treatment.

As an example of degree of slope that can be used with skatewheel or roller conveyors, the following figures should serve as a guide to the amount of slope that may be required when using standard roller conveyors. It is suggested, however, that experimental runs be made if the conveyor is to be maintained in a fairly permanent installation.

Weight in Pounds	Inches of Fall per 10 Feet*
9-15	6-7
15-50	4-5
50-120	3-4
120-250	2-3

*Curves will increase the amount of slope required by 75%.

Changing the slope between conveyor sections should be done cautiously since the load can wedge itself against the next roller conveyor section. Sometimes, if the load is such that it would not travel well on a roller conveyor, a flat board such as a piece of masonite can be used on which to place the package. The boards are accumulated at the bottom of the slope and then returned en masse to the top of the slope for the next batch of items that are to be conveyed.

Gravity roller conveyors are normally manufactured in 10-foot lengths which can be linked together to form a continuous track. The same thing is true of skatewheel conveyors and there are stands that are specifically designed for both roller and skatewheel conveyors.

They have a certain amount of flexibility in that the stand is telescopic within a predetermined range, usually from about 22 inches to about 42 inches in height.

The carrying capacity of the conveyor is related directly to the diameter of the roller. Conveyor rollers will vary from slightly more than one inch to three or four inches in diameter. Usually the larger the diameter of the roller, the heavier the load to be transported upon the conveyor. In the physical distribution center it is doubtful that conveyor rollers of over a nominal two inches would be required. The standard is 1.9 inches in diameter.

NOTE: The pitch of the rollers should be such that at least three conveyor rollers are always under the load.

NOTE: Both skatewheel and roller conveyors can be obtained with the side frames above the level of either the rollers or skatewheels; however, where nonstandard package sizes are concerned, it is preferable to specify either type of conveyor with the wheels or the rollers above the side frames so that packages of almost any size can be readily handled on the conveyor. The advantage of having side frames is that the material will stay within the bounds of the conveyor and will not slide off and fall to the ground.

Powered Conveyors

Powered roller conveyors are made of steel tubing and can range from the relatively simple chain-driven or snubbing belt-driven conveyor to the accumulation type. There are two main types of powered roller conveyors; one is the ordinary powered roller conveyor that we see in illustration Figure 10-3, in which a diverter is palletizing case goods at the end of this roller conveyor line, and the accumulation type powered roller conveyor, shown in Figure 10-4, which will permit packages to accumulate on the conveyor up to a certain point and then it will disengage the rollers beneath the packages so that they will not bunch up and tumble off the conveyor.

Photo courtesy FMC Corporation, Hoopeston, IL

Fig. 10-3: A powered roller conveyor and case palletizer.

Fig. 10-4: An illustration of an accumulation type powered roller conveyor.

Some of these accumulation type conveyors are called zero-pressure conveyors because you can readily stop the package by hand manually, or by letting the packages accumulate on the conveyor. The advantage of having an accumulation type conveyor is that packages can be made to queue up in front of a workstation where it is impossible to take the packages as they come singly and they begin to back up when the movement or velocity of the conveyor is greater than the speed of the operator processing the package at the workstation. In other words, it amounts to giving the operator a backlog of work and keeping a continuous stream of material in front of the operator. In some situations a stop is placed on the conveyor so that the packages cannot go beyond that particular point. In this instance the diverter or stop, on the conveyor, forms the barrier against which the packages will accumulate. Either packages or bin containers, or the like, can be held up at any point on the conveyor without causing a pile-up.

Any type of load having a fairly rigid, smooth base can be moved on roller conveyors but sometimes small irregularities on the transportation surface can prevent free movement, and the item will hang up. As an example, a wood box with steel strapping, which is placed at right angles to the rollers of the conveyor, might be entirely capable of being transported; however, if there are any nail heads protruding from the strapping, or if perchance the conveyor is a large one and it is conveying a wood pallet load, then the irregularities of the bottom deck boards might cause it to hang up on the conveyor. In general, any carton composed of fairly substantial corrugated board which is well-sealed and taped will form an ideal package for conveying on a conveyor. If, on the other hand, the carton has become softened by either repeated handling or moisture, or if its bottom flaps are not properly secured, it might present difficulties and make conveying difficult, if not impossible.

Flat Belt and Slider Bed Conveyors

Flat belts are usually rubberized canvas belts that are set to run over roller conveyors. The advantage in the flat belt is that it can take virtually any package size that would not run too well over the pitch of the rollers.

In overall appearance the slider bed conveyor does not look any different than the flat belt conveyor. The only difference between the two is that the slider bed is a conveyor in which the rubberized flat belt travels over a section of sheet metal, usually stainless steel in food processing plants, but ordinary sheet steel in package conveyor or physical distribution warehouses. In general, belt conveyors have a problem with the belt tracking on the crown and pulley stock of the drive motor. The head stock of the conveyor has a slight taper from the center to the outward edges that is barely perceptible. However, it assists the conveyor belt in remaining centered on the conveyor path. If the head stock is not completely parallel to the length of the conveyor belt, the belt will have a tendency to drift off the head stock, and the edges will become frayed and the fiber threads will begin to peel off the belt and, in general, a mess will result that sometimes can jam the conveyor into a stoppage. For the most part, slider bed conveyors are somewhat less expensive than the flat belt conveyors that are mounted over rollers. There are limitations, however, in the slider bed conveyor in that heavy packages will require more power on the part of the drive motor than will the flat belt which runs over rollers. Part of the PM program for flat belt and slider bed conveyors will be to have a technician true up the parallelism of the head stock so that the conveyor belt will track evenly without fraying along the edges. People working on the conveyor should be made aware of the situation that arises when the belt is not tracking properly and should notify maintenance immediately.

Steel Slat Conveyors

Steel slat conveyors can be manufactured with very wide widths, sometimes as wide as 12 feet, and the composition is either carbon or stainless steel. This type of conveyor is ideal for the food, chemical, or metal fabricating industry, where very hot, acidic, sticky, or wet materials have to be conveyed, or when cleanliness is of primary importance. The slats of these conveyors can be operated in temperatures of 500° Fahrenheit and more. The minimum diameter of the end pulleys on these types of conveyors is normally a great deal larger than that required for the ordinary rubber belt conveyor. The slats of a steel slat conveyor are very similar to the tank treads that you would see on a bulldozer or army tank, since they are articulated between the slats.

Woven Wire Belts

Woven wire belts are used mainly in processing industries and very rarely in a physical distribution operation unless it is part of such an enterprise. Many of these conveyors are fitted with mesh belts that are woven from stainless steel, mild steel, Monel metal, and other metals. They are used primarily for carrying materials through ovens and quenching baths, since hot air can be readily passed through the mesh and circulated around the article being conveyed. It can also be applied to washing and drying of items.

Vibrating Conveyors

Vibrating conveyors are usually manufactured in sections of 10-foot lengths, which can be fastened together to form one continuous conveyor. It is also possible to cause material to travel up slopes of about 10 degrees in the maximum and also to travel in a spiral migratory fashion to elevate certain types of materials. In general, vibrating conveyors can be classified into two broad groups:

- vibrating conveyors with a high-frequency wave form, which is usually imparted to the conveyor by means of electromagnets or unbalanced pulleys.

- oscillating conveyors operating at slow speeds with the pulsations of the vibratory motion induced by an eccentric linkage or crankshaft.

Vibratory conveyors can also be fitted with metal or plastic troughs which may have a top cover or may be in the form of a large tube.

The action of vibrating conveyors is usually gentle with only the trough being in contact with the material. The trough can be relatively smooth and clean and thus may be used for handling food items or materials that must be kept from contamination; however, if the material consists of fragments of varying sizes down almost to dust-like particles, some separation is likely to occur and the larger particles, of course, may travel at a different speed than the smaller ones, which, depending entirely upon the operation, may be detrimental.

In specifying vibratory conveyors it is important that you accurately describe the characteristics of the material to be handled, since any change in its bulk, density, grain size, or other elements may seriously affect the efficiency of conveying. In some physical distribution setups that are part of a processing facility, it sometimes happens that materials must be packaged or boxed, therefore, they must be conveyed to hoppers that will store materials for the filling operation. In this manner, the vibratory conveyor makes itself useful for this application.

Gravity Chutes

Gravity chute conveyors can be used in physical distribution operations where the plant is multistoryed; or, they can be used to convey packages from a mezzanine level to the main floor of the warehouse. When we think of chutes we usually think of coal chutes which were simply straight sections of cold-rolled steel with the edges turned up several inches, and the use of the chute was to get the coal from the ground level on the outside of the building into the basement coal storage bin. The spiral chute has been extremely useful in conserving space and it is similar in many respects to a spiral staircase, where you condense and compact the area utilizing all the air rights that are available.

Chutes can be of many different widths and they can be curved or straight. Also chutes can be either flat-bottom troughs or have curved troughs to conform to the loads being carried, such as bagged materials or sacks. The chutes can be manufactured of steel, wood, plastic and lined with various materials, and they can handle packages or loose items. While the gravity chutes are simple in concept, the behavior of packages traveling down the length of the chutes may vary greatly. Except in some very small installations it is generally desirable to obtain the advice of manufacturers who specialize in this type of materials handling equipment, since satisfactory application depends entirely on controlling the speed of travel and the delivery.

NOTE: Packages should always be fed and discharged from a straight section of the chute.

It is best to use a chute (spiral or straight) when the sizes, shapes and weights of packages will not vary very much; the heavier packages will travel very rapidly, and the lighter packages will tend to come to rest and may cause jams in the chute structure. Also, the center of gravity of a package must be sufficiently low to prevent the possibility of its tumbling while descending the chute, as this could lead to further problems and, depending upon the fragility of the item, could cause damage. These concerns notwithstanding, Figure 10-5 shows that there is a wide variation in package sizes which does not seem to affect the efficiency of the chute despite the fact that there has to be a combination of coefficient of friction, package size, and elevation.

Photo courtesy Jan Tec Incorporated, Traverse City, MI

Fig. 10-5: Packages descending along a spiral chute conveyor.

11

How to Derive the Greatest Benefit from High-density Storage

HOW THE SYSTEMS APPROACH APPLIES TO HIGH-DENSITY STORAGE

Throughout this book, I encourage a systems approach to tackling problems in warehousing and physical distribution where the entire operation must be viewed as a whole in order to develop the *least total cost* and maximize profitability. Therefore, in attempting to obtain the maximum benefits from the systems approach to high-rise/high-density (HR/HD) storage, there are seven factors to consider:

- location
- cost
- flow
- time
- equipment
- throughput
- labor

Taking each of the above factors in turn will permit us to piece together the entire system concept.

Location—Deciding Where to Put the Storage System

When contemplating the installation of a high-rise/high-density storage system one of the first things you have to decide is where to put it. We call this the *location factor*. It should be located in an area that is convenient to all of the subareas that it has to serve. It should be readily accessible and should not block access to, or in any way interfere with, other working or production areas.

Cost—Justifying the Expense of a New Storage System

Make a comparison to determine whether the space about to be utilized will be more densely populated than the previous storage area. It will take a considerable amount of increased utilization, naturally, to justify all of the moving and installation labor, new equipment and material costs to be incurred by the new storage system. If the present storage area is eating up costly production space, how much value will be produced by a condensation of this space into a high-rise/high-density storage area? Also, if manufacturing space costs $70 or more per square foot, what sort of cost avoidance can be obtained by returning this valuable space back into production?

Flow—Determining How to Route Materials

Another component to consider is the routing of materials into and out of the storage area or the so-called *flow* factor. When deciding upon the location of a particular area the technician should provide a straight line path for materials to travel to their prescribed destinations.

NOTE: Remember that provision must be made for load set-out areas in the principal storage location and at the several production points served by the HR/HD storage system. Allocate enough space so that loads may be placed and taken away without creating bottleneck conditions and blocking pathways.

Time—Setting a Schedule for Installing the Storage System

In every substantial project there is a necessity for establishing a time frame that will pinpoint the beginning and end of a project. The groundbreaking and beginning of the project may very well be determined by the time or date of occupancy and the lead times associated with the installation. If the project is fairly large in size and dollar amounts, a Gantt Chart, which is a way of showing progress of a project and tells where each element is from a time standpoint, or a PERT Chart, which shows both progress of elements and their chronological relationship, may be necessary to carefully describe each event that is required. To illustrate some of the elements and possible time frames required, prepare a plan like the one shown in Table 11-1.

Table 11-1. A list of project elements with completion times.

Element	Time Factor in Months
Feasibility study	4
Specification preparation	3½
Fund allocation & approvals	2
Site selection	5
Engage contractor	2
Order equip. & storage racks	2
Construct warehouse	7

Pour floor slabs	3
Inspect, test, accept bldg.	3
Install racks	3
Install rack quadrails	2
Debug system	3
Final acceptance	2
Total	41½

If each of the above elements could only start after the completion of the preceding element, the entire project would take 41 months; however, by starting an element simultaneously with another, and by overlapping elements, the above project can be condensed into the space of 18 months as shown in Table 11-2.

Table 11-2. A Gantt Chart of project elements

Elements and Time in Months

	1	2	3	4	5	6	7	8	9	10	11	12	13	14	15	16	17	18
Feasibility study																		
Specification preparation																		
Fund allocations and approvals																		
Site selection																		
Engage contractor																		
Order equipment and storage racks																		
Construct warehouse																		
Pour floor slabs																		
Inspect, test, and accept building																		
Install racks																		
Install rack quadrails																		
Debug system																		
Final acceptance																		

Equipment—Calculating the Cost of Related Materials Handling Equipment

There is a wide range of materials handling equipment that will lend itself to HR/HD storage; for example, turret and rotating mast trucks, sideloaders, rack-type, standup riders, and stacker cranes. Considering equipment in the light of the ROI or *cost* factor, not only the initial acquisition cost, but also the cost of repair and maintenance is significant. Sometimes the annual cost of maintenance, especially of some of the more complex equipment such as sideloaders, may run as high as 20% of the truck's acquisition price. This equipment is described in detail later in this chapter.

Throughput—Assessing the Volume of Materials Handled by the Storage System

Throughput has to do with the volume of merchandise or materials that is placed into and taken out of the storage system. Throughput determines the average cycle time, the number of storage rack openings, and the height and length of aisles. In establishing the above parameters we can see an interrelationship with some of the systems approach factors that have been discussed above. For instance, cycle times depend on the speed and effectiveness of the equipment used (the *equipment* factor) as follows: speed of horizontal travel and lifting speed, and the speed with which the loads can be moved in and out of their storage rack openings. The number of storage rack openings, and the length and height of the rack storage system are related to the cost factor.

Another element of the *throughput* factor concerns the size of the loads to be handled. If we are handling only full loads in and out, it vastly simplifies the inventory control process. On the other hand, if the stock selector is picking from bulk loads (i.e., a break-bulk operation) inventory control and restocking become much more complicated.

Another aspect of throughput has to do with how materials are stocked in the storage racks. It would be appropriate to view the storage rack system as a vastly enlarged bin system where the main difference would be the quantity of the items to be selected. Thus, in all storage systems items should be stocked in terms of popularity, i.e., frequency of issue. The fastest moving items should be located closest to the front end of the HR/HD installation. *This not only decreases the average cycle time, but it also saves wear and tear on the equipment.*

NOTE: Periodically, usually not less than semi-annually, review the items stocked in the storage system from the standpoint of the frequency of issue. Weed out the slowest moving items, if at all possible.

Labor—HR/HD Tradeoffs in Labor Input

Where turret and rotating mast trucks, sideloader trucks, and other variations of forklift trucks are used in high rise/high density storage, cycle times of putting items into storage and retrieving product usually slows down the productivity of this type of picking operation. The compensation when storage racks are 30 and 40 feet high is that the storage cube, or air rights utilized, will in part offset the additional labor costs involved. However, when stacker cranes are used, productivity will increase in proportion to the degree of sophistication of the installment, i.e., computer driven AS/RS (automatic storage and retrieval system) where multiple stacker cranes are employed brings us closer to the ultimate goal of a completely mechanized warehouse by minimizing the number of persons required to run the plant.

USEFUL MATERIALS HANDLING EQUIPMENT

Sideloaders

While maintenance costs can be a significant part of the expense where sideloader trucks are used in HR/HD installations, there are other cost factors involved in such installations. As an example, the most effective method for preparing the storage rack aisles to receive the sideloading truck is to place guide rails on both sides of the aisle so that sidewheels (rollers) mounted on the sideloader platform can self-steer the vehicle once it has entered the aisle. Additionally the front end of each rack should have a concrete pad with a rounded steel face to guide the vehicle into the rack aisle in as smooth a manner as possible without hesitation on the operator's part. The guide rails and the steel reinforced concrete entrance pads are necessary in order to prevent damage to the pallet storage racks.

Another useful device that will make sideloader operations more effective is the addition of a *height selector* on the sideloader. With each tier numbered all the operator has to do is press a button for the proper tier and the forks will elevate automatically to the proper tier height. The operator advances the forks into the loaded pallet to retract the load from the storage opening.

NOTE: The higher the rack installation, the more important "height selectors" become. They make the operation faster and safer and lessen operator fatigue.

As an illustration of a typical HR/HD sideloader installation see Figures 11-1 and 11-2.

While sideloading trucks are usually larger in overall configuration than a standard industrial forklift truck, they do possess the same type of mobility in that they can go directly from the storage rack aisle to wherever else in the plant they are required. Unlike the stacker crane that is captive to the aisles of a storage system, the sideloader can bring material from the storage location to the point of use.

CAUTION: When making a sideloader truck layout, remember that the truck can service only one side of the aisle at each pass. If the material to be picked is on the wrong side, the operator has to re-enter the aisle with the forks (or loading platform) on the proper side.

Turret, or Rotating Mast Trucks

There is a certain similarity in the use of turret or rotating mast trucks and sideloaders. Usually reinforced concrete entrance pads and guide rails are required, unless of course electronic or embedded guided wire forms the guide path for the vehicle.

When laying out the storage rack area for a turret-mast truck operation the planner has two options: one is to view the rotating-mast truck as a sideloader that may work only one side of the aisle, and the other option is to leave enough working room in the aisle that the truck has room to rotate the load in the aisle. Figure 11-3 is a plan view of a rotating-mast truck showing the clearances required for either one-side-only operation or for rotating the load in the aisle.

NOTE: The space required for rotating a load in the aisle is considerably greater than for one-side-only operation!

Courtesy Crown, New Bremen, Ohio
Fig. 11-1: Sideloader truck in HR/HD aisle.

Bridge Cranes

There are numerous installations of stackers that are mounted on double-girder bridge cranes. A turret or rotating head on the stacker permits up to complete (360°) rotation of the stacker forks. The telescopic mast of the stacker provides the vertical travel component for the forks as well. This is a device suitable only for heavy industry and would not be considered practical for light loads; however, it may have some applications where a plant manager may wish to convert an existing bridge crane for order selection operations. This conversion process is discussed in the next section.

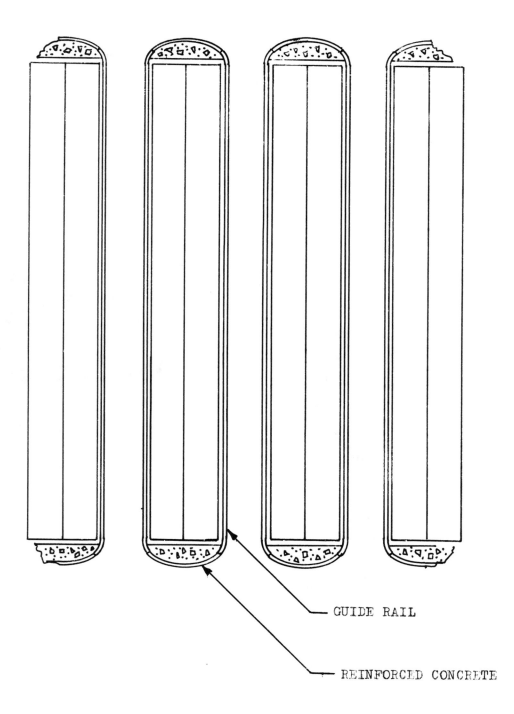

GUIDE RAIL

REINFORCED CONCRETE

Fig. 11-2: Plan view of HR/HD storage rack layout showing steel reinforced concrete front end section and guide rails.

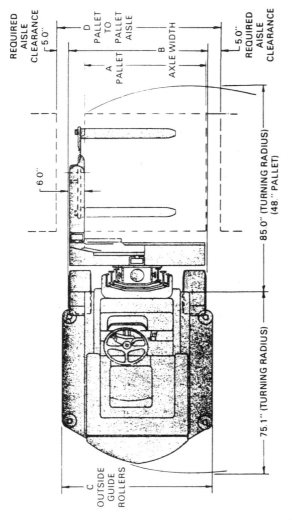

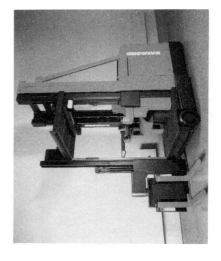

Fig. 11-3: Aisle clearances required by a typical rotating-mast truck for one-side and for rotating the load in the aisle.

Courtesy Harnishfeger Corp., Milwaukee, WI

Fig. 11-4: Bridge crane used with stacker-crane showing operator's cab and forks.

As you can see in Figure 11-4, there are no ground rails, and all of the coordinate X, Y, and Z movements are controlled by an operator in a cab contiguous to the forks on the stacker.

NOTE: It is seldom advisable to have more than one stacker-crane on the same set of craneways; however, under certain conditions a stacker-crane can operate with a hoisting crane on the same craneways.

Steel mill coil storage and handling have been improved by the use of a coil prong instead of forks on the stacker. (See Figure 11-5.)

Courtesy Harnishfeger Corp., Milwaukee, WI

Fig. 11-5: Stacker crane suspended from bridge crane with coil-handling prong.

Coil racks provide a way to achieve random access to each coil instead of pyramiding coils leaving only the top coil accessible. Pyramiding coils, or any material for that matter, is a labor-intensive, order picking nightmare. Despite the high cost of coil storage racks, the racks can be readily amortized through increased picking rates and improved response to customer orders.

Converting Bridge Cranes to Order Picking

Double-girder bridge cranes can be converted to stacker-crane use by adding:

• a telescopic mast

- forks or prong
- a cab for the operator

It was just such a conversion that led to the development of the original stacker-crane. There are a few drawbacks to converting a bridge crane to stacker-crane use. One such disadvantage is that it usually leads to about a 25% downgrading of the capacity of the crane. As an example, a 25-ton bridge crane conversion would probably be downgraded to about 18-tons capacity. Nevertheless, 18-tons is still a respectable amount of capacity and it may be extremely worthwhile to effect such a conversion, depending on the circumstances. (See Figure 11-5.) Despite the loss of capacity there are many products that may be safely handled using the converted bridge crane such as:

- plate
- pipe
- nonferrous coils
- barstock
- lumber

NOTE: Any long, hard-to-handle item could probably be handled more effectively with a converted stacker-crane; however, remember that the stacker-crane is a piece of captive equipment that can be used only in the area serviced by its overhead bridge-crane runways.

RACK STORAGE FIRE PREVENTION

It has been standard procedure for a very long time to use wood deck boards set into step-ledge-design shelf beams in storage racks where they perform very well. The National Fire Protection Association (NFPA) in Natick, Massachusetts has demonstrated, however, that fire tends to spread horizontally under the decking and to jump from pallet opening to pallet opening when wood decking is used and the pieces of lumber are set fairly close together with little or no gaps between boards laid between the shelf beams. The NFPA tests have indicated, also, that for certain classes of materials used with wood decking, the fire will jump clear across aisle spaces.

CAUTION: Avoid wood decking in storage racks whenever possible due to the above fire protection judgments. (This same evaluation can be extended to plywood, particle board, or any other flammable material.)

How to Minimize Fire Risks

Establishing uniform codes that will cover the fire prevention aspects of high-rise/high-density storage racks has been difficult for the insurance underwriters.

In the past decade, the NFPA has been fire testing HR/HD racks up to 25 or so feet in height in order to obtain useful data. Because of the expense involved in this kind of testing, the best that can be expected for heights much beyond this limit lies in the realm of computer simulation. Through the perseverance of NFPA, however, the 231-C manual now covers storage rack applications, classes of combustibles, flue spacing, and so forth. You can obtain this document by writing to:

National Fire Protection Association
470 Atlantic Avenue
Boston, MA 02210

NOTE: If your storage racks are over 12-feet high consult this manual and your fire insurance underwriter.

Some of the provisions of the NFPA code are, as follows:

- If you plan on placing racks over 12-feet high back-to-back, you must use a row spacer that will maintain a flue space between the racks of at least 6 inches. (This may vary with the application, but most flue spacers permit you to provide from 6 to 8 inches of flue space.)

- The NFPA requires an upright post or frame section flue space of 6 inches also. Usually this space is readily obtainable since the upright post width (i.e., cross-section) is approximately 3 inches; thus, there is no real difficulty in providing this clearance between the pallet storage rack openings that begin or end at the upright post.

Use Sprinkler Systems to Protect Your Storage Space

When you store combustible materials such as: wood boxes, crates, corrugated board containers (cardboard), and similar packaged items in storage racks 12 feet or lower in height, your main source of fire protection consists of overhead sprinklers usually suspended 18 inches below the ceiling in black iron piping.

CAUTION: For pallet storage rack heights greater than 12 feet the regulations become much more severe and restrictive. As an example, in some HR/HD storage rack installations it is necessary to provide standpipes and sprinkler heads in the flue spaces between the racks. In addition it may be required that sprinkler heads be staggered between intermediate storage rack levels.

NOTE: To my knowledge, there has been no general policy statement or other regulation concerning the storage of unitized, shrink-wrapped (plastic film) loads in rack installations. Review this with your underwriter. In certain instances, underwriters have permitted shrink-wrapped loads to be placed in racks if they are separated at various intervals; however, from personal observation regarding shrink-wrapped loads stored in pallet racks, it would seem reasonable to assume that when a fire causes overhead sprinklers to release water, unprotected palletized corrugated boxes would become waterlogged causing the containers to collapse, damaging the contents in most instances. The shrink-wrapped loads would disperse water thereby extinguishing the flames and leaving the contents of the containers virtually unharmed.

Use Rack Decking to Your Advantage

Front-to-back Members

There are many pallet storage rack installations that do not use decking as such, but use instead two roll-formed-metal, front-to-back members upon which the palletized load rests. Thus, each pallet opening has a pair of these members to support the load and they are simply laid on a pair of shelf beams, which is no doubt the simplest and cheapest way of providing a surface upon which to place material. (See Figure 11-6.)

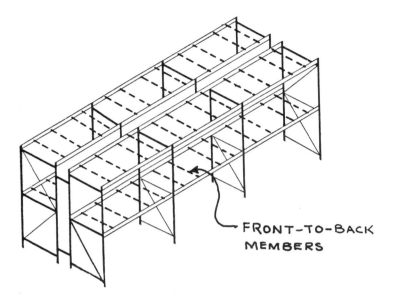

FRONT-TO-BACK MEMBERS

Fig. 11-6: Illustration of storage racks with front-to-back members in place.

Some of the disadvantages of the front-to-back (F-t-B) members become evident if the fit between the shelf beams is loose; there is danger of the F-t-B member becoming dislodged, thereby dropping the load. A method of avoiding this problem is to have F-t-B members welded as part of the shelf beam structure. Then expense of installation begins to escalate, because installation will require a two-person crew. If F-t-B members are simply laid in place it is possible also for loose or broken pallet bottom boards or loose nails to dislodge the F-t-B members.

CAUTION: Never use loose F-t-B members in HD/HR pallet storage racks; if F-t-B members are used they should be safely pinned or welded to the shelf beams.

Front-to-back members permit the free dispersal of fire-extinguishing water. Thus, in addition to their relatively low cost they are a relatively safe fire risk.

Wood Decking

Wood deck boards set into step-ledge-design shelf beams are satisfactory storage platforms in low storage racks. However, as explained, do not use wood decking in HR/HD storage installations over 12 feet high because of fire hazard. (See Figure 11-7.)

Wire-mesh Decking

Wire-mesh decking has been used in many pallet storage rack installations over the years. (See Figure 11-8.)

Despite its fragile appearance it is quite strong and can be set into place easily; where a fit becomes difficult it can be pounded into place without much effort. Several types of wire-mesh decking are made to fit virtually every type of shelf-beam configuration. It has good fire protection properties since it permits water penetration and dispersal unlike other types of solid steel or wood decking. One of the disadvantages of wire-mesh decking, however, is its inability to withstand heavy point loading such as an unpalletized heavy load

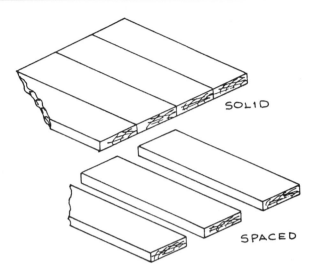

Fig. 11-7: Examples of wood decking.

with feet or mounting blocks, such as unpalletized engines or pieces of machinery, machine-tool dies, and the like. Nevertheless, it does extremely well when uniform loads are placed on it. If the loads are extremely heavy the decking should be reinforced with steel channels or angles welded on its bottom side.

NOTE: The type of merchandise to be stored will determine the type of decking to be used in any pallet storage rack installation.

Solid Steel Decking

Solid steel decking, which is usually sheet steel with the edges bent downwards as shown in Figure 11-9 performs as satisfactorily as solid wood decking.

It does not burn, of course, but depending upon the types or classes of materials stored on its surface it tends to spread the fire and does not readily permit the penetration of water from the sprinklers, which is immensely important in fighting storage rack fires. The solid steel decking usually comes in sections and is laid across the shelf beams of the rack. It is relatively inexpensive and it can be easily reinforced to accept heavy loads. It is the perfect decking for storing heavy dies and fixtures that must be slid across its surface during loading and unloading operations. It makes extremely good decking for installations below the 12 feet mark but must be considered carefully for heights above 12 feet.

Grate-type Decking

There are several types of grate-type decking, one of which is shown in Figure 11-10.

Almost all grate decks are composed of materials that are used primarily in steel stair treads, or storage mezzanine surfacing, or in machinery walkways, catwalks, and the like. The openings, or perforations, aid in fire protection because like wire mesh it permits virtually unrestricted penetration of extinguishing water. Grate decks can sustain relatively heavy loads without reinforcement; however, they are usually very expensive and remain noncompetitive with other decking materials.

Photo courtesy Nashville Wire Products, Nashville, TN
Fig. 11-8: Wire-mesh decking used in pallet storage racks.

Perforated Metal Decking

The concept of perforated metal decking was conceived as a way to utilize coiled steel scrap resulting from steel washer manufacturing. Most washers are produced from coils of steel which are fed automatically into multidie, stamping presses; thus, the staggered hole spacing is uniform throughout the material. Shelf beams made from perforated metal were first manufactured in Illinois by the Heft company. It has all of the advantages of wire-mesh decking, in terms of fire protection since this type of decking permits water penetration, but it has the added ability to withstand point loading and sustain relatively heavy loads inasmuch as it can be obtained in various gauges and hole configurations. (See Figure 11-11.) It is my understanding that it is competitively priced.

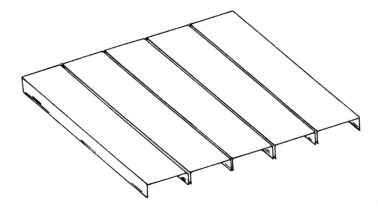

Fig. 11-9: Solid steel decking showing bent-down edges for stiffness.

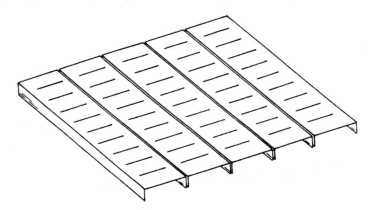

Fig 11-10: Grate-type decking used in storage racks.

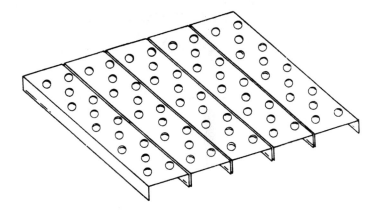

Fig. 11-11: An illustration of perforated metal decking with the edges bent downwards for added stiffness.

12

Using Nonpermanent Buildings for Temporary Storage Space

STRUCTURAL TYPES OF NONPERMANENT BUILDINGS

When there is an urgent requirement for additional storage space—space that is not readily available locally or in a specific location—you should know that at a relatively low price, nonpermanent type of structures may be erected with a lead time measured only in months. There are two basic types of structures that fill this specification:

• Air-supported
• Rigid frame

The air-supported type was developed for the Department of Defense after World War II as radomes primarily for use in the Arctic. The harsh climatic conditions of the Arctic fully attest to the durability of the materials and methods of constructing these so-called nonpermanent buildings. Also, the rigid frame structures were a natural outcome of development that followed the radomes inasmuch as similar synthetic fabrics are used. The following discussion gives a frame of reference for selecting either type.

AIR-SUPPORTED STRUCTURES

The radomes cited above were temporary shelters with a life expectancy from 10 to 15 years. They were composed of a tough, vinyl plastic, laminated envelope (two layers), supported by air blown into the structure, or bubble, at about 5 lb./sq. ft., about ½-inch of water-gauge pressure. (See Figure 12-1.)

The blowers used with air-supported buildings are usually paired so that either one or both blowers can be running at the same time. Alternate blower use can prolong blower life and in some larger units, say where football field size bubbles are concerned, a third standby blower is used. Heating units are also used in northern snow country climates not only for comfort levels for workers inside the structures, but also to prevent ice and snow buildup on

Photos courtesy of William Wheeler, President A-O-S Inc./AIR-O-STRUCTURES, Monmouth, ME

Fig. 12-1: Interior and exterior views of an air-supported structure.

the vinyl fabric surface. Using full instrumentation as described, ambient atmospheric conditions can be monitored. Temperature gauges and an external anemometer (wind gauge) hookup can make the air-supported structure virtually fail-safe. For instance, if internal temperatures fall below a certain safe level the heaters will kick in and snow will be melted from the external surface, thus eliminating the possibility of a collapse of the structure; and if wind velocities pick up to gale force (i.e., 40 mph), the blowers will automatically pump the structure up to a pressure of 10 to 12 lb., making the structure more rigid. With pressures in this range the structure can withstand wind velocities of 90 mph and more. (For the details of construction, see Figure 12-2.)

It is even possible to control humidity in this type of building, something that is not easily achievable in ordinary warehouse structures. A major automotive manufacturer houses metal stampings in two large 40,000-square foot structures south of Chicago without signs of rust or corrosion. These buildings have been in service at least four years.

Recent advances have been made in quilting the laminated vinyl fabric of the air-supported structure to make it possible to use air conditioning methods to lower the temperatures

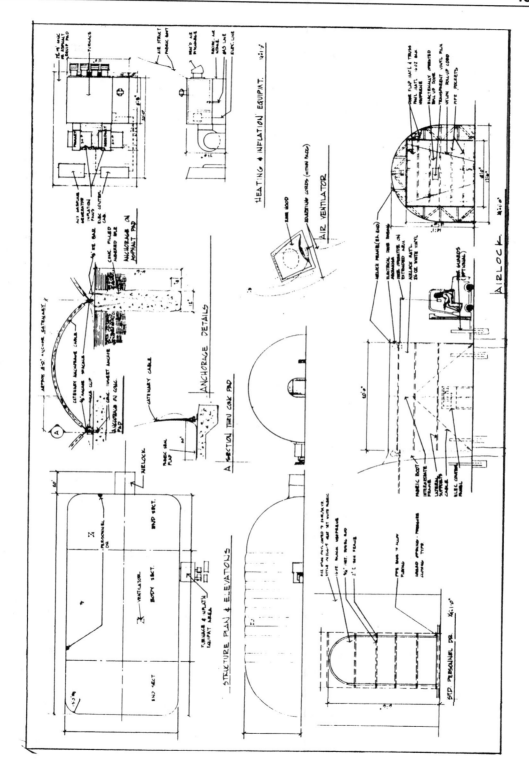

Fig. 12-2: Details of construction for a standard air-supported structure.

within the structure for the storage of produce and other perishables. The quilting technique puts a dead air space between the fabric layers in much the same way as thermopane glass is insulated.

Advantages of Air-supported Structures

- If capital dollars are tight, it is possible to lease or lease-purchase these structures.
- The buildings are considerably lower in cost than any other type of structure.
- They can be erected anywhere that a flat surface can be made available. Air-supported structures have been placed in open fields, on asphalt parking lots, and on concrete pads.
- The structures are easily relocated; as an example, they may be taken down and shipped to another site when required. They may be taken down, stored, and re-erected during peak loads. The Seahawks football team puts up its huge playing field bubble in the month of October and takes it down at the end of March as protection for the team during the Seattle rainy season.
- They can be erected in less than one week's time.
- The inside, being free span, provides excellent storage space.
- The structures require a minimum of maintenance.
- If their cost per square foot is amortized over their useful life, the cost is generally under one dollar per square foot.

Disadvantages of Air-supported Structures

- The inflation system, which is the heart of the system, requires automatic controls, a standby blower, and a reliable power source which may be provided by a standby generator. If maintenance schedules for this equipment are not rigorously applied, it is possible to lose the structure.
- The structure being a laminated vinyl fabric is subject to vandalism; however, tears in the fabric may be easily repaired.
- They are relatively unsafe at winds over 70 mph, although auxiliary blower capacity can be used to add another ½-inch of water gauge pressure, bringing the internal pressure up to 10-12 lb./sq.ft.
- Air locks, short tunnels with doors at both ends to retain the internal pressure, must be provided for the passage of heavy equipment in and out of the structure. They are fairly simple to install.
- Heat is required in the building to minimize snow loads.
- New fabric is required every seven to ten years, although fourteen years has elapsed since putting new fabric on one large structure in mid-California.

NOTE: I have been involved in four projects involving air-supported structures in Illinois and the State of Washington with very good results.

RIGID-FRAME STRUCTURES

Rigid, steel-framed structures generally use a laminated vinyl plastic fabric similar to that developed for air-supported structures. A welded, braced, steel frame structure supports the vinyl fabric which is stretched over the rib members of the building. The end result is a building that appears similar to an air-supported structure but is much stronger and costs approximately $2 to $3 more per square foot. Clear spans of up to 120 feet are now possible using this type of construction. Figure 12-3 illustrates the interior and exterior of a rigid-frame structure.

Photo courtesy of "Cover It," Ansonia, CT

Fig. 12-3: Interior and exterior views of a rigid-frame structure showing open sides. While this type of structure can serve as a shed, the openings may be covered, also, to obtain totally enclosed space.

The rigid-frame structure can provide long-range storage or manufacturing space at less cost than a comparable stick-built structure and at only slightly higher cost than for an air-supported structure. While the vinyl fabric material must be renewed at intervals that approximate those of the air-supported building, say 7 to 10 years, maintenance considerations are less demanding. Figure 12-4 illustrates some of the construction details of a rigid-frame structure.

Advantages of Rigid-frame Structures

- Rigid-frame structures will withstand winds of 110 mph and snow loads of 30 lb./sq.ft.

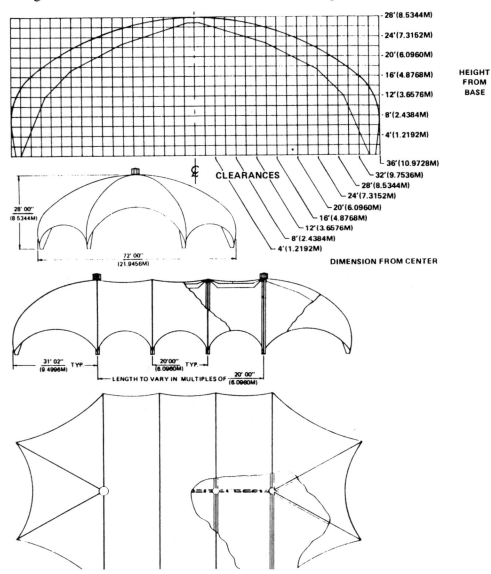

Fig. 12-4: Construction details of a rigid-frame structure.

- If you have a slab upon which to erect the structure, the cost per square foot will be approximately $6 or higher due to inflation.
- Rigid-frame structures do not require blowers or control instrumentation.
- The buildings do not require heat unless the snow loads build up beyond the design limitations of 30 lb./sq.ft.
- Lights, heaters, sprinklers, and signs can be hung from the interior steel trusses.
- Similar to the air-supported structure a rigid-frame structure can be erected in a matter of days.
- Similar to its air-supported counterpart, it can be readily dismantled and reassembled.
- Maintenance costs are minimal.

Disadvantages of Rigid-frame Structures

- The free span limitation is 120 feet.
- The cost per square foot is somewhat higher than for air-supported structures.
- The fabric skin must be renewed every seven to ten years.

13

Packaging
for Receiving

APPLYING A SYSTEMS APPROACH TO PACKAGING

I've emphasized the systems approach throughout this book because it is important to view the whole picture—from the raw material source, through production and the physical distribution chain to the ultimate consumer. With environmental concerns so prominent, it is even necessary today to look beyond the end user and consider the methods of disposal of both the product and its packaging. Some of these concerns are:

- Can the materials of the product be recycled?

- Can the item, including packaging, be safely incinerated without producing toxic by-products?

- After the product's useful life, can some further benefit be derived from its chemical and physical properties?

Packaging is such an integral part of most products that one of the leading economic indicators is the quantity of corrugated, kraft, and fiberboard material sold. The more of these packaging materials sold, the healthier the economy and vice versa. This indicator is on a par with rail car loadings, and motor freight tons hauled.

While packaging is often used to promote the sale of soft goods, in the main, it is the bulk container in which the retailers' product is packaged that concerns us since it is used to protect the fancy internal, display packaging from in-transit damage and warehouse handling. Thus, "bulk" containers and the unitized loads that form part of the systems approach are necessary ingredients of a coordinated effort in every packaging program. To a large extent, a great deal of the rehandling, repalletizing, the picking up of loose pieces, and broken, torn, damaged, or loosely held materials in motor trucks and railway cars can be prevented if there is an operable packaging program in the company.

A two-pronged approach to achieving the benefits of the systems approach to packaging requires the cooperation of the purchasing department, traffic, the warehouse management and related personnel in the physical distribution network. It may also require the efforts of the sales and marketing departments, because they are often the ones initially responsible for setting up promotions that will require preparation for large quantity purchases.

The second portion of this systems concept is its effects on manufacturing or production operations, because we must enlist the cooperation of engineering, scheduling, inspection, and quality control, together with the accounting functions in order to properly evaluate the cost of packaging and the effect that different methods of handling various types of packaging have on departmental costs, as we shall see in later sections.

In the receiving department, expediting the materials handling of (incoming) receivables, three things are necessary:

- Space
- Equipment
- End-use criteria

SPATIAL ARRANGEMENTS FOR INSPECTION OF O.S.D. INVESTIGATION OF INCOMING GOODS

All incoming merchandise must be placed in a prearranged area so that all of the clerical and physical receiving functions can be performed, such as:

- processing documents related to the shipment:
  —checking of packing lists
  —checking of bills of lading
  —piece or weigh count
- inspection

Then the material must either be placed into storage, or transported to the first point of use.

Another spatial consideration concerns material which does not pass inspection or has to be held for an over, short, or damaged (O.S.D.) investigation, which requires that the shipment be placed into a holding area until the problem can be resolved.

Since space is a valuable commodity in any business, you can achieve faster handling and better utilization of space if you specify that your receivables be packaged in unit loads that are as large as your storage racks or bins will permit.

NOTE: The larger the unit loads, the less time and space will be required to handle the total shipment.

If pallet storage racks are not part of your materials storage system, then packaging specifications should be such that the materials can be block-stored. Block storage requires that merchandise be stacked on itself, otherwise the storage space is underutilized, and becomes exorbitantly expensive. Thus, block storage requires that unit loads, containers, or pallet loads be of a type suitable for stacking one on top of another.

CAUTION: The following caveats should be observed in block storage:

- Avoid packaging that is subject to carton fatigue and will not stack for reasonable periods of time. (Carton fatigue occurs when a poor grade of corrugated board is used for the outer, or bulk shipping containers, such as a 125-lb. test instead of 200-lb. test board; or, the carton is stored in a very humid environment. Excessive humidity over long periods of time will tend to degrade most corrugated board.)

- Eliminate void spaces in the bulk shipping (outer) container, especially if it is composed of corrugated board. (The bulk container should fit the inner materials snugly, i.e., without void spaces. If there are void spaces in the shipping container it will not stack well, causing the stacked unitized loads to lean or collapse completely.)
- An inexpensive, or poorly designed container may cause so many problems that it may become more expensive than the best possible packaging from the standpoint of **total cost.**

EQUIPMENT REQUIRED FOR EFFECTIVE PACKAGING

If your company has an AS/RS (automated storage and retrieval system), or stacker-crane, it becomes very necessary that a measure of standardization be included in your packaging program. There are, in the main, three important considerations that you must not neglect:

- Dimensions of the unitized load
- Weight of the unitized load
- Packaging integrity

Dimensions of the Unitized Load

The length, width, and height must be carefully delineated in the packaging specifications due to AS/RS limitations. The dimensions of the conveyors required to receive incoming materials, the stacker-crane shuttle or transfer car, the elevator dimensions, and the storage rack opening sizes will all have to be capable of accommodating the unitized load. A unit load that does not conform to the L × W × H criteria will be rejected by the AS/RS system, and placed in a bulk storage set-out area, or some other holding space. Then if there are no provisions for special handling of nonstandard loads, the load will have to be broken down, and repackaged into a size acceptable to the AS/RS mechanization scheme. All of this added effort means labor and packaging costs that detract from the profitability of the enterprise.

Weight of the Unit Load

The latest AS/RS systems contain weigh scales or load-cell platforms that sense the weight of the load, and reject overweight loads that must be handled in much the same way as L × W × H errors. If a load exceeds the design load deflection of the system, the shuttle or transfer device would collide with the storage rack shelf beam or cantilevered supports of the rack opening, and it could damage the AS/RS mechanism.

Packaging Integrity

This must be retained throughout the entire AS/RS processing cycle, i.e., from input to output of the load. Examples of this lack of integrity are: trailing steel wrapping bands, plastic shrouds, or stretch-wrap dangling from the unit load, broken pallet deckboards sticking out during the various transportation elements during the input or output cycles of the AS/RS. Even corrugated box flaps that bend over into the path of the AS/RS structural members, are conditions that may cause problems or damage and must be corrected, or otherwise resolved.

NOTE: Order picking in AS/RS systems may give rise to problems which do not occur when you receive and ship full loads only. If during order picking you must break-bulk (i.e., remove only one or two cartons of a unit load) and strapping or banding must be cut, care must be exercised with respect to maintaining the integrity of the unit load. A carton or more may be removed from a **shrink-wrapped** load without destroying its capacity for retaining the load intact because it has been shrunk to the contours of the load and will remain as an envelope; however, it is vastly different with **stretch-wrapped** loads where care and discretion must be used on the part of the order picker to ensure that the stretch-wrap will not unravel and destabilize the load.

NOTE: It has been found helpful where shrink wrapping is not used, to specify strip-gluing the cartons comprising the unit load with a "high-shear, low-tensile" packaging adhesive, such as may be obtained from the H. B. Fuller Co. of St. Paul, Minnesota.

For companies that do not have AS/RS systems, the packaging requirements that specify L × W × H and weight are still very valid considerations. The efficiency of the materials handling operation improves in direct proportion to the uniformity of package size and weight. Size is a significant criterion, since outsized loads that will not fit in pallet storage racks, or other preassigned spaces require additional and unnecessary handling. Also, incoming unit loads of greater density than specifications allow cannot be handled safely if they exceed the capacity of your forklift truck.

PROTECTING MATERIALS DURING INDOOR OR OUTDOOR STORAGE AND IN TRANSIT

Product packaging that generates unnecessarily large quantities of dunnage requires additional labor and effort for disposal. Thus, it should be understood by the supplier, that only sufficient packaging be used to guarantee that the product arrives at the distribution center undamaged. Anything else in the way of packaging results in additional costs to the recipient, and should be avoided!

If you are contemplating (or dependent on) outside storage for your receivables (see Chapter 3), then the packaging should be of sufficient integrity to provide the proper protection against exposure to the elements.

Packaging can be obtained to protect various types of receivables from the effects of:

- sunlight, ultraviolet rays;
- rain and moisture;
- corrosive sulfur in the air; and,
- oxidation.

Plastic film opened up a whole new age of packaging. The advent of styrofoam, expanded polyurethanes, foamed-in-place types of plastics has brought about packaging innovations in myriad ways. Of the plastic films, polyethylene and polystyrene are the most common, with a preference being shown for the less expensive polyethylene, although it is not as transparent as the polystyrene.

Clear plastic films, such as the polys may be heat-sealed thereby providing a measure of moisture protection that is sufficient for most packaging needs. Desiccants (drying agents) like silica gel may be added to sealed packages to absorb entrapped moisture, thus protecting the product from rust. VCI (vapor controlled inhibitors) can also be used to prevent corrosion. They work by placing a VCI chip (a paper impregnated with a VCI) or VCI granules in a sealed container with the item. The VCI releases a vapor within the container which coats the product with a thin film, thus ambient entrapped air does not have to be exhausted from the package since the inhibiting shield of vapor is deposited on the part.

Ultraviolet ray inhibitors can protect products from sunlight, this is especially necessary where consumer packaging is concerned, because it prevents less stable colors from fading, and keeps certain plastics from becoming brittle. Plastic films may be colored to opaqueness as an ultraviolet inhibitor, the usual color is black. There is an added advantage of covering some products with black plastic, in that the contents which may be pilferable cannot be readily viewed without damaging the plastic shroud. The fact that the contents are invisible is another deterrent to theft.

By heat-sealing plastic liners in shipping containers, the effects of corrosive fumes, odor penetration, and oxidation can be minimized. Although most plastic films have a degree of permeability, this is not generally regarded as a disadvantage.

OBJECTIVES FOR A PACKAGING PROGRAM

It is necessary to develop a packaging policy that will assure that products arrive at your company destinations damage-free and in packaging or unitized loads that are economical for your company to handle.

There are three main reasons for spelling out the objectives of your company's packaging program:

1. The receivables should be compatible with your company's material handling equipment and handling methods. As an example, if the receivable is too large or heavy, you may not have sufficient forklift truck or stacker-crane capacity to handle it and you would have to lease or rent the proper equipment.

2. The receivable should be compatible in size and weight with your storage racks and bins. If it is too large, you will incur the additional cost of repackaging the material. If the receivable is too small, it may waste your storage space; and it may require a number of additional handlings in order to consolidate the load. Also, if it is not unitized or palletized it may require you to use your own pallets to handstack from the carrier and to stretch-wrap the load after it arrives at your plant. This is always a costly and time-consuming operation, especially if a large shipment is concerned.

3. Ecological considerations must be one of the objectives of your company's packaging program. Packaging requirements must take into consideration disposal and recycling of dunnage and packaging materials, such as corrugated board, strapping, fiberboard, and the like.

14

Developing a Company Packaging Manual to Help Cut Costs and Increase Effectiveness

HOW A PACKAGING MANUAL CAN ELIMINATE PACKAGING PROBLEMS

Even a small company can profit by formalizing its packaging requirements. This codification may consist of only a few duplicated sheets of paper, or it can be a bound volume; the necessary instructions to suppliers should contain the minimum requirements that the company will accept for its receivables. Of course, the degree of compliance on the part of suppliers is often based on how much volume is generated, and/or how valued a customer the company has become to the supplier. Whether your company is large or small, a company packaging manual will help to standardize materials handling methods and equipment, and will

- reduce the cost of operations, and
- increase the effectiveness of the receiving function.

Since the systems approach requires that every facet of the operation be questioned in order to improve the effectiveness of materials handling and reduce the cost of the receiving activity we must eliminate the problems caused by poor packaging. Improper packaging causes:

- excessive handling;
- wasted time;
- unsafe practices; and
- disruptions in the orderly flow of materials through the system.

One of the underlying causes of interrupted work flow and a disorganized activity on the receiving floor is the way in which merchandise arrives in the receiving department. The best way to tackle the packaging problem is to involve in the packaging program all of the departments of the company that are affected by packaging. In this way, the vested interest of each department can be protected. The result of this program will be the compilation of a packaging manual that reflects the best thinking of all the concerned departments. This hopefully will assure the further cooperation of each group, since these groups have become part of the program.

NOTE: Without the cooperation of each involved department, the packaging program may never fully succeed.

Another good reason for obtaining input from traffic, purchasing, inspection, quality control, and so forth, is that their expertise will make the program practical and realistic.

In addition to in-house cooperation, support from your company's vendors is vitally needed. Supplier support is necessary because the packaging manual will indicate such elements as:

- the requirements for the items to be supplied;
- the kinds of packaging; and,
- the suppliers' contacts within your company in order to get specific information.

Therefore, it is necessary that these elements be completely described in the manual so that they can be properly achieved in practice.

In any event, the above discussion does not relieve the supplier of its responsibilities for providing adequate protection for the materials or products it is supplying. The supplier must comply with all laws and regulations concerning the transportation of the product, such as:

- the railroads' Uniform Freight Classification; and,
- the trucking industry's National Motor Freight Classification.

Since carriers' regulations and requirements are relatively complex, there is every need to establish a sound basis for communication between the supplier and your company in order to obtain the best possible packaging for your company at a price you can afford to pay. Therefore, in most companies, the purchasing department has the sole responsibility for communicating with the supplier and the packaging manual should spell this out in no uncertain terms. This should eliminate the interference of gung-ho materials handling and packaging engineers which can create problems for both the supplier and your company.

In any good packaging program, give the supplier an opportunity to make suggestions and recommendations based on its experience with the materials being sold to your company. Establish a climate between the supplier and your company that will make it easy for you to obtain packaging savings and improvements that will contribute to the lowest total cost in terms of labor and materials. Thus, the packaging manual should provide guidelines by which each vendor may use standardized packaging methods and materials within the constraints of load weight limits, packaging materials, and dimensions provided in the manual.

In a formalized packaging program, every supplier should be capable of indicating how its materials will be packaged for shipment, *prior to shipment*. For this purpose a standard form should be used which will provide all the necessary information that will enable you to determine whether or not the receivables conform to your company's requirements. See Figure 14-1 for an example of a "Packaging & Shipping Data Sheet" that your company can use.

PACKAGING & SHIPPING DATA SHEET

Supplier Name and Address   Return to: _____

_____   _____

_____   _____

_____   _____

Date _____ Part/Model No. _____ Description _____

Status: New ☐ Revised☐ Note: For any changes to be made in Packaging or
Shipping Methods, see Plant Purchasing Dept. for prior approvals.

Part or Model	Length	Width	Height	Weight	Materials	
					☐Metal	☐Rubber
					☐Glass	☐Fiber
					☐Plastic	☐Other

Packaging Data

When manually handled packages are unitized with mechanically handled unit loads,
complete both sections.

Manually Handled	*Mechanically Handled*	*Closures*	*Banding*
☐Loose	☐Palletized Boxes	☐Glue	☐Metallic
Bundle	Pallet Tray Pack	Tape	Nonmetallic
Bag	Pieces on Pallet	Staple	Wire
Drum	Pallet Box	Wire	Other

Corrugated Box:	Corrugated-Wood	Cord	*Rust Prevention*
Reg. Slotted	Wire-bound	Other	Type:
Telescopic	Crate	_____	(Explain)
Full Flap	Returnable Company-Owned	*Interior*	_____
Material _____	Returnable Supplier-Owned	Wrapped	_____
Bursting	Other Type _____	Loose	_____
Strength__ lb	Send drwgs, specs, photo	Cells	
Other _____	*Load Size:*	Liner	
Load Size:	L _____	Diecut	
L _____	W _____	Nested	
W _____	D _____	Other	
D _____	Gross Wt. _____	__ _____	
Gross Wt. _____	No. of pieces _____		
No. of pieces _____			

Description of Pallet Design:
☐2-way   ☐4-way   ☐Block   ☐Stringer
☐Other _____

Size L _____ W _____

Fork Entry: Width _____ (Min 22 inches)

Height _____ (Min 3¾ inches)

Container Charges:
☐Supplier Returnable: Type _____

Deposit required: $_____

☐Expendable (one-way): Type _____

Pallet cost: $_____ Packaging Cost $_____

continued

Fig. 14-1: Example of a Packaging & Shipping Data Sheet.

Type of Carrier to be used:
☐Rail ☐Truck ☐Other _____
If part or model cannot be packaged by means of existing container types: (Explain)

_____
_____

Additional Comments: _____
_____
_____

Supplier's signature _____ Title _____Date __
For Company Use Only:
   Purchasing _____ Date _____
   Matl. Handling Engineering _____ Date _____
   Packaging _____ Date _____
(Note: An instruction sheet should accompany this form, but this can be placed on the back of the form.)

Fig. 14-1 continued

It contains all of the necessary elements to ensure that you will receive properly packaged materials with a minimum of "grief," save the company money, and protect the environment.

On the other end of the stick, is a form of communication with the supplier when things are not going so well; for this we have a "Packaging Deficiency Notice," see Figure 14-2.

In the event that materials are received in poor condition, or if they have been packaged in a way that does not conform to the packaging manual (and, will not fit in with your company's requirements for L × W × H, or weight, etc.), then the *deficiency notice* completed by your materials handling or packaging engineer, should be sent to the supplier by the purchasing department.

NOTE: It should be a company policy that any deviation from the packaging manual and the "Packaging & Shipping Data Sheet," should require prior approval by both the plant materials handling engineer and the purchasing department. Exceptions to this rule should be made only when emergency shipments or special handling are involved, and then only upon prior notification by the purchasing department.

Inasmuch as a systems approach in warehousing and physical distribution cuts across company lines, packaging affects the productivity of materials handling, and vice versa. The materials handling component of packaging takes many shapes, especially since the excessive handling of a product, whether it is a purchased part, or manufactured in-house, and becomes an undesirable and unnecessarily expensive part of plant operations. Thus, in order to reduce the quantity of excessive handling, which costs money and causes product damage, the goal for the packaging program is *to develop a high degree of standardization in the way products are packaged.*

THE BASICS OF A COMPANY PACKAGING MANUAL

If you have any hesitation about whether or not your company needs a packaging manual, you should take into consideration two things:

- it is necessary to formalize packaging procedures in order to have them work well; and,

PACKAGING & DEFICIENCY NOTICE

Date Rec'd _____ Supplier _____ Date
                       Name and _____ of Notice _____
                       Address _____
Part or Model No. _____

Gentlemen: The packaging of a recent shipment received from your company resulted in the arrival of the materials in poor condition. Please complete and return two copies of this form indicating the action you have taken to remedy this situation.

            Buyer _____ Location _____

1. Unit Load:
   ___ Incorrect size for storage $L \times W \times H$
         Load size we require L _____ W _____ H _____
   ___ Material loaded in carrier poorly.
   ___ Part numbers mixed. Please consolidate.
   ___ Excessive carton void spaces.
         Pallet too small _____ too large _____.
   ___ Container failed
   ___ Improperly marked
   ___ Banding defective
   ___ Other

2. Identification/Packing List:
   ___ Improper location
   ___ Not available
   ___ Incomplete information
   ___ Other

3. Transportation:
   ___ Unit load failed because of improper loading/handling
   ___ Fragile items not protected
   ___ Dunnage between tiers missing
   ___ Excessive weight on bottom load

4. Pre-shipment Test:
   ___ Container/unit load failed
   ___ Packaging failed
   ___ Pre-shipment test recommended
   ___ Certified pre-shipment test required

5. Comments: _____
   _____
   _____
   _____

6. Supplier Action Taken:
   (To be completed by supplier)

   _____
   _____
   _____
   _____

   Packaging/Material Handling Engineer _____
   Photo Attached ☐

Fig. 14-2: Example of a Packaging Deficiency Notice.

- it is necessary to have a reference source for suppliers and plant personnel in order for them to do a good job, and save money for the company.

A good manual should contain the following information, as well as the "Packaging & Shipping Data Sheet" (Figure 14-1), and the "Packaging Deficiency Notice" (Figure 14-2), together with any pertinent information specific to your company and/or which has been discussed, above.

All packages, palletized unit loads, and containers can usually be grouped into two rather broad categories, as follows:

- *Manually handled packages*—These are packages that cannot be readily or conveniently handled by an industrial forklift truck, or other mobile materials handling equipment, and that weigh 50 pounds, or less.

NOTE: According to OSHA regulations, women are allowed to lift items weighing 35 pounds, or less; men can lift up to 50 pounds.

- *Mechanically handled packages*—These are unit loads that are palletized, slip-sheeted, skidded, shrink-, or stretch-wrapped, containerized, and the like, such that they can be readily handled by a forklift truck and other types of mobile materials handling equipment.

Packaging Guidelines for Manually Handled Packages

- Corrugated boxes are the most acceptable type of manually handled package, depending to a large extent upon the type of product or parts to be contained.
- The packaging must provide proper protection for the parts so that they may arrive safely at their destination.
- The gross weight of the package must not exceed the OSHA limitation of 50 pounds, and it must be of a configuration such that it can be readily handled by a single individual.
- The package must be sealed or closed so that the contents will not spill out, and the closure method must not be a safety hazard. For this reason staples and other metal fasteners are to be discouraged, unless they are the result of the supplier's automatic packaging line and a changeover would be prohibitively expensive. When glue is used as a carton closure it should be applied in strip or dot application only to the point where the carton has sufficient adhesion to withstand the rigors of shipping and handling, so that the carton may be readily opened at the receiving plant.
- The packaging materials may be capable of being recycled, but unless prior approval has been obtained from both materials handling and purchasing to the contrary, the container must be an expendable or one-way type.
- Parts that are a meter in length, or longer, must be removable from the end of the package.
- Eliminate void spaces when using corrugated cartons. Voids cause container collapse.
- Bundles are to be used only when the configuration of the part makes other types of packaging prohibitively expensive.

- Re-used, i.e., second-hand, corrugated cartons can be used only after obtaining prior approvals from the materials handling and purchasing departments.
- A supplier's packaging may require testing prior to shipment, especially when fragile parts are to be transported; these might include ceramic parts, electronic components, glassware, and the like. (See Pre-shipment Testing in of this chapter.)

Packaging Guidelines for Mechanically Handled Packages

This section applies to all packages, not to be manually handled, that require some type of mechanical equipment to move them satisfactorily across the receiving platform and within the plant or distribution center.

- Unit or unitized loads, unless containerized, must have a reasonably strong pallet base in order to assure that the load arrives at its destination without damage and may, in addition, be handled safely from the receiving platform to the first point of use within the plant.
- Establish pallet standards for expendable (one-way, or one-use-only) pallets. (This is discussed later in this chapter.)
- Containers and packaging materials must be expendable, unless prior agreement and approval has been obtained from materials handling and the purchasing department for use of a "returnable" container. (In some instances a returnable container program is very cost effective.)
- Drums, barrels, bags, and salvaged containers that are reused may only be used with prior approval from purchasing since these materials are more difficult and costly to handle because of the labor cost involved.
- The gross weight of palletized or unit loads must be within the capabilities of your company's materials handling equipment.
- Every palletized load should have a minimum underclearance of 3-5/8-inches and a minimum width for fork entry of 24 inches. (Underclearance is not required for slipsheeted loads or BOP sheets; however, prior approvals from purchasing must be obtained when either of these "pallets" is used.)
- Material should be stacked on pallets with an interlocking pattern whenever possible.
- Palletized loads should be securely banded with edge protectors when necessary.
- Strip gluing with a high-shear, low-tensile adhesive should be used whenever practicable.
- Pallet overhang is to be avoided, because of potential product damage.
- Palletized loads should be shrink-wrapped when more than normal protection is required; stretch-wrap must be used on all palletized loads that are not otherwise held in a compact module.
- Corrugated board containers are preferable to wire-bound or wood boxes, since they may be recycled more easily.
- Palletized unit loads should have only one part number, unless this is impractical, since this speeds up the receiving paperwork.

- Rust-prevention and anti-corrosion methods should be used if the parts could be adversely affected during transportation or storage.
- The company's packaging manual should include definitions of all of the types of containers that might conceivably be received, such as:
  —pallet boxes, either corrugated, wire-bound, or wood
  —pallets with loose parts
  —boxes on a pallet
  —pallet tray pack
  —pallet shrink-, or stretch-wrap
  —crates
- Instructions should be included so that piece parts are packaged correctly.

Guidelines for Heavy Small Parts Packaging

Small, heavy parts such as nuts, bolts, washers, and other fasteners should be packaged according to the fastener industry's "Adopted Container Type Standards," which may be obtained from:

Industrial Fastener Institute
1717 E. 9th Street, Suite 1105
Cleveland, OH 44114-2879 (216)241-1482

and applicable carrier regulations. The company manual should reference the above sources and the Fibre Box Handbook which is published by the Fibre Box Association:

Fibre Box Association
224 S. Michigan Avenue
Chicago, IL 60604

This handbook is available through local fibre box suppliers who are members of the association. The handbook includes descriptions of:

- box styles
- interior packaging forms
- closures
- carrier regulations (motor, rail, air, express, parcel post, and other information extracted from carrier regulations)

Small, dense parts should be packaged in fiberboard boxes and then packed into double- or triple-wall corrugated containers. The following represents fastener carton sizes:

Container Style	Size in Inches
1/16 keg	$6\frac{1}{4} \times 6\frac{1}{4} \times 3\frac{1}{8}$
1/8 keg	$6\frac{1}{4} \times 6\frac{1}{4} \times 6\frac{1}{4}$
1/4 keg	$9 \times 9 \times 6\frac{1}{2}$
1/2 keg	$9 \times 9 \times 13$
3/4 keg	$11 \times 11 \times 12$
Full keg	$11 \times 11 \times 17$

Specifications for double-wall, and triple-wall corrugated containers should be included in the manual, as described and illustrated in the Fibre Box Handbook.

In order to properly support palletized containers of dense small parts, the pallets should conform to the specifications for expendable pallets described for mechanically handled parts as shown in Figure 14-3.

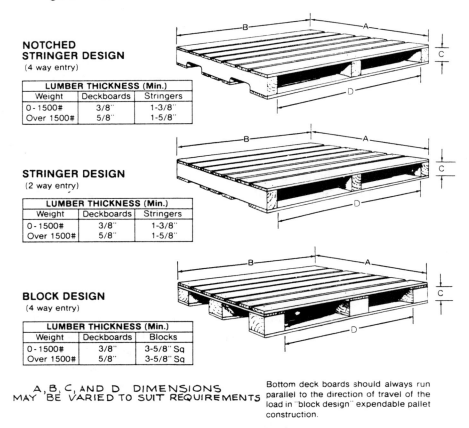

NOTCHED STRINGER DESIGN
(4 way entry)

LUMBER THICKNESS (Min.)		
Weight	Deckboards	Stringers
0 - 1500#	3/8"	1-3/8"
Over 1500#	5/8"	1-5/8"

STRINGER DESIGN
(2 way entry)

LUMBER THICKNESS (Min.)		
Weight	Deckboards	Stringers
0 - 1500#	3/8"	1-3/8"
Over 1500#	5/8"	1-5/8"

BLOCK DESIGN
(4 way entry)

LUMBER THICKNESS (Min.)		
Weight	Deckboards	Blocks
0 - 1500#	3/8"	3-5/8" Sq
Over 1500#	5/8"	3-5/8" Sq

A, B, C, AND D DIMENSIONS MAY BE VARIED TO SUIT REQUIREMENTS

Bottom deck boards should always run parallel to the direction of travel of the load in "block design" expendable pallet construction.

Fig. 14-3: Illustrations of expendable wood pallets with minimal specifications included.

Further information and data on wood pallet construction and usage are contained in the following handbooks, "Pallets and Palletization," and "Wooden Pallet Containers & Container Systems," which may be obtained from:

National Wooden Pallet & Container Association
1619 Massachusetts Avenue, N.W.
Washington, D.C. 20036

For very heavy loads where even the heaviest of corrugated containers are not suitable, wirebounds may have to be used. A handbook entitled, "Wirebound Boxes, Crates and Pallet Boxes," may be obtained from:

Wirebound Box Manufacturers Association
1211 West 22nd Street
Oak Brook, IL 60525

As another source of data on packaging dense small parts, or even not so small parts, another handbook, "A Guide to Good Construction of Nailed Wooden Boxes, Bulletin No. 102," and "The A-B-C of Good Crating, Bulletin No. 101," may be obtained from:

Association of American Railroads
Freight and Loss Damage Prevention Section
Freight Loading and Container Bureau
59 East Van Buren Street
Chicago, IL 60605

THE ADVANTAGES OF PRE-SHIPMENT TESTING

When your company has insufficient data or experience with shipping certain parts, or the supplier would like to demonstrate the cost benefits of a new type of packaging, you should require that the supplier submit its packaging to Pre-Shipment Testing. The company's purchasing department in coordination with either the packaging engineer or the materials handling engineer should review the information provided by the supplier on the "Packaging & Shipping Data Sheet" (Figure 14-1) to try to determine whether the packaging will be sufficiently durable to withstand the harsh treatment of:

- materials handling from the supplier's plant;
- materials handling at the receiving company;
- in-transit shipping; and,
- unloading and loading at transfer or consolidation terminals.

It is not always possible to determine from the information provided on the Packaging and Shipping Data Sheet in what condition the product will arrive at its destination. Thus, it may be necessary to require the supplier to certify that its packaging is sufficient for the protection of the materials to be shipped. Pre-shipment testing is one of the best methods (outside of actually shipping the product) for discovering potential package design deficiencies. Approved test methods can pinpoint:

- *underpackaging*—which leads to product damage; and,
- *overpackaging*—which increases packaging costs unnecessarily with no improvement in product safety.

Almost every major city has at least one certified testing laboratory, so that this type of package testing can be performed in every region of the country. The laboratories use standardized test procedures and equipment that serve to isolate packaging deficiencies. Some of these tests are, as follows:

- vibration;
- drop;
- incline-impact;
- compression; and,
- various tests on the packaging materials, themselves.

As an example of the basic components of a certification of pre-shipment testing, see Figure 14-4.

CERTIFICATION OF PRE-SHIPMENT TESTING

Part No. or Model No. _____ Date _____
Name or Description _____
Supplier's Name _____
         Address _____
Shipped From _____
Packaging
Laboratory Name _____
         Address _____
    Package Design   Date of Prior Test _____ ☐New ☐Revised
_____

Description

Dimensions

Interior Packaging

No. of Parts/Container   *Gross Weight* _____ lb
                                                          _____ kg
COMMENTS:
_____
_____
_____

We hereby certify that the package and contents described above have passed the
Shipping Container Pre-Shipment Test as prescribed in the "X" (your company)
Packaging Manual.
Signature of
Authorized Supplier Official _____ Title _____
Date _____

Fig. 14-4: An example of a "Certification of Pre-Shipment Testing" which, when properly
used, guarantees the safe arrival of a product at its destination.

HOW TO GUARD AGAINST CORROSION

Rust, and various types of chemical action on metallic surfaces that result in the deterioration of the product can usually be prevented with only slight additional care and expense. It is the ounce of prevention that generally rewards the prudent manager many times over. For this reason, the packaging manual should specify the preservative processes that may be used with particular types of product. The necessary elements to be included in the manual are, as follows:

• Specify the most desirable cleaning method for the part before the application of any type of preservative. Naturally, some parts may not require cleaning or preservation.

• Specify the preferred method(s) of applying the preservatives, viz: dip, spray, or brush.

• VCI (volatile corrosion inhibitors) may, on occasion, be specified to minimize deterioration. VCI may be used as chips, precut disks, or as VCI impregnated paper wrappers.

To be most effective, containers should be taped, glued, or otherwise sealed. The inhibitor works by slowly releasing a vapor which places a light, hardly noticeable film over the metallic part, and although moisture may be present, the part will not be affected over long periods of storage.

- Vacuum sealing is another effective way of preventing corrosion. Packaging the part (usually, small metallic parts) in a plastic bag, exhausting the air with a probe, then heat-sealing the bag, assures a fairly long shelf-life.

- Heat sealing the part in a plastic bag partially filled with preservative oils is another good method of preserving fine machine finishes of such items as ball-bearings and some tools. Depending on part size and weight, the plastic film, usually polyethylene, should be at least 3 or 4 mils in thickness.

GETTING THE MOST BENEFIT FROM SHIPPING CONTAINERS

Your company's decision whether or not to invest in shipping containers should be based on the particulars of each situation. In many companies the question of whether to use *expendable* (one-way, or non-returnable) containers, or *returnable* containers is never fully settled.

As an indication of the unresolved question of whether to use one type of shipping container versus another, you have only to look at the combinations of containers that are used in most companies. Since there are advantages and disadvantages to either type of container, you must carefully examine the cost of doing business with either one of them.

One of the problems with returnable containers that are not nestable or KD (knock-down) is that they require a great deal of storage space when they are not being used. Sometimes they are of such poor quality that they are hardly worth returning. Then again, if the containers are of the KD-type, they may require an inordinate amount of expensive labor effort to collapse them. This is especially true after the containers have been in service a while and have made a number of roundtrips between the customer and supplier. In some instances, it becomes virtually impossible to collapse the containers and the tendency, then, is to leave them assembled, with all of the storage and shipping problems that this entails.

NOTE: It is a general rule of thumb that the point of diminishing returns for the use of a returnable container is approximately a 300-mile radius of the distribution center. Beyond 300 miles, freight rates make the use of either captive or returnable containers uneconomical.

The 300-mile range for the most effective use of returnable containers is based on motor truck transportation. Most railroad companies, however, will return empty shipping containers to the shipper at no charge to the user, thus, expanding the effective distance of this logistic method well beyond motor truck transportation range.

Tender rates or preferred rates may often be obtained from trucking companies that could offset some of the disadvantages that occur when using returnable containers.

NOTE: A desirable type of returnable container should have a *low tare weight* and be *knock-down* (collapsed) or nestable. Another goal when steel shipping containers are used is to obtain maximum payloads of up to 40,000 pounds per shipment.

Accounting for containers and memo charges concern both the accounting and receiving departments. In general, when returnable containers are shipped, the invoice should indicate the cost per container. This could be either an actual charge or a memo charge; thus, if the container is destroyed, or used in-house, then the customer must pay the cost of the container.

CAUTION: Careful monitoring and controls are required to stop this hemorrhaging of company funds. In comparison to steel containers, wood containers are more often discarded, damaged beyond recognition or inadvertently incinerated.

Container Identification

Whether the shipping container belongs to your company or the supplier, each container must be stamped, marked, or tagged in a satisfactory and permanent manner with the following information:

- the supplier or company name of the owner;
- Return to (location/plant name or address); and
- "Returnable Container" in large letters so that it is clearly visible from a distance.

In addition to the above, the supplier should give the same information on all packing lists and invoices presented to your company. At original costs of $60 to $100 per unit, these shipping containers represent thousands of dollars of assets which must be protected.

NOTE: The packaging manual should emphasize to each supplier that if the containers are not properly marked, or if no reference is made to them on packing lists and invoices, deposits or payments for the containers *will not be made*.

Captive Containers

In order to obtain the best price for a supplier's merchandise, and to protect the product in transit, it may be in your company's interest to lend the vendor your company's containers. Therefore, to promote the exchange of containers with suppliers, you should formalize exchange agreements by making this known in the packaging manual. In following through on this concept, let suppliers know what types of containers are available. Another important facet of this program, if the containers are owned by your company, is to decide in the early stages what container types you wish to use, and after considerable experimentation and practical use, standardize on the container type, size, and style.

CAUTION: If there is more than one plant involved in the program, make sure that storage space and materials handling equipment at all sites are compatible with the unit loads being contemplated.

LABELING METHODS ARE IMPORTANT

If you want to have a cost-effective receiving operation, then it is necessary that all incoming merchandise be quickly and easily identified. In order to further this consideration, the packaging manual should have specific instructions as to what is required on all supplier shipping labels and tags, as follows:

- Ship to: (give plant name)
- Part No.: (give the complete number together with applicable modification number or letter.
- Quantity: (the number of pieces in each package)
- P.O. No.: (purchase order number)
- Model or Change No.: (this may be a portion of the Part No., above; however, if there is an engineering change no. give the latest number; if a model no. give the latest no.)

- Date packed: (show the date by month, day, and year in which the material was packed; this may be necessary for the turnover of inventory and/or inventory control)
- Weight: (give the gross weight in pounds and metric measure)
- Supplier's name: (give the supplier's name and shipping plant address)

NOTE: The methods of labeling should be standardized as much as possible to your company's requirements with only few exceptions, and these are: if the supplier has its own company standards that fulfill all of the above requests for information; and, if both your company and the supplier are set up for bar-coded labels.

Your packaging manual should contain forms showing what your company requires in the way of labels and tags. The forms should illustrate specific sizes with dimensions clearly indicated, so that the supplier will have no doubts as to what is expected. Some very small suppliers may not be able to comply with printed label requirements; therefore, the manual should be specific in accepting handwritten labels under the following conditions:

- Labels should be hand-lettered legibly using waterproof ink. A plastic overlay, of clear packaging tape will help preserve the label.
- When tags are used they should be made of 110-lb. card stock.

Special Instructions

Specific unit loads may require special instructions whenever it is felt that the safe arrival of the material at its destination may be in any doubt.

CAUTION: These instructions should not be made a part of the shipping label, but should be clearly marked on the load, as indicated below:

- SPECIAL HANDLING to prevent damage should be in large letters at least 2 inches high, in black or other contrasting colors.
- DO NOT BOTTOM TIER should be used to prevent heavier loads from being placed on top of your materials in transit, especially since less-than-truckload (LTL) shipments are usually consolidated at transfer points and inside truck terminals.
- Direction of travel of the material in transit is sometimes very important. This is especially true when some types of expendable, block-design pallets are used, because they are stronger in one direction than in another at right angles to the first. As an example, the bottom deck boards of this type of pallet should always run parallel to the direction of travel of he load in transit. A large clearly visible arrow should be used to indicate the direction of travel of the load.

Bills of Lading and Packing Lists

A carrier completes a bill of lading whenever it accepts goods from a shipper and gives both the consignor and the consignee copies. The bill will contain the shipper's (consignor's) and the receiver's (consignee's) name and address. It will include a description of the goods and the quantity being consigned to the carrier, together with the freight classification and the shipping charges. The receiving department should have tight control over this document: it is used (1) in pursuing in-transit damage claims, and (2) as the proof of receipt required by your accounting department before they pay for a shipment. By and large, the bill of lading is not a necessary element of the packaging manual, but its mention is made so that it will not be considered an omission in the text.

Packing Lists

The packing list (P.L.) is a vital part of each shipment on the receiver's end. Without a packing list checking receivables can be extremely difficult. The P.L. informs the receiver what has been shipped and what must be received. The P.L. is an important part of packaging, because it is customary to place this document on one of the packages of an LTL shipment, and on full truck loads it is placed as close to the tailgate as possible so that it is available when the carrier doors are opened. The packaging manual should assist in describing the characteristics of this document, as follows:

- Every shipment should have its own packing list.
- The P.L. should be easily found in the shipment.
- The P.L. must be clearly visible on the outside of the package, container, or load.
- Place the P.L. on the side or end of the load.

CAUTION: Never place the P.L. on top of the load, because if another load is placed on top of it, it will either be lost, or destroyed.

- Whenever possible, place the P.L. on the load that is nearest the loading door.
- Use a colored, highly visible, plastic packing list envelope with a pressure-sensitive adhesive backing.

The packaging manual should, also, indicate that the P.L. should contain the following information:

- Supplier's name
- Part or model number
- Purchase Order number
- Receiving plant address
- Number of units, or packages per pallet, or skid
- Total number of pallets, skids, or bulk containers comprising the shipment
- The number of pieces ordered
- The number of pieces shipped
- Engineering change number, if applicable
- A description of the material
- And, if returnable containers are included in the shipment, all of the information mentioned in Sec. D,4, above.
- Individually wrapped parts are not desirable since this requires additional labor and packaging material disposal.
- Some parts may require added packaging protection; therefore, cellular and die-cut corrugated egg-crates may be necessary.

NOTE: Your company may have certain unique handling and/or point of use requirements that should be emphasized in your company's packaging manual.

15

The Importance of Plant Layout in Manufacturing and Warehousing

INCENTIVES FOR IMPROVING LAYOUT

Good plant layout provides three major benefits to your warehousing operations

- least total cost of materials handling
- increase in productivity of your work force
- improved morale

It doesn't make any difference whether we are talking about manufacturing warehousing, or about the materials handling of a physical distribution center, the problems and solutions are virtually the same.

There are many incentives for improving layout, not the least of which is the high cost of factory and warehouse space which is a direct result of the increases in building material, labor, and land cost. Thus, when a layout has to be changed, or a plant expansion has to be undertaken, it is necessary to minimize the effects upon the dislocation of stock (materials) and equipment. The transition from the old to the new has to be made quickly so that a satisfactory level of production can be sustained to maintain the customer base without alienation.

A more cogent reason for striving to obtain the best possible layout is the fact that almost all materials handling operations are performed repetitively throughout the working day, year in and year out. Thus, if the shortest and most direct manner of routing and handling is not practiced then each individual worker's increment of wasted time and effort is multiplied many times over to detract from the total effort and profit of the company. Escalating direct and indirect labor costs in warehousing coupled with excessive and unnecessary wear on materials handling (MH) equipment and increased maintenance costs will force profits down.

A poor plant layout has the tendency to increase the need for storage space, and very often management succumbs to the task of fighting fires rather than biting the bullet and getting down to the basic cause of the problem which is poor planning.

Good plant layout is essential to productivity and growth. At some companies, plant layout is a process that never ceases and they are continuously arranging and rearranging sections and departments on a very current basis. This type of company has the size and funding to make this ongoing process possible. In other words, they are staffed for this activity and they realize that nothing is static, and there is no operation that cannot be improved; for the sake of the argument, let us say, there is hardly an operation that cannot, at some point, be changed for an improvement in methodology, equipment, process, or outright elimination.

PLANNING PLANT LAYOUT FOR A NEW SITE

An obvious reason for preparing a plant layout is when a new building is going to be built or occupied. If the building has already been leased, or purchased, then the challenging task is to fit the activities of the company into the allotted space as efficiently as possible. When making a space layout in an existing building, the primary regard should be to provide for a flow of materials such that backtracking and wasted movements are minimized, or eliminated.

CAUTION: When a layout is being prepared it is advisable to keep in mind the effect of expansion on particular activities. In other words, try not to box in important operations that may need to be expanded, between operations or equipment that may be difficult or expensive to relocate.

If the site has already been selected, but the building dimensions have not been decided, then the layout planners are in a better position to obtain a layout with a good materials flow than in the situation, where the building is already in existence. Another problem that is sometimes experienced by planners is the procrastination by management to arrive at a decision to build, to lease, or to arrive at an amount to be allocated for the new structure. Usually this problem is compounded in the larger companies with "design and construction" (D&C) groups that realize the longer the delay, the more expensive the project will be, thus they proceed to develop plans for the new building from educated guesses supplied by the various departments to be housed in the new facilities. Since they may already have had budget approvals for D&C efforts for the new facility, they start to draw the new plant on paper, and may even obtain the services of an architectural-engineering firm (A/E) to execute structural drawings. The D&C and A/E's may be well along in their project before they realize that the layout planners have not yet finalized their layouts, and in this respect the project is off to a poor start.

To stave off the impasse that results from uncoordinated planning, appoint a project committee in the initial stages of the consideration for a new facility so that as soon as a management decision is made to allocate funds for a new facility the work of the various planning groups may begin.

The six planning stages of a new facility project are:

1. Allocation of funds
2. Site selection
3. Site planning
4. Facility planning

5. Plant layout

6. Equipment selection

These six steps are interrelated in many ways, and it is the responsibility of the task force or project committee to see that these phases receive the complete attention of every department involved in the planning process. It is important to remember that a choice made on one level of planning inevitably affects other steps. Short-sighted decisions can have long-lasting negative effects on the future productivity of the enterprise, for example:

- a site that does not permit expansion in one direction or another may limit future profitability.

- a site that has limited railroad or truck access may cause future problems.

- poorly thought-out routing of water or sanitary lines may inhibit, or make more costly, the rearrangement of internal departments of the facility.

- Locker rooms and toilets, column spacing and column locations may prevent the best possible arrangements of materials and equipment, conveyors, and the like.

Thus, the need for a plant layout which can anticipate future growth and future changes is both a challenge and a necessity for plant management.

Facility and Site Planning

During the past several decades there has been a proliferation in construction materials, and even new methods of building have come into vogue. The many choices of combinations of materials and methods have been both frustrating and rewarding. Since you cannot be expected to have the necessary expertise in these matters, you will have to depend on the task group for the new facility which must oversee the work of the D&C, and the A/E responsible for the actual construction of the facility.

The type of facility, certainly, has to fit in with the terrain of suburban, or rural settings. If the facility is to be located in an urban area, then it should reflect the kind of public image your company wants to present to the neighboring communities, and this will be influenced to a large extent by the restrictions and requirements prescribed by the local planning and zoning commission, who sometimes may make very arbitrary demands on the company wishing to locate in its jurisdiction.

CAUTION: Before committing the company to any site, the plant management should assure itself of any arbitrary restrictions or requirements that may be involved with the erection of a facility in the particular area under consideration. For this purpose, the D&C group should prepare a preliminary drawing of the facility, just a line sketch of approximate dimensions, and seek a hearing before the city's department of construction and land use. Request a certified record from the city's planning group of the results of this meeting(s), which may be useful in the event of future disputes with city regulators.

The high cost of land in urban areas may preclude the erection of a single-story structure. While a multi-storied building is generally considered inefficient, in some areas and within certain industry segments, this building concept has a great deal of merit. For example, pharmaceutical manufacturing and warehousing and appliance manufacturing and distribution are prime models for this type of facility. The General Electric Company has several such buildings in its most recent Appliance Park in Columbia, Maryland, near Baltimore.

On the other hand, some companies are forced into the use of the older, loft-type buildings because of the relative availability or affordability of these facilities. This type of structure requires the layout planner to use a considerable amount of creativity and imagination, especially when elevators of limited size or capacity have to be used in handling materials.

You should be particularly concerned with the following in selecting a loft-type building:

- Size and capacities of the elevators.
- Elevator replacement, or overhaul costs.
- Column spacing.
- Ceiling heights of all floors.
- Sufficient floor load capacity of all floors.
- Configuration and weight of materials handling equipment to be used on each floor of the building.
- Whether the elevators conform to the building, safety, and fire ordinances.
- Whether the elevators are automatic, or require an operator.
- Elevator downtime and repair/maintenance history.
- Whether the building has an adequate fire protection, sprinkler system.
- Whether the building is adequately lighted throughout.
- Whether the electric service is adequate.
- Whether the floors are in serviceable condition.
- Whether there is adequate heating and ventilation.
- Whether stair wells and handrails are in good condition.
- Whether truck and rail facilities are adequate.
- Whether receiving and shipping dock heights, doors, and lighting are adequate.
- Whether there is sufficient office space for the staffing of the plant.
- Whether there are sufficient and adequate toilet and washroom facilities for the staff and work crew.
- Whether there is adequate water pressure for fire fighting and sprinklers.
- Whether there is a sufficient number of drinking fountains.
- Whether fire extinguishers are available according to code.

If the answers to the above questions are satisfactory, then you have a fairly satisfactory building. It is not unusual, in these multistoried buildings to find that the main floor upon which receiving and shipping functions are carried out, will have as much as 14 to 18 feet of headroom. Occasionally, however, water mains, or sanitary lines, will be hung from these ceilings in critical locations, thus minimizing effective ceiling heights, and making high lifts of industrial trucks hazardous. Another serious drawback of these older buildings is the relatively small size bay—usually only 20 ft. × 20 ft. The relatively low rental or acquisition costs of these buildings must be compared with the wasted space, expensive elevator maintenance, downtime, and extra labor costs to determine value and least total cost.

While facility planning is important to successful project completion, the site planning effort is no less critical. Site planning is usually performed by architects, land surveyors, A/E's, developers, and the like. Contour maps of the property may be required so that drain water may be properly relieved. It is sometimes required even in urban areas where paving, parking lots, and so on, may create drainage problems for sewer take-offs. Since preparing site plans is normally the highly specialized work of the A/E's, your material handling expert should work side-by-side with them to make sure that the architectural and aesthetic aspects of the site do not outweigh the more practical and prosaic factors of materials handling. In suburban and rural areas established railroad lines and truck access roads are costly to relocate: unless potential future expansion is factored into the planning the orderly growth of the plant will be impeded.

The project planning group should meet with the A/E's on a periodic basis to keep in touch with progress of the site planning effort in order to avoid surprises where utilities, sewer lines, drainage, impinge on the layout of the plant. The same caveat applies to the way fire walls, load-bearing partitions, washrooms, processing equipment foundations, and so forth are treated in the overall layout. A million-gallon water storage tank, a transformer building with high-voltage gear, and fuel or cryogenic tanks are very permanent structures, and their locations should be carefully determined.

The same reasoning applies to sprinkler system layouts. Insurance companies do not like to see large open areas, they prefer a compartmentalized division of space that will contain a fire and prevent its spread. One of the ways of resolving this impasse is by the use of ceiling fire curtains, and ceiling monitors that will exhaust the air in strategic locations.

There are other challenges to the site planning A/E's and the project staff which in urban situations, can include getting trucks into and out of the facility and handling traffic flow, and providing for off-street parking, which may be required by local ordinance. Also, most city building codes have a three-foot-wide fire aisle between storage areas and exterior walls of the building.

To save your company time and money, use the following site planning checklist.

- The land area selected should be large enough in width and depth to adequately accommodate the building.
- The site should permit full expansion.
- The selected site should have suitable soil, load-bearing characteristics for a building to be erected without extensive, special construction, footings, pilings, and so on.
- Soil tests are essential.
- Water should be available in sufficient quantities to supply the needs of the plant.
- Electric and gas utilities should be readily available.
- Rail and truck access should be readily available.

There are two elements which must be given careful consideration in planning new warehouse or factory construction.

- Column spacing
- Materials handling equipment to be used.

Column Spacing

Spacing of columns is extremely important, because it affects the movement and storage of merchandise. If columns are placed too close together in either direction, they will restrict the movement of materials handling equipment and the placement of merchandise, parts, and the like, in storage equipment (whether storage racks, or bins). Also, space will be wasted if pallet sizes, or unit loads cannot utilize the full floor area between columns.

A lower, initial cost of construction may not be as cost effective as anticipated if storage and handling are forever restricted by poorly spaced columns.

NOTE: *Rule One*—Eliminate as many columns as possible within the floor area of the building. *Rule Two*—Enclose columns within walls, dividing walls, or partitions, wherever possible.

Materials Handling Equipment

When planning the new, or expanded, facility, the type of materials handling equipment that will be used should be an integral part of the study. What equipment you use will affect such elements as ceiling heights, the size of doors, slopes of ramps (if any), aisle space, pallet sizes, and the like. If a forklift truck and pallet system are to be the main handling method then the door widths and heights must accommodate the loads passing through them, especially if pallet loads are transported two high (one pallet on top of another), and if forklift trucks are required to pass each other within the doorway. In addition to this, adequate aisles must be planned for each storage area in the facility. Ceiling heights will be determined by two factors:

- cost
- the height with which palletized loads will be stacked.

Along with this latter factor is the decision that must be made as to whether the unitized loads will be block stored, or will be placed into pallet storage racks.

Other considerations are the placement of sprinklers, ducts, fan units, utilities, and water, steam, and gas lines.

Lighting is especially important in storage areas. Never plan the lighting system before the storage system has been planned, otherwise you will wind up with ceiling lights being blocked by stored commodities. Plan the lighting system *after* the storage bays have been delineated so that the lighting fixtures will be hung over aisles, and cross-aisles (intersections).

CAUTION: Wherever possible have service lines, i.e., utilities, ductwork, lights, etc. protected by the rafters, trusses, and bar joists so that they are not in the way of loads being lifted in the air.

NOTE: The size of pallets should be determined prior to beginning the storage plan, so that floor space will be determined in multiples of the pallet dimensions in order to provide for the best possible layout.

HOW TO GET THE DATA YOU NEED TO OPTIMIZE PLANT LAYOUT EFFECTIVENESS

The task force charged with the responsibility of laying out the new facility should be composed of experienced employees who know the characteristics of their operations. Select a project leader who has intelligence and that rare leadership trait—the ability to compromise. This individual should be close to you in authority so that, together, you can select the remaining members of the project group, who will respect the project leader's authority to make decisions.

Your task force should reflect the great amount of information your staff may have already acquired through membership in trade and technical societies and subscriptions to trade journals. If your company pays for memberships or subscriptions, your personnel files should have data on the organizations that these employees have joined. Since these employees are in touch with their peers in other companies through their association with technical societies they are familiar with current methods and, to some extent, the non-proprietary processing that is practiced in competitors' plants. Such employees would be invaluable members of your task force.

The purchasing department has developed contacts with equipment manufacturers and suppliers who are only too eager to talk about competitors' latest innovations in order to promote their own products; therefore, the purchasing department should also be represented in the project group to lend their expertise to the fund of knowledge that is available on the subject of the new facility. The same types of data are available in the more technically oriented areas of the company, as well as the materials handling staff and this cross-referencing will confirm and verify differences in methodologies across your particular industry segment.

In order to obtain the best possible layout for the new facility, the task group must weigh the advantages and disadvantages of methods and equipment with the project leader assisting in the selection process. They should review the present plant and operations and solicit suggestions and recommendations from each department in order to avoid the mistakes and pitfalls that may have plagued the present facility.

The next two steps are important:

- Step 1—Determine what capacity the plant is to be designed for—The data required in Step I will come from the marketing department indirectly, as it is evaluated by the company's top management, and would more than likely comprise short-term estimates of the marketplace, (i.e., from one to five years after the new facility comes on stream.)

- Step 2—Determine what growth is anticipated—In Step 2, your task force must assess the changes that are taking place in their industry and predict how these changes might affect the new plant so that they can build into the new facility the flexibility needed to adapt to the requirements of the longer term.

In order for your planning group to start the actual business of laying out the new plant, they need to know a good deal about the quantities and types of materials to be handled, stored, processed, packaged, or worked on in some form or other in your facility. In looking at the subject in only bits and pieces, or studying only small segments of the operation at a time, materials handling problems can remain unresolved. The systems approach requires that your task group regard preceding and succeeding phases of materials flow over the complete range of activities within the plant, from raw material source to final destination, in order to obtain *the least total cost of materials handling.*

The task group should question every facet of the present method of operation, especially in regard to the way in which merchandise is received from the mill, or supplier. This should be done in order to determine whether the way the material is presently packaged will be advantageous in the new facility. If it is not, then one of the responsibilities of the group would be to have the purchasing department contact various suppliers to see what cost benefits might be derived from having the material properly graded, marked (bar coded?), and packaged for your use. As is often the case, changes in packaging , or handling method, may benefit the supplier as well as your company, without any additional cost to either party.

If the suppliers should demand higher prices due to the changes, then it behooves the task group to make a cost benefits study to determine if there is a significant cost advantage, either in labor effort required, or time, by changing the packaging or handling method. The same systems approach would apply in physical distribution as in manufacturing, where the plant materials handling engineer would examine packaging and handling at typical suppliers' plants to determine whether these functions could be properly integrated in the systems network that the task group is implementing.

Some of the packaging and handling parameters that must be studied are:

- size
- shape, or configuration
- weight
- density
- crushability
- stacking or nesting characteristics
- shelf-life

Your materials handling engineer and the project staff must determine which of the above factors are important in the scope of your processing operations, noting them, and even tabulating and coding them so that they can be examined and decisions made that will direct the course of the planning activity. After all of the information is coded it may be stored in a computer file, or it may be manually posted and manipulated as the occasion warrants. If computer time is unavailable at your company it is always possible to purchase computer time and expertise, usually at a very reasonable cost. The scope of these data will dictate the equipment to be employed in working with them.

Adjusting Volume of Materials and Work-in-process

Your task force should subject the quantities of materials to be handled to very intensive analysis. The data to be examined, in this stage, should be categorized, as follows:

- Input/output quantities
- Internal processing (types of operations)
- Flow of materials within the plant

A valuable source of information is found in developing a "From-To" chart. (See Figure 15-1).

By making this type of chart a number of important criteria can be determined, not the least of which is to establish the density or number of moves made between departments, or activities. Another facet of this data is the tonnage of loads moved and handled. In addition,

FROM-TO CHART

Location: *Jamestown Plant*   Date: *4-1-8_*   M.H. Engr: *Bill Smith*

Dept. *18*

FROM \ TO	Unformed Steel	De-coiler	Shear	Blank	Brake	Storage	Weld	Chip & Clean	Subassembly	Storage	Assembly	Shipping	Totals
Unformed Steel	3												3
De-coiler		5											5
Shear				8	5		3		1				17
Blank					3	9							12
Brake						3	2						5
Storage							12		4				16
Weld						5		10					15
Chip & Clean						3			6				9
Subassembly						2				4			6
Storage									3		4		7
Assembly												3	3
Totals		3	5	8	8	22	17	10	14	4	4	3	98

Remarks:

Investigate need for additional shear capacity.

Fig. 15-1: A "From-To" chart used to indicate the movement of materials through the plant.

by observing other variables it is possible to assign costs between departments, time consumed per total moves (per workshift), and the like.

Using the "From-To" chart, it is possible, also, to illustrate the information from the matrix, graphically, in the form of graphs or bar charts, as shown in Figure 15-2.

The primary purpose in preparing bar charts from From-To data is to present this type of information during presentations to management, wherein plant relationships become increasingly important in justifying equipment purchases, staffing, and the like.

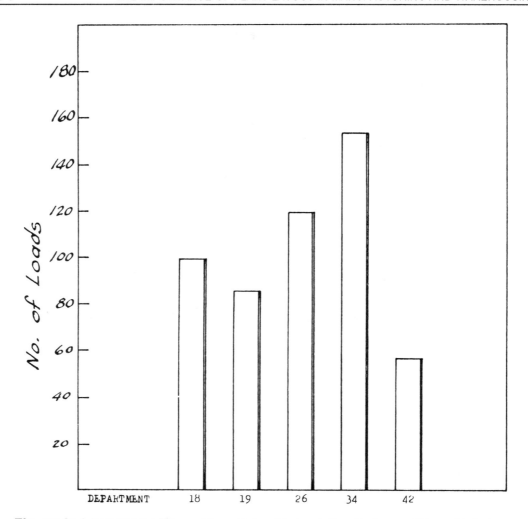

Fig. 15-2: A bar chart prepared from data obtained directly from a "From-To" chart.

As the plant manager, you should insist on weekly meetings with the new facility project group. In this way you will determine whether they are doing the type of exploratory digging that will turn up and permit the evaluation of the latest concepts and state-of-the-art equipment that might be used effectively in the new facility. Our goal is to insure future profits by using handling methods and installing equipment that will keep the plant reasonably abreast, and even ahead of competition. As happens to some roads, you do not want to see your plant become obsolete even before construction is completed! Thus, the task force must continue its probing to ascertain that both methods and equipment together with production processes and layout are definite improvements over past practices.

NOTE: The task group should base all, or almost all, decisions regarding new equipment upon returns on investment (ROI) studies.

NOTE: The task group should obtain the most advanced processing equipment commensurate with budgetary limitations.

Analyzing Materials Flow

In the area of materials movement and flow analysis, the task group should make use of From-To charts in order to develop reliable measures of the size of storage areas and processing departments. Thus, when reviewing the work of the task group in your weekly meetings you should evaluate the methods and data used by the group to derive the dimensions of each area of the facility, bearing in mind that each bare square foot of the new plant will cost, at the very least, $70 in most parts of the country, and perhaps more, where your new facility is located.

Work Simplification

The task group should try to eliminate all useless and unnecessary processing and handling movements of materials. Therefore, every operation from receiving to shipping must be examined minutely in order to determine the following:

- Is it necessary?
- Does it add value?
- Can it be combined with another operation?
- Can we obtain the same results at less expense by having a supplier do it?
- Is it packaged by the supplier in such a way that it will save us time and money?
- Can we dispense with the packaging?
- Are we receiving materials in the correct quantities?
- Can the task group think of any other ways to simplify the operation? (Have the group make a list, then evaluate the ideas at the weekly staff meeting where follow-up action may be taken.)

Balancing Operations

Physical distribution and warehousing operations are somewhat akin to manufacturing production in that line balancing is sometimes necessary. For example, whenever two or more operations occur simultaneously or in sequence they should take approximately the same amount of time so that one operator is not waiting for the next operator to finish a task before commencing his/her own. Line-balancing is quite common in the automobile industry upon the introduction of new models; also, in any large-volume production operation, line-balancing is necessary in order to achieve the maximum effective use of tools (i.e., equipment), and labor input. For this reason, to obtain the maximum productivity it may be necessary to observe every operation and add, or subtract, elements from each of the functions so that a balanced operation is achieved.

In a manufacturing plant it is sometimes possible to use new equipment, or to substitute one machine tool with another that has faster cutting feeds and speeds in order to achieve line balance; however, in a physical distribution activity, the substitution of one powered industrial truck with another that has:

- greater capacity,
- higher lifting capability,
- faster traveling speed, and,
- faster lifting speed,

may achieve the effect of better line balance and promote the efficiency and productivity of plant operations.

Processing and materials handling should always be integrated; therefore, as the task force proceeds through the various phases of processing the materials handling elements must be considered as part of the processing. The containers (or, lack of them) may become an important part, even a critical part, of subsequent operations.

CAUTION: Try to keep materials out of containers until the final consolidation or shipping stage is reached.

Any wholesale use of containers during the production process is likely to generate unnecessary rehandling—and, should be avoided.

NOTE: Never let the paperwork dictate the handling method. Many times, a procedure with an elaborate paperwork structure is perpetuated, almost unquestioningly, until it is discovered that it is the paperwork that has corrupted a fairly simple handling into something absurdly complex.

Decide on the best materials handling method, then make the paperwork fit the processing and handling. Better yet, eliminate the paperwork, if possible.

As the task group begins the chore of layout, it will be of value to remember that every day, for more than 200 days each year, there will be many repetitions of the way the materials are moved through the plant. The layout planner, therefore, has to have a conceptual visualization of the travel paths for all materials. Concrete evidence of this are:

- written instructions outlining the movements of materials.
- detailed description of the types of materials handling equipment to be employed.
- sketches of any containers that might be considered.
- layouts showing the travel paths of materials.
- staffing required of the methods.
- alternate proposals, with a cost comparison of each method.

The Effect of Variations in Productive Capacity

Factory *burden* consists of all manufacturing costs except those for materials and labor which are applied directly to the cost of goods that are manufactured. Typical items included in factory burden are:

- indirect labor
- manufacturing supplies
- heat
- light
- power
- repairs and maintenance
- depreciation
- property taxes
- insurance

In the case of physical distribution, all elements of cost except manufacturing supplies (which are included in the above list) apply to the enterprise. In some instances even this element of cost may be included in the burden; however, in addition to the difficulty of accounting for a large number of different kinds of expense, accounting for burden by operating units and by products or product lines involves many cost allocations. Some costs can be clearly identified with specific departments or cost centers; but, other costs must be allocated to various operating units on some manner of equitable basis. In addition, in factories or distribution centers of fairly large size, there may be service departments, such as: maintenance, personnel, medical, cafeteria, power plant, and the like, whose costs must be prorated equitably to direct producing departments, if the complete costs of output of these departments are to be realistically computed.

In short, when a variety of products is either manufactured or stored within each of several departments it is generally impossible to identify specific, actual burden costs with the specific goods which are contained therein. Therefore, it is often necessary to compute the burden to be allocated to these products by the use of an across-the-board burden rate.

Thus, in arranging production equipment in a plant layout, or in laying out storage areas it is well to keep sight of the following fact:

The higher the productive capacity is for a given floor area, the lower the overhead (burden) cost for this production.

This means, in short, that the fixed costs, or burden, for each unit of output will decrease as the productive capacity increases. The challenge for the layout planning group is to provide as much production per given square foot of floor area as possible while maintaining good materials handling practices.

HOW YOU CAN REDUCE THE COST OF MATERIALS HANDLING

The best materials handling is the least materials handling, and that is the goal you should set before your entire organization. This section discusses some of the ways you can achieve this result.

Controlling the Design of Processing Equipment

To make the most effective use of both space and the human factors, equipment used in the production areas should be properly designed. The *human engineering* factors are: standing, sitting, reaching, grasping, and lifting.

All of the above are characteristics applied to the human being, the worker who toils at his/her task eight or so hours daily, minus a few time breaks. As examples of a few simple improvements that can be made, consider conveyor heights and widths, and storage bin shelf heights.

Conveyor Heights and Widths

If an employee is very tall, stooping over to place materials on a conveyor that is too low can induce lower back pain; a conveyor that is too high for a short person means that he/she will be similarly stressed. The solution is to adjust conveyor heights to the individual worker; if several workers are assigned to one conveyor line then the shorter workers should be given stations equipped with platforms. Usually the shorter individual will have a reach that is, also, shorter than a taller individual; then this condition must be dealt with by reassigning the employee to another work station where his/her shorter arm length does not interfere with the satisfactory performance of his/her task nor does it contribute an undue measure of fatigue in the job setting.

Shelf Heights

In some bin picking operations, where standard, 87-inch high storage shelving is used, the bottom of the top shelf may be 77-inch or almost six and one-half feet from the ground. Imagine the short, 5'4" individual reaching for stock items on this top shelf! Sometimes, in a single floor operation, replenishment items are kept on top of the shelving. Needless to say, the small order picker will use the first one or two tiers of the bin shelving as a stepladder, unless the cart being used to gather bin items has self-contained steps, or a small, order-picking ladder is available. Besides the danger involved in using the bin shelves as a step ladder, there is the damage that occurs to the shelving when it is used repeatedly in this way.

Controlling Travel Distance

When the plant layout is being made, it should be realized that if the distance between operations is shortened, the time required for performing the entire task, or transporting the part, will also be shortened. This one factor alone, will significantly increase the productivity of the operation. Also, if various pieces of transportation equipment, other than conveyors are used in the foregoing operation, it will substantially reduce wear and tear of the equipment, thus lowering maintenance and replacement costs.

Controlling Materials Movement

Since the least amount of materials handling is best, observe *line of flight* handling. This means you should take the most direct line, between two operations in order to transport materials more economically and with less damage. The mathematical principle that "a straight line is the shortest distance between two points," should be your slogan because it reduces the amount and cost of materials handling.

Increase Your Profit by Maximizing the Use of Labor and Equipment

Since a good plant layout enables you to make use of labor and equipment effectively, here are some ways of accomplishing this:

- eliminate crowded aisles;
- provide enough storage space between operations, but not too much; and,
- avoid crowding the space around processing equipment so that the employee will have enough space to work safely.

Another way you can maximize profit, also involving the *least total cost of handling,* is the *critical time phasing* of materials in process. Thus, when we have provided the proper arrangement and design of equipment and materials in our plant layout, there will be a steady and continuous flow of work-in-process (WIP) throughout the production cycle. This is achieved by integrating the production scheduling with the materials handling method(s).

Therefore, by eliminating or minimizing line imbalance and cushions of WIP between successive operations, several things happen:

- there is a steady flow of work through the plant;
- there is a reduction of the length of time it takes to process materials;
- inventory is turned over faster, so that capital dollars are not tied up unnecessarily;
- the employees are more responsive to schedule changes; and,
- there is much better utilization of labor, equipment, and plant space.

Improve Safety and Working Conditions to Lower Costs and Raise Morale

The layout planner is generally concerned with the overall view of plant operations, but he must also pay attention to the operator safety and good working conditions of the individual work station. A fire extinguisher that is neatly marked, and placed, on a painted board at eye level near a work station communicates a company's concern with safety. If an operator must remain standing for lengths of time in a relatively small area, then a rubber mat underfoot can ease the shock of concrete on the skeletal structure. Even a simple improvement like wood planking underfoot, shows the employee that he/she is more than a number on an employee badge, and morale is boosted in this manner.

A first aid station, adequately equipped eye baths and safety showers, if hazardous materials are being handled, or if there is an electric storage battery charging area nearby, are part of the psychology of achieving significant improvements in safety and employee morale. Drinking fountains and restrooms maintained in a sparkling clean manner, strategically placed throughout the plant, are other additions to morale that will improve materials handling effectiveness.

If the new distribution facility involves materials handling equipment of a type that has not been used before, then the preparation and training of the workers in the use and proper care of the equipment should be initiated prior to completion and occupancy of the new facility in order to assure worker safety.

APPLY MATERIALS HANDLING PRINCIPLES TO INCREASE PRODUCTIVITY IN YOUR PLANT

If your materials handling engineer and the task group keep specific materials handling principles uppermost in their thoughts, they will greatly improve the possibilities of obtaining a smooth materials flow through the system that will produce the least total cost of materials handling.

Economy of Operations and Continuous Flow

Achieving the largest measure of materials handling economy in a plant occurs when materials are:

- moved in direct lines;
- moved through a minimum distance; and,
- moved by mechanical, or automatic, means.

Since processing time and costs are minimized when the product passes through the several processes in a continuous flow with a minimum of backtracking or crosshauling, another set of principles are:

- Avoid batching or lot processing (these practices should be minimized or eliminated).

- Always remember that the slowest process will become the bottleneck, and will pace the rest of the plant operations.

- Since materials handling is an integral part of processing, it should be closely scrutinized in order to improve or eliminate it as an element of the process.

- While you should try to obtain as direct a line of materials flow as possible, you should remember to mechanize the routing of materials as much as possible, using conveyors, chutes, silos, robots, and other devices including special containers where required.

Building Flexibility into Plant Layout

The plant layout should be developed with a certain degree of flexibility that will enable future planning to provide for growth and changes in product and process. In order to do this, the following guidelines should be observed:

- Design expansion plans into the initial plant layout.

- Examine all of the critical operations of the plant that could eventually become candidates for expansion, and determine how these units will be provided for in the future.

- Eliminate, or hold to a minimum, all obstructions that may cause future problems, such as:
  —obstructed floor areas;
  —column spacing that is too close n either direction;
  —elevator shafts and pits;
  —stair wells;
  —toilet and locker room facilities in awkward places;
  —expensive laboratory plumbing;
  —sanitation lines; utility lines;
  —certain subfloor equipment;
  —in-floor drag-chain conveyor systems; and the like;
  —cafeterias;
  —maintenance and battery charging areas; and,
  —miscellaneous areas, or processes characteristic of your industry segment.

Allocating Areas for New Facilities

In the realm of physical distribution, the building and planning for a new facility will be a once-in-a-lifetime experience for most employees. Therefore, the task group may have only a few, if any, employees who have been through this exercise before. It will come as no surprise to a veteran of planning plant layouts, that the subject is considered part science and part art, and a subtle combination of the two, at that. Fortunately, there are some basic approaches to plant layout that may make it seem a little less imposing. We can express the approaches for allocating areas in new facilities, as follows:

Determine Space Requirements

Make use of data obtained by means of the From-To charts, and any other data that will indicate the square feet of area that each department of the plant will require. Take heavy paper, or card stock, using a scale of ¼-inch to the foot, cut out each departmental area on its own piece of paper. Initially these areas may be squares containing the necessary dimensions indicating the size of the department. For example, if 400 square feet are required for an operation or process, then the rectangular piece of paper would be 5 in. × 5 in. representing a square of 20 ft. × 20 ft. which has been scaled down in this manner.

Create a Variety of Layout Models

The next step is to arrange these squares in a logical relationship as indicated by our From-To charts, and other data. The scaled-down squares of paper can be arranged and rearranged, as though there were no walls in the facility, since at this stage there have been no determinations of this kind. (See Figure 15-3.)

Choose a Layout Model

After satisfying yourself that the arrangement is somewhat satisfactory tape the paper squares together on the drawing board using pieces of masking tape.

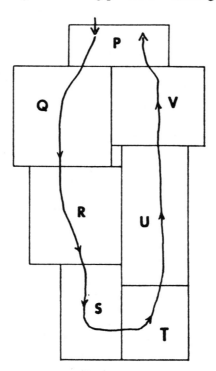

Fig. 15-3: One method of obtaining a building shell to house each department, given flow data, department size, and the use of paper templates.

Adapt Your Model

Position a large piece of transparent plastic or acetate over the entire collage of paper squares. When this is done, taking colored grease pencils, trace the flow of the major components and/or components of parts with high dollar volume on the plastic as they make their way through the plant. (See Figure 15-4.)

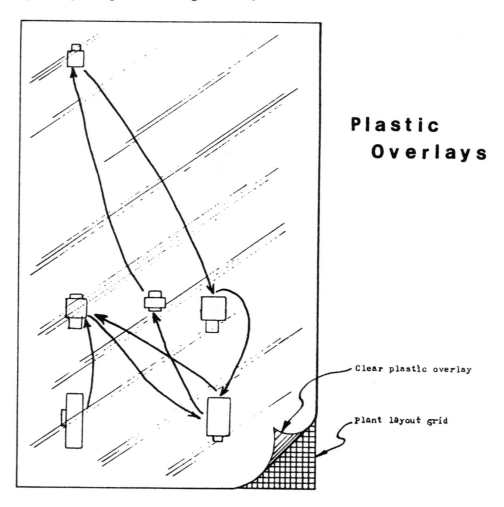

Plastic Overlays

Clear plastic overlay

Plant layout grid

Fig. 15-4: Using a transparent plastic overlay, colored grease pencils can be used to trace and improve material flow of high-dollar-volume items.

Rearrange Your Layout, if Necessary

As you look at the pattern of flow, it may become necessary to rearrange some of the departments to obtain smoother flow paths, remembering always that straight line flow is best. Thus, some areas, or blocks of space may have to be redrawn, in their scaled-down versions in rectangles that are not square, and some may even have to be L-shaped, or U-shaped in order to make the walls of the building shell more uniform in appearance. (See. Figure 15-5.)

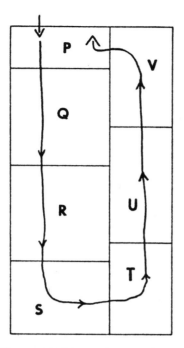

Fig. 15-5: The templates in Figure 15-3 have been adjusted and rearranged to obtain a workable building configuration.

Finalize Your Layout Model

As a final phase, configure the building size and add interior walls, as required. From this point on the receiving and shipping docks, storage areas, maintenance, and service areas may be added, prior to turning the layout over to the A/E's.

Discuss and Review the Plant Layout with the A/E's

This may require additional rearranging of the blocks of space, but at least a logical, spatial plan has been developed that the planning group can be proud of, knowing that they have provided flexibility and room for expansion where possible.

Allocating Areas for Existing Facilities

When a new facility has been leased or purchased, the task group has the difficult and often frustrating task of making departmental requirements fit into existing space. It may not always be possible to fit every requirement well, and what usually results is that a compromise is achieved between what is required and what is available. Here are some guidelines on how to allocate areas in a leased facility.

Obtain Building Blueprints

One of the first things the task group should do is obtain a set of the latest revision of the drawings of the building from the owner.

Check the Accuracy of the Blueprints

The second step is to check out the blueprints on the site to make certain that what is on the drawing and what is in the building agree 100 percent, and vice versa. The drawings should correspond in every detail, otherwise you are off to a bad start. (in one large industrial building constructed for WWII shipbuilding, which was also used as a war plant during the Korean conflict, the drawings were not in accordance with the building inasmuch as column bracings were added and extra steel was installed to raise load-bearing requirements and never shown on subsequent drawings. Discrepancies such as these can upset storage rack placements, or processing equipment locations.)

In order to further assure the accuracy of the blueprints of the building, the following items should be clearly marked on the prints:

- columns
- posts
- interior walls
- stairwells
- ladders
- elevators
- doors
- windows
- railroad tracks
- rail docks
- truck docks
- roadways

Check the Load-bearing Capacity of the Floor

Determine that the load-bearing capacity of the floor(s) is certified in writing by the architectural firm whose name is on the blueprints; or by a structural engineering firm if the A/E company that drew up the plans for the building is no longer in existence.

Track Materials Flow

Every two or three years trace the path of materials flow using the transparent plastic overlay described in the preceding section of this chapter. This will reveal what is actually happening to materials flow through the plant, especially when new equipment is added, new products are introduced, and when storage areas are shifted around, and the like.

How You Can Use 3-dimensional Models to Improve Plant Operations

The previous sections of this chapter, show how 2-dimensional templates and layouts that are scaled ¼-inch per foot can be used to assist in visualizing space and the flow of materials in both new and leased facilities. Unfortunately, there is a limit to what can be done graphically in the above manner, especially when the plant is rather complex, has thousands of items, and has several processing operations in addition to large storage areas. It is then that you should turn to 3-dimensional models for the visual affects and computer simulation to determine flow and throughput, since they complement each other.

Figure 15-6 is a 3-dimensional scale model that helps planners visualize spatial relationships that exist among several departments, building elements, and equipment. Models such as shown in Figure 15-3 can help sell management on the necessity for investing capital in a project.

A 3-dimensional model made to a -inch scale can be very expensive, from several thousand dollars to $25,000, or more. Despite the cost, however, there are a number of advantages to be gained by this type of model making.

By applying this technique to work station arrangements in physical distribution operations, or processing, it is possible to obtain an efficient placement of equipment that is directly related to:

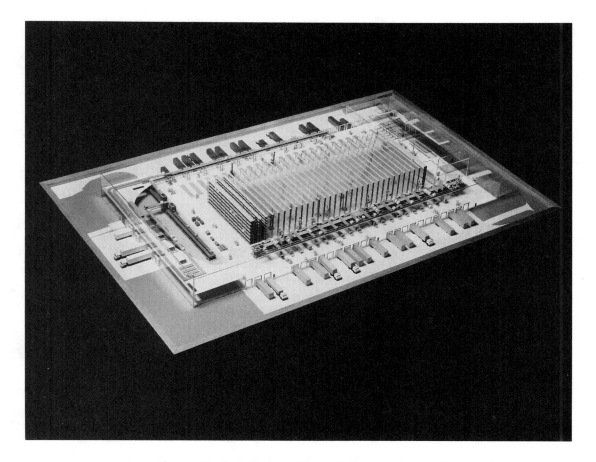

Courtesy The Austin Company, Cleveland, Ohio, consultants, designers, engineers, constructors

Fig. 15-6: A 3-dimensional scale model of a high-density storage and order filling complex.

—productivity;

—morale; and,

—safety.

In every planning group there is bound to be at least one model builder. Some homemade models can be very effective in showing spatial relationships despite their lack of polish, and their effectiveness in depicting an order picking, bin area layout, as an example, can equal professional model-building skills. Bins and pallet storage racks can be properly scaled, and can be constructed of simple blocks of wood. A large measure of realism can often be obtained by using 3-dimensional figures which can be obtained from a number of companies that sell scaled replicas of every conceivable type of machine tool, bin shelving, storage racks, male and female figures, and the like. See Appendix B for a list of companies that manufacture supplies for layout planners.

AN EXAMPLE OF A TYPICAL WAREHOUSE PLAN

The layout planner has several choices in drawing materials. Cloth or vellum (relatively tough tracing paper), depending on whether a long or short shelf-life is expected of the layout, were formerly the main choices. If the drawing is microfilmed then it makes little difference which type of drawing material is used, except that the cloth will withstand fairly rough treatment and many handlings a good deal better than the vellum, which tends to get brittle with age. Recently cloth has been largely supplanted by mylar, a strong, fairly thin polyester sheet that is highly resistant to tearing; in addition, it doesn't become scratched or marred, even with extremely rough treatment, and it makes excellent prints. Mylar sheets can be erased easily, without ghosting, and it is the material of choice for layout planners.

The "Perfect" brand of mylar, marketed by the Dietzgen Company, is cross-sectioned $10 \times 10 = 2\frac{1}{2}$ inches giving a scale of ¼-inch to the foot, which is recommended for most plant layout work. The "Perfect" mylar can serve as the base upon which to place the layout templates. Every tenth line of this mylar is dotted, representing a distance of 10 feet on the ¼-inch scale. The layout planner can use other pieces of mylar and make scale models of equipment, racks, bins and work station arrangements that can be manipulated on the mylar base to come up with the final configuration of the warehouse or distribution center. These scale models can be mounted on the mylar base using a 3M double-backed transparent tape.

Another aid for the layout planner is the use of "Chart-Pak" tapes, which are available at any good art and drafting supply store. These preprinted tapes can be used to denote aisles, conveyors, direction of travel, bridge cranes, and so forth. Any changes that need to be made to the layout can be made simply by peeling off the cutout models and tapes and replacing or relocating them.

While vellum, cloth, and mylar bases are often used for layout work, most warehouse layouts, unlike machine production lines, are so infrequently changed once they have been laid out that they are quite often drawn on vellum. Subsequent changes, which are usually only minor ones, can be made with red pencil on the blueprints.

A layout for a portion of a large warehouse, showing the receiving and shipping truck docks and the auxiliary areas is illustrated in Figure 15-7.

The lines with directional arrows represent the towconveyor system that services various areas of the warehouse. (A complete plan would show that the towconveyor makes a full circuit around the periphery of the warehouse.) Towconveyor spurs at convenient locations have been provided throughout the facility so that towcarts may be sent to various areas, automatically, by setting an indexing mechanism on each towconveyor cart. In addition, a *towconveyor crossover* (not shown in this layout) can be strategically placed in the dragchain system in order to eliminate the unnecessary travel of towcarts to the far ends of the warehouse. Figure 15-1 shows set-out spurs in the receiving and shipping areas. Orders are accumulated in the shipping setout area, and as these are outloaded, empty carts are placed back on the dragchain for transportation to the receiving area where they will await incoming merchandise.

NOTE: The general direction of the towconveyor dragchain line should always be from shipping to receiving in order to provide empty carts for the receiving operation.

Another objective of good towconveyor installation practice is to divide up the warehouse floor area so that the towconveyor guide path slot is equidistant to both sides of each area. As part of the planning layout process, it must be realized that warehouse walls and partitions will affect the accessibility of the towconveyor line to operators. This is especially true if the facility was constructed initially without a towconveyor system.

Fire safety practices will dictate fusible links be installed to hold the large, sliding doors between warehouse segments. In case of fire, if the path of the door is blocked a Klaxon will sound, requiring that the obstruction be removed to permit the door to close. When fire erupts in a warehouse, the towconveyor system is immediately shut down, thus personnel will have ample time to remove towcarts or any other obstructions in the doorways as standard operating procedure.

Another important feature to note in Figure 15-7, is that of the location of service facilities. Inspection and quality control (QC) laboratories, and the like, should be readily accessible to the departments they serve. For this reason, the inspection and QC laboratory and office should be fairly close to the receiving activity in order that samples of incoming materials may be taken, inspected, and analyzed conveniently.

The maintenance area and the electric battery charging areas (if electric forklift trucks, or electrically operated, automatic guided vehicles are used in the facility) should be located near the center of the vehicle population of the warehouse. Also, locker rooms, a cafeteria (if there is one), swing-rooms (canteen), and the like, should be centrally located.

NOTE: Consider mezzanine locations for these service and convenience areas since they will help utilize nonproductive space, which you are paying for anyway.

Fire extinguishers, drinking fountains, and personnel fire exits (minimal in some facilities) should be considered not only because they are required, but because they are good for morale.

CAUTION: Fire exits can be avenues for pilferage, however, they may be safeguarded by alarms.

It is better to err on the side of too many, as far as these essentials are concerned, because they make a statement for the integrity of the organization.

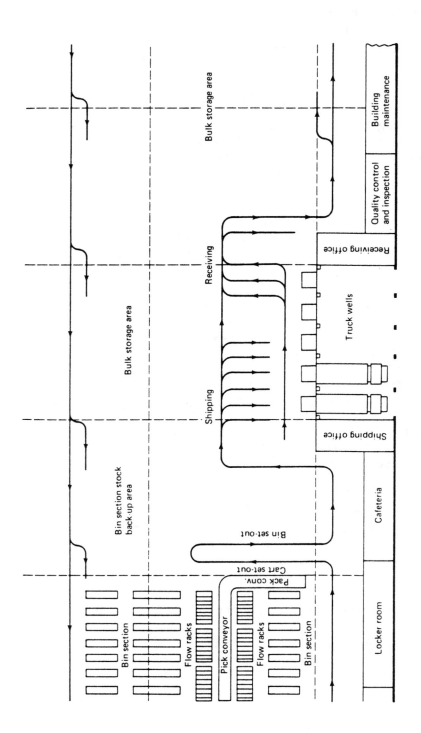

Fig. 15-7: Large warehouse layout showing portions of an in-floor, dragchain conveyor line and conveyor spurs, used to service different areas of the warehouse.

16

Better Work Station Arrangements for Humans and Industrial Robots

PLANNING HUMAN WORK STATIONS

A large portion of business profit is generated at the work station. This is true from the largest manufacturing or physical distribution operation to the smallest. The work station, whether a single installation or part of a multiple grouping, is the basic building block of the company's productivity, and as such has an impact on the organization's service functions, computer controls, software, and paperwork systems.

At the time of this writing, there is no completely automated factory, although the Allen-Bradley company's Milwaukee facility (the Industrial Automation Systems Division) which manufactures motor starters comes as close to being fully automated as any plant in existence. Nevertheless, even the manufacturers of automatic assembly machines like to break up the sequence of completely automatic operations with a human operator, someone who is quite capable of pushing the panic button when required, and who can visually monitor the assembly process.

The human being is the most valuable resource of any company, yet most companies spend more time and effort in justifying capital dollar expenditures than in training workers properly, or in providing them with the *proper tools, place, or environment in which to work.*

Sometimes workers who are barely more than five feet tall are working at conveyors and benches set at levels for taller workers. Also, light levels may be unbelievably low for some types of work. It is not unusual in some plants for workers to spend an entire shift standing on concrete. Changing conveyor and bench heights or providing platforms, increasing light levels, placing rubber mats (or, similar floor padding), or making better footwear available to the employees are rather inexpensive measures that can be taken by any plant's management to remedy the basic complaints that have been cited. Attention to details such as these is a fundamental element of designing human work stations, and will do much to eliminate employee absenteeism, vandalism, and labor conflict.

In addition to the more humanitarian aspects, there are, essentially, five steps in planning a work station:

- Survey physical factors.
- Compile data.
- Analyze spatial arrangements.
- Implement the work station plan.
- Follow up.

Survey Physical Factors

The first step in planning a work station is to survey all the physical factors affecting this particular area, such as:

- all details regarding environmental conditions
- the type of activities being performed in the area
- sizes of parts to be handled
- quantities of parts
- temperature and humidity requirements
- light levels
- size of the area
- ceiling and truss heights, if applicable
- capacities of trusses, if overhead handling is involved
- electrical service available, if applicable
- the availability of water service, if applicable
- other utilities required, and,
- other specifics which are an integral part of the particular job function

As your physical distribution center is being staffed, or reviewed from the standpoint of improving productivity and lowering costs, it will be found that each new and different work station may require a new set of parameters, but eventually the astute manager and his/her staff will develop a *checklist* of items to be covered in order to develop the optimum work station arrangement at the most economic cost.

In this initial, or exploratory phase, the project manager should clearly define the objectives of the work, as follows:

- what is to be accomplished
- how it will be accomplished
- who will be responsible for each part of the project (in other words, assign responsibilities)
- specify beginning and ending dates for each step of the project

Compile Data

While there is much that can be done in the way of data collection during the physical survey (which involves numerical and environmental data) there is also the necessity to obtain a knowledge of the products to be handled, including the quantity of product to be handled in a given period of time.

Other data involve:

- what operations are to be performed
- what equipment is to be used, and how much of it

In reviewing and determining the operations to be performed at the work station, it may be found that some operations may be combined with others, or even eliminated.

Analyze Spatial Arrangements

In physical distribution operations there are not as many requirements for developing the work station arrangement as there are in most manufacturing establishments; however, consider the following tasks as potential candidates for this type of planning:

- Receiving clerical
- Dispatcher
- Quality control inspector
- Laboratory technician
- Shipping clerical
- Packing person

In each of the six categories above, there may be one or more tasks that are performed by different employees, thus enlarging the scope of the work station development. In addition, many physical distribution centers have tasks that are unique to their particular operations. Your supervisory staff will be able to delineate work station activities based upon the job functions of their personnel.

Almost all work station arrangements require that you take into consideration the activity area and the space required for each activity. Space and its relation to the individual employee are critical elements in designing both sitting and standing work station arrangements, and each requires an understanding of *human engineering factors* in order to achieve a good solution that will produce a satisfactory place to work.

Implement the Work Station Plan

Since repetition of most tasks in the factory and warehouse takes place many times during the course of one nominally 8-hour work shift, and thousands of times per year, small incremental time savings become formidable when considered over the period of a year. Therefore, you and your project engineer should not overlook any detail of the employees' job function when scrutinizing the work station plan. When all of the preceding steps have been taken, it may be necessary to schedule the proposed changes even to the extent of utilizing a Gantt chart to make certain that nothing important has been overlooked. A typical Gantt chart for the schedule of events for a work station arrangement project is illustrated in Figure 16-1.

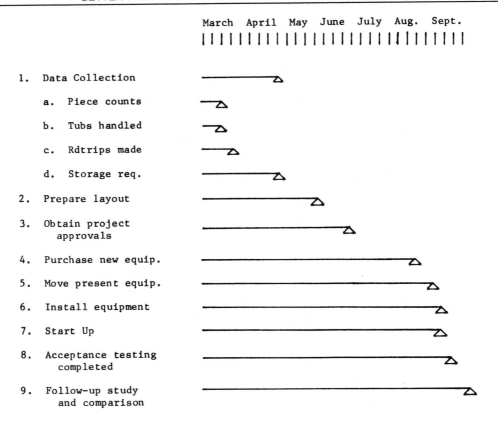

Fig. 16-1: A Gantt chart showing how various parts of a work station arrangement project may be implemented.

Figure 16-1 shows the various events, such as, data collection which has been divided into four elements:

- piece counts
- SKUs handled (SKU is a stock keeping unit, or line item)
- roundtrips made
- storage required

As shown in the chart, some of the above data elements can be collected simultaneously, other data, such as storage requirements might depend upon the results of preceding data, marketing information, factory scheduling, and the like.

Item 2 in the schedule is to prepare the layout, and the justification. Next, make a presentation to management and obtain project approval.

If the changes are sweeping, or if the concept being advanced is very new and innovative, this may be the largest hurdle faced by the project engineer. If the project is not canceled completely then it may require modification; when step 3 is repeated and approvals are obtained, the rest of the scheduled events are relatively easy.

New equipment may not always be a necessary part of the project, thus do not infer that this is characteristic of a new project involving work station arrangements; however, if new equipment is part of the project then an ROI must be prepared to accompany the presentation.

Follow Up

As shown in the Gantt chart of Figure 16-1, step 9 is a follow-up period in which the performance of the new work station arrangement is carefully monitored. In order to validate the new work station efficacy, data are compiled during the follow-up period to compare the new with the old work station.

NOTE: Any successful work station implementation should be widely publicized throughout the company in order to make future projects easier to sell to top management.

MAKING COMPARATIVE PHYSIOLOGY WORK FOR YOU

There is a wide range of individual physical characteristics in the labor force. Some of the diversities appear in the areas of:

- physical size; and,
- male/female differences.

When designing a work table work station, certain physical limitations must be recognized, especially since you should assume that the operator is required to perform satisfactorily throughout an 8-hour shift, plus or minus one hour for breaks, and so on. Figure 16-2 illustrates the reach of an average male seated at a work table.

Figure 16-2 assumes that the average male is approximately 5 feet 9 inches in height with a body weight of 150 to 160 pounds. Since this is presumed to be an average male, the reach dimensions used must frequently be adjusted downward for women, or smaller men. In this illustration, the reach distances are assumed to be made without any movement of the man's body.

Another human engineering factor must be considered when the work station involves the employee in a standing position. The limitations in reach will determine how heavy a load can be handled by either one hand or two, depending on size and shape of the object.

When a human is working in either a standing or sitting position, the coordination of hand and eye movements can be critical. Fortunately, in the physical distribution environment there are not too many areas in which this aspect of human engineering becomes a decisive factor. Nevertheless, it has been included in this discussion, because it may be of value in certain circumstances. Figure 16-3 indicates the areas of reach for both hands, and the shaded areas show the variation in the areas where the eye must follow the hands.

Work Station Equipment

Since large amounts of money are usually required in equipment purchases, i.e., capital dollars that cannot be expensed for accounting purposes, but must be depreciated over relatively long periods of time, you must take a cautious and conservative approach to the matter. A piece of equipment selected by the project engineer or by the task group can be a

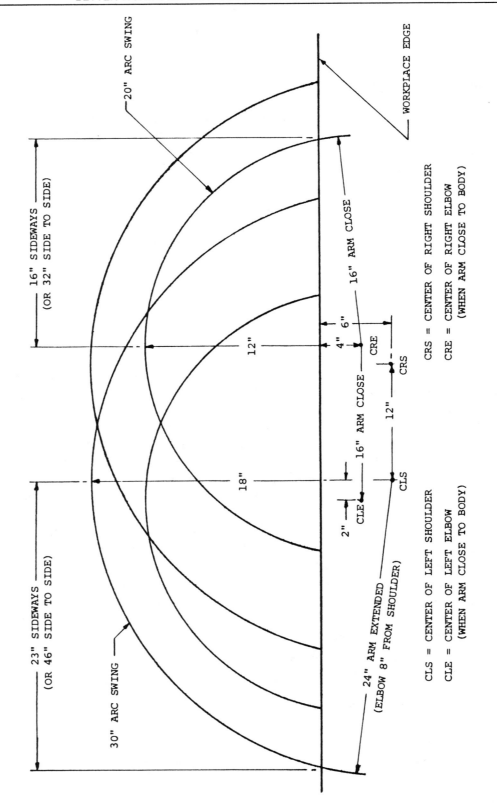

Fig. 16-2: Reach of average male seated at a work table.

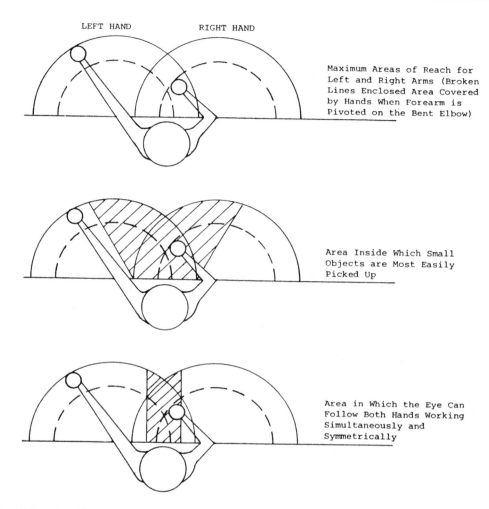

Fig. 16-3: Variations in the coordination of hand and eye movements for critical areas.

vital component of the handling process in a plant, or it may turn out to be an upsetting influence that causes labor disturbances and other problems.

You should obtain the broadest possible view of equipment selection; to this effect you should encourage the project leader, who is the key person in the group encharged with the responsibility for determining equipment needs, to obtain as much information from equipment manufacturers and suppliers as is humanly possible. This is necessary in order to obtain a firm conception of what is currently the best available from all sources.

Where *equipment systems* are concerned, if the in-house capabilities are not sufficient to the task, for one reason or another, then a professional materials handling consultant should be employed.

Conventional Work Places

The project leader should first obtain data that will enable him/her to make certain basic assumptions as to the type, the size, and the quantity of equipment required. Primarily, these data are concerned with:

- the volume of material to be handled;

- how far the material must be transported;

- the way in which the material is, or is not, packaged;

- where and how it is to be stored; and,

- whether or not the volumes handled vary from day to day, during the day, week, or month.

INDUSTRIAL ROBOTICS FOR WAREHOUSING OPERATIONS

The 1980s could, in all honesty, be called the coming of age of the industrial robot. Many advances were made in laying the groundwork for productively applying robotics principles in many manufacturing, and in some warehousing situations. Yet, a great deal of the pioneering work in robotics was accomplished during the 1960s and 1970s when the term "mechanical manipulator" was euphemistically substituted for the word "robot" in order to allay the fears of some unions, particularly in the automotive industries, that the robot was to replace the human worker on the production line. During the 1970s industrial robotics was finally recognized as management's attempt to fight competition, especially the cheap labor companies overseas.

There is another form of robot, called a "put and take" mechanism, that is designed for only one repetitive task performed a large number of times. As an example, feeding a stamping press where a slug or a piece of sheet metal is placed into a die. This machine differs from a robot in that the robot may be programmed to perform a number of different tasks, and to be reprogrammed to perform other operations.

While there are infinitely more applications for a programmable robot in manufacturing than in physical distribution, it is only the imagination of the practitioners that limits the scope of application. In physical distribution operations, some of the potential areas for the use of robots include the following:

- palletizing cartons

- placing materials in tubs or bins on a conveyor line

- placing different materials in cartons on a conveyor

Using the Robot Intelligently

Essentially, an industrial robot consists of a stand or base, upon which the mechanism rests; a trunnion about which the whole mechanism revolves; an arm that can be telescopically extended, or retracted, and a hand or claw with which to grasp an object. The hand can be made in many different configurations, such as: gripping jaws, or it can be equipped with vacuum cups or pads, magnets, and the like. In addition, the base of the mechanism does not have to remain stationary, but it may move down rails or alongside a conveyor to keep pace with a production line, or it may be suspended from the ceiling or any overhead structure.

Naturally, since the industrial robot is different from a "put and take" mechanism that feeds a press, or similar machine, it must be capable of being programmed for each task. There are two main systems for programming a robot at this time, these methods are:

- continuous path; and,

- point-to-point.

When the *continuous path (CP) method* of programming is used, the business end of the robot, or the hand, can be made to follow a smooth path, rather than move through a series of coordinates. This is the more sophisticated approach to robotics, and the mechanism is programmed by manually leading the hand of the robot through the preferred path of action. For example, on a paint production line, a skilled spray painter (human) would guide the robot's spray gun attachment through the intricate motions required to paint an auto fender, or other part, suspended from a moving conveyor line in a spray booth. The movements, thus described, are recorded on magnetic tape in a digital form. The robot can be stopped, started, and have several programs in its repertoire, so that as different parts pass on the conveyor, it is indexed to perform a choreography that will correspond to the proper part.

The total cycle time in the CP program depends on the length of the magnetic tape used for the program, and the speed at which the tape playback is operated.

When using the *point-to-point programming method,* the robotic hands will move between precise, three-dimensional points that conform to the X, Y, and Z axes, which is somewhat similar to locating an object in gun-fire control. For example, the hand is moved to the desired position from a point of rest, and a button is pushed to establish the location of the (X, Y, and Z) position coordinates on a magnetic drum memory. When the time comes to operate the robot, digital encoders provide feedbacks that compare the information stored on the magnetic drum memory. When the proper coordinates are reached, the correct hydraulic values are blocked off, arresting further motion.

Tooling for Robots

The hands, or the business end of the robot's arms, are the areas in which most of the tooling effort is concentrated. This type of tooling, which is the primary concern of the customer, has led to some very ingenious solutions in the field of mechanism. The robot's hand—or whatever attachment is provided for the arm of the robot—is extremely important as a solution to the handling problem. As an example, the control of gripping pressure, tension, or vacuum must be controlled according to the weight and fragility of the object to be picked up, in contrast to the spray gun application which is an entirely different type of robotics application. Other factors may enter into the computations of the design engineer, because some applications require a certain amount of resistance to heat, impact, and corrosion. Nevertheless, it is the outstanding versatility with a wide range of tooling that permits the robot to be applied in so many different applications in the materials handling field.

There are three general categories of robot hands, these are:

- grippers, or claws that depend largely on compressive and tensile forces to grasp and hold, i.e., they are strictly mechanical in action.

- surface-lift mechanisms that include magnets, or vacuum cups (either singly or in multiple units), arranged so that they can lift and position objects that have relatively flat surfaces like sheets of steel, or glass, or rectangular solids. Some of the objects lifted are cartons, automotive windshields, window glass, and some cylindrical objects.

- tools such as spray-painting guns, impact wrenches, welding devices for either spot-, or seam-welding, and the like.

In materials handling, it has been found that a hand that has finger-like cams that are parallel and opposed to each other, very much like the opposed thumb and fingers of the human hand—to grasp an object—is the most universally applicable attachment. Unlike the human being who is limited to two hands and ten fingers, it is possible to equip each robot with any number of hands and fingers so that extremely complex lifting, grasping, rotating, and positioning motions may be carried out. In addition, the reliability of robots has increased to such an extent that hundreds of thousands of repetitive operations may be performed with a positioning precision of ±1/64-inch (0.0156"), or better, i.e., the robot attachment can return to a position from its preceding stop, within 1/64-inch of its precise location.

To illustrate some of the hand (gripper) tooling, let's look at the following:

Mechanical Gripper

This is tooling that picks up a cylindrical piece from a tray pack and deposits the object into a carton, in a particular sequence or pattern.

Surface-lift Mechanism

This is the pick-up from a conveyor, or edge-grinding operation of a piece of plate glass, by means of multiple vacuum cups, and transferring the glass into a prepared crate or corrugated carton for shipping or storage. A simple "put and take" mechanism could be considered for this operation except that since several pieces of glass are to be placed in each container, the end position of the glass plate must be predetermined and programmed into the robot operating pattern.

In the above instance, programmable robots are more economically employed, since short runs of different pieces require reprogramming, only; whereas, a "put and take" mechanism would not be economically feasible since it would require new tooling after each production run.

Other Tooling

As indicated in the general discussion on robots, it is possible to equip the robot's business end(s) with welding guns, paint spray guns, glue guns, impact wrenches, and the like; however, these features would have very little application in the normal warehousing situation.

Using the Robot for Profit

There are at least four *variables* involved in the application of industrial robots in any given situation. These variables are:

- The weight of the object(s) to be handled;
- The cycle time, or the rate at which this handling takes place;
- The orientation or position of the object at the start and finish of each cycle;
- The quantity of objects required to be handled in each complete cycle performed by the robot.

Let's discuss each of these parameters in turn.

Weight

Programmable robots are capable of handling a fairly wide range of objects weighing from a few grams to several hundred kilograms, i.e., from ounces to 1,000 pounds, or thereabouts.

One difficulty that occurs when relatively heavy objects are handled has to do with the deflection of the arm of the robot. For example, with a heavy object as the arm position travels from a position close to the pivotal point of the robot and is extended out over several feet, deflection of the arm becomes critical if the repeatability of the positioning of the object is of major concern. If the positioning tolerance approaches $\pm 1/64$ of an inch (0.0156"), then the fact that a tolerance of less than two hundredths of an inch is required means that the stiffness or minimal deflection of the arm must be made a design characteristic for the arm. Thus, certain other design relationships are established as a chain reaction to the degree of stiffness of the arm, which affects the operation of the robot. A stiffer, beefier arm means that a larger mass of metal is to be moved and consequently the robot will perform each cycle slower, or to sustain cycle times an increase in the power input will be required. Either effect will increase the cost of the robot.

Handling Rate

Since the weight of the part or object to be handled influences the cycle time of the robot, the industry has evolved the following rule of thumb:

RULE: If the number of cycles exceeds 15 complete cycles every four seconds, then high-speed mechanization should be considered.

High-speed mechanization requires a considerable amount of capital investment, and is not normally considered for physical distribution operations. In other words, the production run of parts must be large and fairly uniform in configuration, as they might be in automotive parts production. In this instance, if several hundred thousand parts are required to be handled, the increased tooling cost would be relatively insignificant when distributed over the total number of parts handled.

Orientation, or Parts Placement

Almost all programmable robots currently in the marketplace are considered second-, or third-generation mechanisms, because of their reliability, i.e., general consistency in repeated tasks, and they can be readily programmed to perform a number of fairly intricate tasks.

As an example of a programmable robot that will detail just how complex a series of operations may be performed by such a device, consider the following: a robot picks up a wax pattern (foundry pattern made by the "lost wax" process) and dips it into a ceramic slurry several times (each with a different angle of immersion), then rotates the part over the slurry vat to assure a uniform coating of the slurry material and to remove excess slurry. After this is done, the robot carefully and gently orients it properly on a drying rack. This then becomes the first step in the investment casting process wherein the robot coats the wax pattern in much the same manner as a skilled worker. The repeatability of this task is much more precise than would be possible with a human operator over the course of an eight-hour work shift, since the robot is not influenced by the sheer boredom of the job, and since it has been programmed by a highly skilled artisan, it produces high-quality parts, part after part.

Unfortunately, this particular robot was not equipped with machine vision, and unseeing as it is, the tray load of wax patterns must be precisely oriented on a conveyor within its production cycle, or reach. In addition, it is necessary that the patterns be oriented in such a way that the robot's program can always start and finish a tier in the same position. Thus, a *dwell time* must be included in the robot program to permit the first tray to be removed automatically and the succeeding tray to be positioned for the robot's production cycle.

It is extremely important, therefore, that any part to be handled by an industrial, programmable robot be properly oriented in regard to position so that the repeatability of the production cycle can be maintained. There are several ways of doing this ranging from the simple to the ingenious. For example, an operator may place a part on a conveyor face up, face down, or on its side, and so forth; the conveyor can be equipped with pockets that will accept the part in only a certain way; guides, gates, and chutes can also be used to orient parts. Plastic trays can be designed with specially positioned cavities that can hold parts in only certain ways.

RULE: In automation mechanization you must never let go of the part; in industrial robotics you must keep the parts properly oriented.

Quantity of Objects

Finally the quantity of objects to be handled in each complete cycle of the robot must be considered. There is a parallel in physical distribution between a complex machining center and a programmable robot; for example, a machine tool that is tape controlled has the versatility to handle a number of very short production runs in rapid succession simply by changing the tape program and the fixture that holds the part. In the same manner, this versatility can be achieved by a programmable robot in the physical distribution environment by simply changing the robot's program and the hands and fingers of the robot to accommodate the new part.

This is in sharp contrast to a high-volume parts operation where a specially designed mechanism may provide a satisfactory rate of return; however, most physical distribution mechanization in carton handling, for example, requires greater flexibility; therefore, it is possible to design a robot's hand mechanism with built-in adaptability to a whole family of parts that may be sensed and handled by the robot. For instance, a photo-electric cell, or limit switch on a conveyor can activate a subprogram of the robot to handle a new or different part with different fingers, or rotate the part, or position it in a different manner, ad infinitum.

It is possible, also, to design hand mechanisms to grasp one part, or several parts simultaneously; however, keeping the correct orientation and positioning of the parts in the proper, prescribed pattern becomes of critical concern, in this instance.

The distribution centers of many food processing companies palletize outgoing loads of packaged foods either for shipment or storage. The wide variation in package sizes means that robotic palletizers must be capable of adjusting to the different box dimensions, and to the pallet patterns that will make efficient and satisfactory use of the pallet, as in the case where an interlocking carton pattern is required. (An interlocking pallet pattern for containers assures the maximum stability of the pallet load provided that each carton has been filled to the point where there are no void spaces in the box to present undue crushing of the container's corrugated board.) The robotic adaptability factor is important in captive distribution centers where production runs are relatively short and product dimensions are often changed, even during the same work shift.

The following is an example of the use of a PR-110 robotic palletizer developed by Pacific Robotics of San Diego, California, for a food processor and distributor. The PR-110 unit has an eight-foot reach and can pick up loads weighing up to 110 pounds. The average cycle time for a roundtrip is 10 seconds. The robot can handle one, two, or three boxes at a time by means of twelve suction cups, four for each box, on its pickup hand. Two ejector-type vacuum generators are hooked up to the vacuum cups by means of plumbing. The robot's generators are supplied by shop air through independently actuated solenoid valves so that the hand can be programmed to pick up the proper number of boxes at each cycle.

The purpose of the robot is to transfer shipping cartons from a conveyor line to a pallet and to load them in an arbitrary pattern. The robot was designed with four axes: a vertical linear drive, and shoulder, elbow, and wrist pivots. These axes use DC servo-motor drives with a digital-motion control card and an analog amplifier. The general system control and the downloading of selected pallet patterns are provided by an industrial-type computer. Limit switches are provided in order to prevent over-travel movement of any of the four axes. Furthermore, five sensors were provided for robot control, in the following manner:

- Three sensors are located at the box pickup station on conveyors to indicate the presence of the boxes to be picked up; all three boxes (of a three-box pickup) must be at the station when the robot prepares to make the pickup. If, due to any delay, the boxes are not all there, then the robot pauses in its cycle until all of the boxes have arrived at the location.

- Two sensors have been provided at the pallet station, one to ascertain whether the pallet is in its proper place, and the other to determine that the pallet is not loaded.

All of the five sensors are monitored by the computer prior to making the initial transfer of boxes from the conveyor for each loading of a pallet.

Since the robot is programmable, all that has to be done to teach it a pallet pattern is to use the *teaching pendant* to locate only the individual boxes of the first layer on the pallet, and the next successive tier of boxes if the pattern happens to be interlocking. After the teaching program has been completed, normal operational control is established by switches and indicator lights in the control panel located in the door of the control cabinet. The working speed of the robot can be regulated in a range from 10- to 100-percent of programmed speed. In addition, the robot can be stopped at any point in the cycle by the operator, and then can be reactivated using a pause control button. (Safety aspects of robot stations are discussed in detail later in this chapter.)

Robots and Machine Vision

The most customary application of the robot for physical distribution is that of a floor-mounted unit in a palletizing mode. Instead of being floor-mounted, however, it is possible to have the robot mounted on a traveling gantry crane. An advantage of this application is that, since grippers can be of various sizes, a large amount of flexibility may be built into the system due largely to the programmable feature of the robot. When this advantage is added to the possible use of automatic identification equipment, i.e., bar coding and scanning devices, it is possible to have the robot change its pallet-stacking pattern(s) to handle different sizes of boxed materials as they proceed along a conveyor line. Furthermore, additional flexibility may be obtained by having the robot serve a number of palletizing stations on several different conveyor lines.

While palletizing operations are relatively mundane operations in warehousing, it sometimes happens that assembly operations must be performed as part of the combined manufacturing-distribution operations. Thus, when a machine vision system is added to the robot's control mechanism, robots can perform precision work that is beyond human capabilities. This type of robotic application is especially commonplace in the electronics industry where both "put and take" and programmable robots have been so equipped.

A programmable robot equipped with machine vision can locate pieces conveyed to it in varying positions and properly orienting them, thus contributing to the productivity of the work effort.

Machine vision is a technology that uses computer capabilities to analyze the configuration of an image. It combines several disciplines: optics, electronics, and digital-signal processing. A fundamental characteristic of machine vision is that it performs its job without touching the object under analysis, therefore, it is usually referred to as *noncontact sensing*. All of the information and data about the object is generally collected using a light-sensitive sensor, such as a camera. Machine vision is like a human eye in that an object is "seen" by light reflected from the object. While machine vision can perform some of the same functions as the human eye, it does not yet have (in its present stage of development) the same degree of sophistication.

As a general rule, machine vision is best suited for operations that are very demanding (for example, measuring), labor intensive, and boringly repetitive. When a human has to inspect a piece part, or any product where it is necessary to examine the same part over and over, visual fatigue and boredom set in and lead to performance errors. When it is possible to substitute machine vision for humans in an inspection situation the following guiding principles should be used if the functions concern the detection of flaws, defects, and other aspects of quality control:

- Machine vision is capable of many uninterrupted hours of inspection.
- Machine vision is not just limited to visible light, but it can use x-rays or infrared to examine an object.
- Machine vision can examine an object and make precise measurements within and beyond a tolerance of ±0.001 inch.
- Machine vision can provide input data to programmable controllers, robots, and other devices.

Since computers can receive only digitalized data, the image that the human eye can see must be converted to a digitalized picture so that it can be "seen" by the computer. In the conversion process a video camera, vidicon, or solid-state camera is used. The camera is placed on the image plane which is an imaginary surface where the images are formed by convergent light rays, in effect, a means of focusing on the subject. The image, or object, is scanned line by line very rapidly, and a video signal is transmitted from the camera to the processor where it is instantly transformed into a digital image. The method of scanning is from top to bottom and from left to right in exactly the same fashion as in reading this page, for example.

A digital image is created by laying an imaginary grid over the object. Each small, grid square is a picture element called a *pixel,* an abbreviation of "picture element." In machine vision terms, a common-sized grid matrix would be a square measuring 256 × 256 pixels. Each tiny pixel (picture) is evaluated and its light intensity, i.e., the amount of reflected light it returns to the vidicon, is weighted or gradated from 0 (which is the equivalent of no light) to 64 (which represents the maximum amount of reflected light). As the grid of the object is scanned, pixel by pixel, the computer begins to visualize an image in this digitalized representation. The fascinating thing about machine vision is that the system has the capability of separating objects from one another, and of, also, delineating features within an object. This is accomplished by analyzing the object and determining the brightness of its various features and casting them into a binary pattern. This type of data is used to describe every feature of the object.

In forming a binary image, it is first necessary to establish threshold numbers as a frame of reference, or reference level. For example, all pixels with gray scale values above or below the threshold are considered black. All pixels that have gray scale values between the two threshold numbers are considered white. Thus, the resulting image has only two values, black and white.

The digitalized image, which has been converted in the above manner to a computer-compatible form, may now be analyzed. This analysis requires four steps, as follows:

- preprocessing to enhance the image;
- segmentation to separate the image into one or more components;
- feature extraction in order to transform the image into a set of useful attributes; and
- interpretation, which is user defined, being unique to each application.

In this manner, machine vision can be used to control robots to do precision assembly work in industries such as electronics component manufacturing, or it can be used as an inspection tool in many quality control applications.

NOTE: The plant manager who is considering the use of machine vision for either controlling robots, or in quality inspection applications, should be aware that the technique of binary threshold imaging is effective only in simple, well-defined applications where illumination and the material or object surface characteristics can be controlled. It is sometimes necessary, however, to use a more complex set of analytical tools to perform the required imaging. For the sake of identifying the technique, it is called mathematical morphology and is a method of analyzing images in full gray-scale representation. The method consists of filtering the image to distinguish the object's shape, orientation, size, and luminous contrast. This powerful tool permits the object to be analyzed despite the fact that there may be uneven lighting over the subject, there may be material surface variation, and there may be other adversities to consider.

Other important, front-end considerations when you are contemplating machine vision applications are: lighting, optics, and sensor selection. A company that has come up with solutions to this problem area is Penn Video of Akron, Ohio. They have developed an excellent expert system[1] called *Lighting Advisor*. The system was designed to assist in resolving lighting and optics problems, primarily in the small-parts assembly area, but their expertise has flowed over to many other areas where machine vision is being applied. The rationale behind the program is that since many plant engineers and plant technicians are not necessarily skilled or expert in the area of lighting and optics for machine vision systems, the packaged Lighting Advisor program forms a good basis from which to operate.

---

[1] An "expert system" consists of a combination of sophisticated computer programs and a knowledge base which duplicates the actions of a human expert in a particular, specialized field.

As an example of how this *expert system* is used, consider the following scheme where output data in the form of conclusions or directions are used to solve any number of problems. Relatively simplified instructions are reinforced through the use of computer graphics, and there are over 300 "rules" in the Lighting Advisor data base. The system uses a PC as its work station and the software is menu-driven to help the user over the rough spots.

How it works is that the user informs the Lighting Advisor about his/her application by answering a series of questions and making choices from the menu. The questions concern the characteristics of the application, the features of the object and background surface qualities, and whether or not the object is moving during inspection (as it would be if it were on a conveyor, for example), and the like.

A typical Q&A of the program:

Question: What is the light technique?

Answer: Front-light, light field.

Question: What is the light source?

Answer: A quartz halogen lamp with reflector.

NOTE: Applying machine vision requires a fairly large amount of specialized experience in several disciplines, and for this reason a packaged program such as Lighting Advisor will not only prove useful in installing such a system, but will make it possible to troubleshoot possible aberrations once the system is installed.

If your company is fortunate to have an enthusiastic training director on board, you might suggest to him/her that the type of Question and Answer procedure as exemplified in the Lighting Advisor program should be considered in promoting various types of training within the company, especially safety and forklift driver refresher courses.

Robots and Cycle Times

The "put and take" mechanism which was mentioned earlier in this chapter is considered **hard** automation and, as such, its cycle time is entirely predictable and capable of being engineered into its design. On the other hand, the use of a programmable robot (Figure 16-4) sometimes makes it necessary to simulate a given procedure in which the robot will be engaged in order to predict cycle times.

Assisting in this cycle time prediction the Silma Corporation has developed a software program called, "CimStation" which is a productivity enhancement tool that describes the design and simulation of multiple devices working simultaneously in a work cell. Programs for a number of different automation devices, such as: conveyors, robots, and programmable controllers, are generated and downloaded to each piece of equipment (either online or offline) without interrupting the main process. Programming on the CimStation is done in the Silma company's interactive programming language, called SIL, which provides the software that links incompatible, computer-controlled equipment into a completely unified automation system.

Before the development of CimStation, robotic simulation systems were incapable of dealing with the complexities found in multiple-device, work cells—such as, communications between devices that work in extremely constrained places, and in overlapping work spaces. The CimStation manufacturer claims that its software program has the capability of

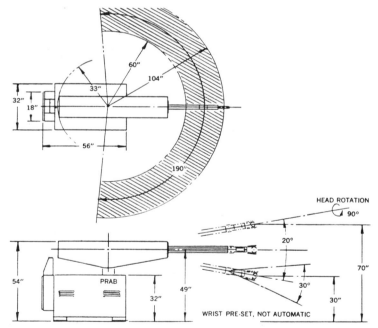

Photo courtesy Reis Machines, Inc., Elgin, IL

Fig. 16-4: Some of the parameters involving an industrial robot.

providing the communication commands that will permit the user to simulate and program more than one device (robot) working simultaneously. Thus, the technician-operator can accurately predict cycle times and determine where the business end of each robot will be at any given time. This consideration permits the technician to use his/her work cell more effectively and prevents possible collisions between robotic arms if more than one robot is used in a tight place.

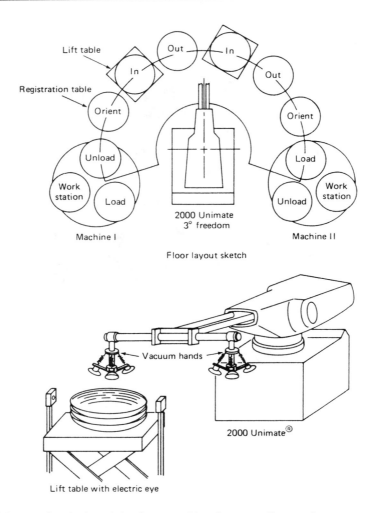

Fig. 16-5: A Unimate Co. industrial robot stocking harrow discs using vacuum cup grippers.

Robotic Movements and Devices

The versatility of the industrial robot has been discussed above, but there is another mechanism developed by the General Electric Co. that should be of especial interest to warehouse and distribution center managers, called a CAMS device (Cybernetic Anthropomorphous Machine System). It is not, in the strictest definition of the term, an industrial robot, but it requires explanation and description, at this point, because of its tremendous versatility. The GE Co. calls the CAMS device a "Man-Mate," because it is a means of amplifying the reaching, grasping, and lifting capacity of the human body. It accomplishes this through a series of electro-hydraulic and mechanical means.

The CAMS machine was originally designed to run in an automatic mode through computer control, in which case it is, indeed, an industrial robot; however, most of the GE CAMS units are run with an operator aboard, hence the name Man-Mate, see Figure 16-7.

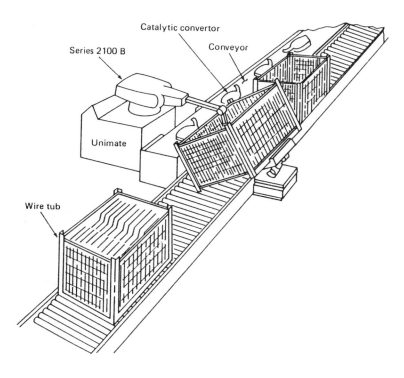

Fig. 16-6: A Unimate Co. industrial robot palletizing catalytic convertors into wire storage tubs from a conveyor line.

Fig. 16-7: Sorting electric range appliances from several conveyors in a distribution center using a GE Man-Mate.

There are a number of advantages in using a GE Man-Mate:

- The Man-Mate may be remotely positioned and the operator's cab completely enclosed and air-conditioned, in order to remove the operator from a hazardous or hostile environment, such as extremes of temperature, toxic dusts, or other pollutants.
- It can extend the human capabilities of reach from 20 to 30 feet; also, it can grasp and lift up to 12,000 pounds and more.
- It can repeat a cycle of activity as long as the operator, who is comfortably (air-cushion) seated remains at the console. The operator's control arm consists of a pistol grip (see Figure 16-8) that controls the operation of the Man-Mate which obeys the operator's commands.

Fig. 16-8: The command schedule used in the pistol grip servos of the GE Man-Mate.

The Man-Mate is not in direct competition with conventional industrial robots, because added to the cost of the mechanism is the payroll expense of the human assigned to it. Since the device has a wide range of activity and is relatively easy to use, it adds interest to the job task and decreases the fatigue element usually associated with warehouse materials handling. In effect, it makes arduous tasks simple and non-stressful, in contrast to unaided human activities.

As an example of a warehousing situation where a GE Man-Mate is employed, one need only visit the General Electric, Columbia Park, Maryland, Appliance Division. An operator seated at the controls of a GE CAM-100 Man-Mate (see Figure 16-7) is centrally located at the convergence point where refrigerators and electric ranges on three assembly conveyors meet. The operator at the Man-Mate controls, sorts the appliances according to a number code, lifts them from the incoming conveyors and places them on several warehouse conveyors. These conveyors transport the appliances from the assembly building by means of an enclosed conveyor bridge into a warehouse and distribution center building.

PREPARING EMPLOYEES FOR THE INTRODUCTION OF INDUSTRIAL ROBOTS IS AS IMPORTANT AS PREPARING THE ROI

When considering the use of industrial robots in the warehouse or distribution center, it is simply not enough to prepare an economic justification that points out the return on investment. Of course, you would require that an ROI be forthcoming in any capital expenditure; however, in applying this type of mechanization, it is critical that the climate be favorable to the introduction of the robot on *all levels* of the company.

It is one thing to have a satisfactory ROI when considering an industrial robot application, but regardless of the euphemisms you employ, the robot will displace at least one human in the work place and is usually considered anathema by labor in general and the unions in particular. So, starting with the departmental foreman in the area in which the contemplated robot is to be installed, you must lay the groundwork necessary to make the project viable. You may rest assured that if your foreman is not wholeheartedly with you or your project leader in this endeavor, the chances are that it is doomed to failure. If the foreman can be won over, then it is his/her task to introduce the robotic application to his/her subordinates, the people who will be working in the general locale of the robot.

You must also direct attention to the general attitude of workers in the department, who by this time, must be thinking that they will all be replaced by mechanical monsters. If this attitude prevails, then actual sabotage, either willful or through neglect, will be one of the silent methods by which the employees will take revenge on management who they feel is trying to victimize or swindle them.

It should be your policy, and one that is widely publicized throughout the distribution center, that as you attempt to increase productivity by means of greater mechanization, i.e., including the use of industrial robots, no worker will lose his/her job with your company because of mechanization. With the cooperation of the personnel department and good planning, attrition in the various departments of the plant will absorb the labor surplus due to robot, and other mechanized applications. Ideally any displaced worker(s) should be relocated at a higher wage scale.

By balancing cessations with accessions, the company can minimize the temporary imbalance brought on by mechanization. The assurances provided by management, even to the point of including a clause in union contracts, that it will be a policy of the company to retain employees will be a major step in improving the climate between labor and management in regard to the effects of technological unemployment. As an example of effective communications, where labor unions are concerned, it is necessary that management consider conferring with union officials prior to placing any orders for robotic hardware. If the proper groundwork has been accomplished then the installation of a robot will not cause shock waves throughout the company. The secret weapon of good labor/management relations is to keep the union informed, even to the point of your project leader taking several union officials on a visit to a robot manufacturer's plant, or a plant using a robot in a fashion similar to the proposed installation. This, alone, will do a great deal towards allaying fears, frustration, and tension concerning new mechanization proposals. The "known" causes fewer problems than the "unknown," and this should be your management philosophy in virtually every aspect of mechanization.

17

OSHA and Safety Requirements in Warehousing and Physical Distribution

THE IMPACT OF OSHA ON WAREHOUSING OPERATIONS

Every employer of more than seven workers throughout the United States is affected by the Williams-Steiger Act of 1970, which is known as OSHA, the Occupational Safety and Health Administration (OSHA). has purview over the application of safety principles in a wide range of occupations throughout both industry and agriculture. While some employers may harbor a certain amount of resentment about the bureaucratic application of and establishment as well as enforcement of some of the regulations, in general the law makes good sense from the viewpoint of materials handling. Conforming to some of these regulations will actually improve the operations of the physical distribution center, since many of the standards that have been adopted by OSHA were taken directly from those standards that were developed by the professional and trade associations in each of several fields, for example the standards of the Industrial Truck Association (ITA), the American National Standards Institute (ANSI), and the National Fire Protection Association (NFPA).

Various Pertinent Provisions of the Law

Subpart N, Materials Handling and Storage, Para. 1910.176, Handling Materials—General: This particular heading is shown exactly as it appears in the Federal Register, which has recorded the OSHA regulations, and we shall parallel each reference letter, number, and heading exactly as it is in the OSHA regulations in discussing this subject, as follows:

Use of Mechanical Equipment

According to the OSHA regulations wherever mechanical handling equipment is used, sufficiently safe clearances shall be allowed for aisles, at loading docks, through doorways, and wherever turns or a passage must be made. All aisles and passageways must be kept clear and in good repair with no obstruction across or in the aisles that could create a hazardous condition. Permanent aisles and passageways must be appropriately marked. While the law is somewhat vague on this point, it is both necessary and advisable from the standpoint of efficiency to clearly mark aisles in factories or warehouses wherever mechanical equipment such as forklift trucks, towconveyors, tractor-trains, pallet jacks, and other mobile handling equipment is used. And the guiding reason behind this regulation is, naturally, safety to personnel. In addition to safety there are other intangible and psychological reasons to mark the aisles of the physical distribution center, since the more orderly and organized a plant appears, the more conducive this appearance of system and order is to the promotion of improved morale and the productivity of the operation. In your plant, safety aisles for pedestrians and clearly marked aisles for vehicular traffic can be more readily controlled by the use of certain aisle designators, whether they be markers or painted yellow lines or yellow tape on the floor.

Secure Storage

Another provision of the law is that storage of material should not create a hazard; such things as bags, containers, bundles, sacks, and so forth, should be stored in tiers which are well stacked, interlocked and fairly limited in height so that they are stable and secure against sliding or collapsing.

Housekeeping

According to the OSHA law the storage of materials should not create hazardous conditions. Therefore, they should be free from the accumulation of materials that constitute hazards in the form of materials that an employee could fall over or that constitute fire hazards and explosion, or that could become infested with pests and insects. In addition, weeds and general vegetation should be controlled around the plant as required and when necessary.

Drainage

Proper drainage should be provided in and around the plant.

Clearance Limits

Wherever there is low clearance, that is, low head room, for either personnel or vehicular traffic, then clearance signs to warn of the height limitations must be provided.

Rolling Railroad Cars

Rail and/or bumper blocks shall be provided on all spur railroad tracks where a rolling car could bump into other cars being worked upon, or enter a building, work or traffic areas of the plant.

Guarding

Another aspect of the law requires that covers and/or guard rails be provided to protect personnel from the hazards of open pits, tanks, vats, ditches, and so forth.

How to Maximize Plant Safety for Profitability

The statistics on safety concerns vary in reliability since there is no central data collection point for accidents that occur in industrial plants and other businesses. Many of the smaller companies do not report accidents, and there is also a problem of a lack of uniformity in describing the accidents themselves. Since there are thousands of small companies, the data collected, for example, by the U.S. Labor Department and OSHA makes it very difficult to derive anything but approximations from the data that is collected. In addition, since plants with fewer than seven employees do not report accident data except in connection with Workers' Compensation claims, only assumptions can be made as to the extent of certain accident rates.

We can, however, extrapolate from the data; as an example, although forklift truck injuries represent only about one percent of the medical cases, they comprise about ten percent of the disabling or serious injuries. This is an indication that, while the number of forklift truck injuries is small, they are usually more severe than other types of industrial accidents that cause injuries.

Another very important area, which concerns damage to property caused by the forklift trucks, does not show up in any data collection system. At every plant in the country there are numerous examples of such damage, even on a daily basis, thus indicating how very costly fork-truck operations can be. In general, the safety record of women forklift truck operators per capita is much better than that of male forklift truck operators. Nevertheless, if all operators can be trained properly to regard safety as the number one concern, then secondary benefits will accrue that will minimize to a large extent any damage to property and personnel.

It is unfortunate that every time a plant has an industrial accident, the Workers' Compensation rate from the insurance carrier will increase in cost. Therefore, in order to maintain insurance costs at a reasonable level, it is important to increase safety consciousness on the part of every employee of the company.

Instilling Safety Consciousness

If your plant doesn't have a safety director, then it is your responsibility to make sure that the foremen and leadmen and other supervisors are aware of the need for a safety consciousness attitude throughout the plant. Safety consciousness begins at the top and then filters down the ranks to your employees. Awareness of safety issues is important to your relationship with the community surrounding the plant and its operation. Your company should send out the message to the community that your plant is a safe plant, and safety is extremely important to you. In order to obtain the type of reputation that will influence your suppliers, customers, and the community, you do have to do more than pay lip service to safety.

The focal point of every plant's safety program should be the forklift truck accident prevention approach. As mentioned above, it was indicated that while the forklift truck injury frequency represents only 1% of the medical cases, they comprise about 10% of the disabling or serious injuries. This is the reason why we have concentrated on the forklift truck since, if your plant supervision is able to cope with the problem of forklift truck safety, then the other plant safety problems will fall into line as these safety problems are better understood.

The nine most commonly occurring forklift truck accidents are as follows:

Forklift Truck Strikes Employee

This potentially fatal type of accident is one of the most common in the plant. Since a two-ton capacity, gas-powered, forklift truck (which is one of the smallest in use) weighs almost 7000 pounds without a load, you can imagine that the kinetic energy will not permit it to stop quickly. Therefore, a pedestrian stepping in front of it is certain to be injured, sometimes fatally.

What usually happens in this type of accident is that an employee will not be paying attention to his or her surroundings and step out into the vehicle path or into the side of the vehicle. When the employee walks into the side of the truck and receives a glancing blow, it may not of itself cause serious injury, but if, as an example, the employee is pushed by the truck and lands on some sharp object or into other material, or the uprights of a storage rack, serious injury can occur.

Another type of injury occurs when an employee is walking alongside a moving truck as the vehicle turns a corner. Either the truck will hit the employee, or the steering wheels will run over the employee's feet.

A Forklift Truck Pushes a Container or Part onto an Employee

A forklift truck operator must always be taught to be aware of accident developing situations such as driving up to an employee who is standing between the forklift truck and a fixed object. The scenario becomes dangerous:

- The operator drives down an aisle with a load.

- A part or container extends partially into the aisle and the forklift truck operator may see the obstruction and think there is enough room to pass it by, but being distracted for a moment and possibly not seeing the obstruction, he/she proceeds and pushes the object into an employee standing behind it. Immediately behind the employee is a fixed object such as a wall or a bench or other obstruction, and the employee is crushed, and severely injured.

- A forklift truck operator is putting material away in back-to-back storage racks.

  When the operator of the forklift truck places a load into an empty space on a rack on the second or third tier, or higher, a clerk taking inventory in the opposite aisle is struck or crushed by material that has been pushed off the higher level by the forklift truck driver, not realizing that the load he/she was putting away was pushing an oversize load out of position. (In a storage location several years ago, instead of one clerk in the aisle opposite the forklift driver, there were two clerks, one counting inventory and the other recording and tagging the merchandise. A pallet-load of materials was dumped upon both of them from a height of approximately 20 feet. Both of these employees were severely injured, and one of them was crippled for life. An unfortunate accident that should never have occurred.) Dividers or safety backstops down the center of back-to-back storage racks can prevent this type of accident from happening.

Manually Handled Parts or Materials Strike the Forklift Truck Operator

When the forklift truck operator manually handles materials from the ground next to the fork-truck and is trying to shift the load into position on the forks, the object may fall off the forks, striking the operator's legs or feet.

The Forklift Operator Is Injured While Climbing Aboard or Stepping Off the Forklift Truck

While the forklift truck operator steps up to his truck and steps down from the truck many times during the course of a working shift, this apparently simple action has resulted in many knee and ankle injuries, and the cause is not entirely clear. In many instances, it may be that the sudden transfer of body weight onto one leg when the person either steps up to the truck or steps down places all the weight on one leg. In some instances the operator may step off the truck and step onto a piece of dunnage lying on the floor or another stray object, severely twisting the ankle or knee. The simple remedy in this instance is to look before you leap, figuratively speaking. Therefore, the forklift truck operator must always be aware of his/her surroundings and pay attention to his/her next move.

The Forklift Truck Driver Does Not Recognize a Potentially Serious Accident Situation Ahead and Fails to Slow Down

While forklift truck overturning accidents are relatively infrequent, almost every operator has had close calls with this potential accident type. This is another serious kind of accident that can result in a fatality and it usually happens to the newer employee or the rookie operator. In each instance of an accident occurrence, it could have been prevented if the operator had sized up the situation and reduced the truck's forward speed. Traveling too rapidly around a corner or down a ramp can be extremely dangerous for both the vehicle and the operator. While three-wheeled vehicles are less common today than they were several decades ago, they are still around and it should be realized that they have less stability than the four-wheeled vehicles; however, exceedingly high speeds can overturn both three-wheeled and four-wheeled vehicles. In addition, carrying a load too high raises a truck's center of gravity and is potentially hazardous, especially when combined with high speed and turning corners.

Vehicle Runs into Another Mobile Piece of Equipment

In a plant with more than a few forklift trucks and other pieces of mobile equipment, the collision between vehicles can occur, especially when one of the units is smaller than the forklift truck. For example, small personnel carriers, carts, scooters, and bicycles which are often used in many physical distribution centers, are not as visible and are quiet in operation. When these vehicles are driven carelessly at high speeds, they become potential accident situations, especially at aisle intersections of the plant. Since supervisors and expediters usually are driving these smaller units, they should be the first ones to realize the potential hazards of their vehicles in the plant and set an example to the forklift operators by pausing at intersections and looking in both directions, just as if they were crossing a busy highway.

Forklift Truck Backs Off or Runs Off the Edge of the Loading Dock

The possibility of running off the dock can occur on both the receiving and shipping docks where the operation is relatively high-speed. The potential for serious injury or fatalities is very high in this type of accident. Sometimes it happens that a truck will move out of position and the forklift operator will fall into the gap. The OSHA regulation requires that to load or unload a truck, you must first block its wheels to prevent movement of the truck. This means dismounting from the forklift truck, or having the receiving or shipping personnel dismount and put chocks under the wheels, or having the motor carrier driver place the chocks under the wheels. Since this is a divided responsibility, an accident is bound to occur sooner or later. City deliveries or small drop shipments, that require only a few minutes to unload, sometimes cause negligence on the part of both the forklift operator and the motor carrier operator who don't chock the wheels. In recent years, a common restraining device which lashes onto the frame of the motor carrier in the loading or unloading position has been successful in preventing many of this type of accident. In many plants, the responsibility for seeing that an over-the-road carrier has its wheels properly chocked has not been clearly defined. Regardless of this fact, it is the forklift truck operator's supervisor who has the final responsibility, and you should inform him/her that he/she must make this a priority in the safety program. While the supervisor may not necessarily place the chocks under the trailer wheels, he/she should make sure that this is done before any personnel enters the truck with a forklift truck or other piece of mobile handling equipment.

Loading and unloading flatbed trailers is extremely hazardous, especially where the forklift truck operator is backing off the trailer onto the loading dock. A second's inadvertent distraction is enough to make the operator misjudge the distance from the edge of the trailer and back right over it.

All of the above comments apply not only to the motor carrier loading and receiving docks but also on the rail side, if the plant has a rail siding.

When a Forklift Truck Operator's Body Parts Protrude Outside the Configuration of the Truck

If any part of the forklift truck operator's body protrudes from the operating lines of the forklift truck, there is a potential for serious accident. The body parts can be severely bumped, scraped, twisted, and sometimes mangled. This type of injury often occurs when the forklift truck driver is running with a load on the forks and he or she is looking outside the load for increased visibility. It is possible for the operator to strike his or her head on a building column, partition, or wall surface.

Boxes and Cartons Falling on the Operator

All forklift trucks in which the mast height can elevate above the driver's head should have canopy guards which are certified, in order to protect the driver from falling objects.

Despite the canopy guard there is still an area between the mast and the canopy guard that requires the exercise of caution. This dangerous spot occurs when the driver is stacking a load and has raised the forks to the proper level and begins inching into position. The driver may have a very cumbersome load or has cartons that are not interlocked properly in their stacking pattern and is relatively unstable. At this moment, if the truck should run over a rough spot in the floor or over a piece of dunnage, it's enough to joggle the truck and the loose parts will fall back behind the mast hitting the operator.

Tilting the mast backward when positioning a load over the second tier may be enough to cause an unstable load to slide back into the operator. A way to prevent this is to have high backrests on the mast and to always make sure that the load is stable, even if it means using stretch-wrap or fiber reinforced tape to stabilize the load.

A vivid example of the seriousness of the situation happened during a warehouse installation. A freak accident occurred in which the forklift truck operator was entering a railroad car and driving over a slightly raised dock plate into the car. The jostling that occurred as the driver went over the plate dislodged several cartons of the load, causing the driver to reach through the mast as he was elevating the forks, and the result was that he mangled his hand between the chain and the lowered backrest. While this is an example of the instinctive reaction of a conscientious employee, it does speak to the necessity for improving safety awareness.

If you do not have a safety director in your plant, then the responsibility for safety rests between you as the ultimate authority and your supervisors who are on the front lines.

It would be advisable to distribute a copy of some of the common forklift truck accidents discussed above to each forklift truck operator in a session in which the supervisor can run through each of the problem areas in order to achieve some degree of awareness on the part of all of these employees. While your ultimate goal is to have a safe plant in which to work with minimal injuries to employees, by following the rules and regulations implicit in the above examples, you can cut down the damage to forklift trucks and other mobile handling equipment, and reduce insurance premiums.

In small companies the severity of accidents can increase insurance premiums to the extent that the profitability of the company is diminished.

You must make sure your equipment functions properly and is in good operating condition. This contributes to morale as well as to plant safety. While mechanical malfunctions account for less than 1% of the forklift truck accidents, they are relatively minor in comparison to operator and employee errors in judgment and awareness.

HOW YOU CAN PROVIDE THE CLIMATE FOR SAFE MATERIALS HANDLING

Accidents usually have multiple causes; however, the other causes are relatively minor compared to operator and fellow employee errors that are committed as a result of a chain reaction in which one thing leads to another and an accident occurs.

Recognize the Causes of Accidents

We have to make a fundamental assumption that no one intentionally causes an accident and, therefore, we often wonder why they occur. In analyzing the situation, we usually come up with three areas of particular concern, which are the underlying causes.

Lack of Skill or Knowledge

On the subject of forklift truck accidents,lack of knowledge and skill is a contributing factor in a large number of accidents and is one of the primary reasons that the OSHA regulations require that forklift truck operators be trained before operating such vehicles.

Inattention

The second contributing factor to forklift accidents in particular is that the operators are not concentrating on what they are doing. Usually when an accident occurs the operator is being inattentive to the job at hand; sometimes this is attributed to on-the-job boredom. Periodically, even the most skilled and best trained operators are inattention, but it usually occurs when his/her resistance is down, the operator has domestic problems, and the lack of attention based on these causes cannot be controlled by the plant supervision. It is the same as saying don't drive a car when you are angry. Unfortunately one of the only mechanisms that the plant management can resort to is the periodic reinforcement of on-the-job training.

Studies of motor carrier drivers indicate that the safest drivers have one thing in common: an intense concentration on what they are doing while they are driving. These same top drivers do not do any better than any other driver in the various other tests required of the drivers, such as knowledge of the rules of the road, but they all did very well in one particular area, and that was the ability to keep their minds completely on their driving, and they were constantly aware of the traffic conditions about them.

Taking Chances

This third factor is one of the most difficult to rectify. The operator takes a chance with full knowledge of the consequences the cowboy instinct prevails and an accident occurs. All of us take certain chances in our daily lives, such as when we walk across a busy street or change lanes in heavy traffic; however, there sometimes is an exceedingly fine line between taking a calculated chance and being careless which can result in injury.

How to Minimize Materials Handling Accidents

Once you have examined the types and causes of accidents with forklift trucks as a basis, it is advisable to review the past history of accidents in your plant and see which operations are causing the most problems. When this is done the possibilities of developing a workable program with the objectives of eliminating, or at the very least, minimizing accidents such as those that have occurred in the past, are quite possible.

Every plant needs a good forklift truck operator training program. In addition, it needs quality training in every department of the plant. The main ingredient of each and every training program should start with the selection of employees. As an example, a potential employee who has lost his/her automobile driver's license certainly does not give any indication of being a safer or more responsible driver operating a forklift truck. The forklift truck driver should be required to take a physical examination in which specific medical criteria applicable to the job of forklift truck driving will be used. Employees who have a history of medical problems such as a heart condition or diabetes, or other ailments that require medication to keep the problem under control, should probably not be considered in filling vacancies for forklift truck drivers or other positions which are relatively critical, simply because of the potential hazard to themselves and to their fellow employees.

Forklift truck drivers require quality training to operate their vehicles, whether they are part-time or full-time drivers. The OSHA law requires that they be trained, and training means a lot more than just gathering a group of potential operators to a classroom training program and then assigning them a truck and letting them start operating in the job situation. In addition to teaching the rules governing the operation of a fork-truck, practical hands-on experience is also required.

In the physical distribution warehouse, you would be advised to require that your supervisory management team develop a training program for each job description it has in its cadre of employees.

There are many by-product benefits that accrue to a sound, quality training program. Despite the fact that the basic objectives of quality training are not safety per se, the fact that it is often mentioned as the best practice, in textual material, such as an instruction manual and through driving practice or on-the-job training, it does have a bearing on the performance and maintenance of fork trucks and other equipment.

As an example of some of the benefits that accrue to you, just regard, for a moment, what happens when you develop a group fork-truck training program. Maintenance costs on forklift trucks drop demonstratively for a period of up to six months after such a training program has been taken. The indications that by-product benefits have occurred are, as follows:

- The quality of the training is such that the operators are motivated to take much better care of their trucks.
- Periodic refresher training helps each employee in that it is an opportunity for reviewing operating procedures and, from the company vantage point, it serves as a motivationally reinforcing tool.

How You Can Start or Revitalize an Existing Accident Reduction Program

Training and safety go hand in hand because a well-trained employee is a much safer employee than one who does not fully understand or know the requirements of his or her job. For this reason you should incorporate a follow-up mechanism in every training program in the plant. For example, you should monitor a new forktruck operator's performance after his or her training period in order to eliminate poor work practices and bad work performance habits. Psychologists often say it requires seven years to break a bad habit; unfortunately operating personnel don't have the luxury of that long a time to change an employee's behavioral aspects.

NOTE: When the evidence of a bad performance work habit is observed, immediate follow-up is required not a day later, or a week later, but within hours of occurrence. You simply cannot wait for a bad habit to develop before trying to rectify the procedure.

For this reason we maintain that your supervisor should correct a problem immediately, before an accident occurs. If any habits are to be formed within your plant, your supervisors should make sure they are good work habits.

A good work supervisor will not make the excuse that he is too busy with paper work, or some such excuse, to take over the task of correcting the employee whose performance can be questionable.

How You Can Provide Quality Safety Training

The enforcement of safe work practices can be adherence to procedures established by management and is essential to controlling forklift truck operations and the other operational processes that take place within your plant. Your supervisors should be instructed to exercise control of their employees' work habits through a combination of both positive and negative reinforcements; this is tantamount to saying that there should be a combination of coercion and reward in order to maintain control.

Negative control requires the use of consistently applied disciplinary measures. If your plant is unionized, it might be advisable to have your supervisors meet with the shop stewards in order to develop the necessary carrot-and-stick approach to maintaining a high level of safety consciousness in the plant. If the plant is not unionized, then the supervisors should meet with the employees of their respective departments and explain that, with their help, they will develop a system of disciplinary measures contrasted with rewards for safe operation. As an example, the employees may agree on a one- or two-hour to one- to three-day suspension, depending the seriousness of the violation. On the reward side, a $25 savings bond or up to a $100 savings bond for a safe record of an accident-free period of time. If the employees feel that they have had a hand in constructing this system of coercion and reward, it may make it more palatable. In any event, you should discuss the requirements and the objectives of the program with the supervisory staff prior to their meeting with employees.

Positive control requires that safe behavioral practices on the part of your employees be reinforced on a continuing basis. If your plant doesn't have a safety director, you should appoint one of your supervisory staff to serve as an acting director. This person will wear two hats; however, a safety program can be developed that will make use of plaques, certificates, and various prizes as safety habits are reinforced and safety records are maintained. A safety bulletin board can be established and, if the company has a newsletter, then a significant amount of space should be devoted to the safety program and the employees who have achieved good operating records over the course of each quarter. The reporting period does not have to be as long as a quarter; it could be monthly, even weekly, depending on the supervisory input into this particular area.

FORKLIFT TRUCK DRIVER TRAINING

Since this book is intended for plant managers operating a physical distribution warehouse, it is important to combine the theoretical aspects of materials handling and materials management with an understanding of the complexities of certain characteristics of distribution center and warehousing equipment. Even if you have sophisticated equipment (e.g., an AS/RS system with a front-end conveyor installation, sideloaders and right-angle and turret trucks; a multiplicity of conveyor systems, both overhead and powered and free; bar-coding and other automatic identification data entry and tracking systems; EDI systems and computer simulation), the basic forklift truck and all of these other exotic high-tech systems require structured training programs for maximum effectiveness.

Almost every forklift truck manufacturer has training programs that you may take advantage of if you do not want to establish your in-house program. The forklift truck manufacturer's representative will come directly to your plant and conduct the training course for your personnel.

After all three parts of the training program have been given, your line supervision must maintain the newly established performance levels and, in addition, must set a good example by their own conduct in order to establish the proper climate conducive to maintaining the attitudes required for forklift truck operation in a safe working environment. This requires that the supervisor enforce the rules for safe forklift truck driving in a fair and consistent manner.

The training program should be designed to instruct not only new operators but their supervisors in the safe, efficient and economical operation of forklift trucks and any other pieces of mobile equipment. The training should be divided into three parts: (1) a seven-hour course, (2) a safety film, and (3) on-the-truck training.

NOTE: When there is a new hire or transfer from another department being considered, there are two preliminary steps that should be mandatory before any classroom or on-the-truck training is given:

- The supervisor should ensure that the employee has developed an acceptable level of safety consciousness by reviewing his/her safety record and history with the company.

- It is important to determine the acceptable physical capabilities of the employee by means of a medical exam in which his/her hearing, eyesight, depth perception, and a review of prior health records is made.

Part One: The Training Course

Require each operator to complete a seven-hour programmed learning course "Forklift Operators' Training Administrators' Guide" developed by the Dupont Company's Education and Applied Technology Division, Wilmington (DE), which consists of five units and is designed to teach safe, accident-free, efficient operation of the mobile materials handling equipment. Complimentary copies may be obtained by calling the Dupont Co. at 302-774-1000. Each unit takes a little over one hour to complete and ends with a review quiz. The sixth unit, a 45-minute written, qualifying examination, which each one of the potential operators should complete, is administered at the conclusion of the training sessions.

The details for conducting this course, including all of the required methodologies, are covered in the Administrator's Guide, which is a significant part of this program. It includes a schedule of presentations, training records, a review of the concepts of instruction, and answers to operator exams. The rules and regulations that are emphasized in the training program are the Occupational and Safety Health Administration (OSHA) standards. Therefore, when you provide this type of training you can be satisfied that you have conformed to the OSHA requirements to the letter.

Part Two: The Audiovisual Materials

Show to all operators the Towmotor (Caterpillar) color film "The Color of Danger," which is available from each local forklift truck dealer of the Caterpillar Tractor Company. Depending on your anticipated usage, you may desire to buy a copy for your facility's use. The Hyster Company also has some excellent training films that may be used in this phase of the instructional program and may be obtained simply by calling your local Hyster dealer.

The trainees should be supplied with paper and pencil so that they can make notes during the training film.

The training instructor should introduce the film by indicating that it is a safety film made by the Towmotor (Hyster) Company showing how carelessness in operating forktrucks can often create serious problems in the day-to-day work. Although some of the examples shown in the films are rather extreme examples of what can happen on the job, it is important to emphasize that they do happen, and that serious accidents or fatalities may occur. The instructor should also indicate that the danger points in the first film, "The Color of Danger" have been indicated by coloring all of them red, the color of danger. The instructor tells the trainees to look for these signs of danger and make a note of them as they occur during the course of viewing the film, so that they may be discussed after the showing.

At the end of the film the instructor should go to the blackboard and list all of the danger points by asking the trainees to enumerate them. The following danger points should be covered:

- driving the forktruck with the forks in an elevated position, unloaded
- carrying loads on the forks that are not properly secured or stable
- the danger involved in a lack of preventive maintenance
- carrying passengers on the forks
- disregarding the important principles of leverage, counterbalance, and steering

- improperly handling loads with the forklift truck

The training instructor should conclude the film session with such comments as: Since the film attempts to point out the danger and assist you in recognizing danger before accidents happen, it emphasizes that operators who take things too much for granted will almost always miss the signs of danger until it is too late to prevent accidents from happening.

Part Three: Training on the Truck

A qualified instructor supervisor, or one of the plant's most experienced operators, should be delegated to perform this type of training in a fairly secluded area of the warehouse. The instructor should reserve from two hours to a half-day, depending on the number of trainees, for the on-the-truck training session. It is important that the training session include the following areas, and as you will note the sequence of the activities parallels the forklift truck operator's functions, as follows:

Inspection

Instructors will have the trainee walk completely around the truck checking for any abnormalities. They will be asked to inspect the general condition of the forks, tires, motor, and cleanliness of the truck before getting into the driver's seat or on the truck. Instructors should point out the nameplate on the truck which shows the model and serial number of the truck, the weight limitations, and the load center as required by OSHA.

This check of the lift-truck should be comparable to the aircraft pilot's pre-flight check, and the instructor should emphasize the importance of this forklift truck pre-use check just as it is emphasized in the aircraft industry. As part of the on-the-job training, the forklift truck instructor should observe the employee each day as he/she begins his/her working shift to make sure he/she carefully conducts the pre-use inspection, and he/she should be graded accordingly.

Starting Up the Truck

The instructor must emphasize the importance of a safe truck start-up. The trainee is asked to neutralize all of the controls and set the brake, and then he/she is shown how to start the motor and then the trainee will actually perform the start-up. The trainee will be shown how to test and operate all of the parts of the vehicle including the following: horn, steering mechanism, hoist, tilt, lights, brakes, and the operation of the motor. Since this is on-the-job training, the trainee will actually get in the driver's seat and perform all of these functions as indicated. When demonstrating the tilting function, the trainee is first shown how to raise the lifting mechanism, then he will operate the forward and backward tilt as far as the mast will travel in both directions. The pre-use inspection of the lift-truck should become a routine before the start of each work shift.

Vehicular Steering

The trainee should be made aware of the fact that the weight of the load is carried by the front wheels of a counterbalanced lift-truck, and that turning of the vehicle is accomplished by means of the rear wheels. The trainee should get the feel of the steering wheel with the vehicle in motion. It should be emphasized that when the rear wheels bounce up and down, it is an indication that too much weight is being carried on the forks. The truck may be overloaded, and this can seriously impair the steering and/or cause the operator to lose complete control of the vehicle.

Operation

The training instructor should emphasize the fact that the forks should be lowered to within a couple of inches of the floor before setting the vehicle in motion. The trainee should be made to practice the smooth operation of the lift-truck, including smooth starts and stops. The instructor should let the trainee test the brakes for positive stopping power and point out the need to plan ahead to avert panic stops, which can be hazardous with a loaded fork-truck. The trainee should also practice driving clear of storage racks, containers, walls, and other obstacles. The instructor should also emphasize that the lift truck should never be stopped by putting the drive control in reverse (plugging), since there will be a considerable stress placed on the motor and drive gears which will result in increased and extraordinary wear and untimely breakdowns of the forklift truck.

Trainees should also practice the slowing-down when approaching main aisles and blind corners in the warehouse. They should practice steering by going in and out of aisles, unloaded to begin with, and then after some practice, they should do the same with a loaded forklift truck. The proper use of the horn, for example at intersections or when personnel appear in aisles, and so forth, is an important aspect of training, also. The trainee should also be instructed in the right-of-way rules which you should maintain in your facility. A plant speed limit of a maximum five miles per hour in the main aisles and three miles an hour in side aisles should be stressed. As a safety measure, the operator trainee should be drilled in the practice of facing in the direction of travel whether going backwards or forwards on the vehicle, and in always remaining alert to conditions within the plant.

NOTE: While the speed limit of the forklift truck or other mobile equipment within the plant is a matter of record and should be widely disseminated among the operating personnel, it is advisable to indicate a difference that exists between the loading and shipping platform operations, which are usually done at fairly high speeds because there are very few pedestrians in this area.

CAUTION: The trainee should be made to remain alert concerning the functioning of a forklift truck from a mechanical standpoint during his entire shift, and to report any potential problem or malfunctioning that may exist with the vehicle.

Handling Emergencies That May Occur

The Truck on Fire (Electric)

The instructor should explain the emergency procedure for this eventuality, and then have the trainee practice the procedure: the trainee will immediately stop the unit, turn off the switch, dismount from the truck, disconnect the battery connector, remove the fire extinguisher from the truck or secure the closest one that may be nearby. The instructor should explain that in the case of an actual fire the trainee should extinguish the blaze and then notify his supervisor and safety personnel immediately.

Truck Catching on Fire (Gas)

Trainees should simultaneously turn off the ignition switch, stopping the unit, and dismount. It should be explained that they should clear the area of bystanders and try to get assistance, to procure a fire extinguisher, if one does not happen to be on the unit, and then the operator should notify their supervisor and safety personnel.

Throttle Stuck, or Accelerator Device Will Not Release

On an electric truck the trainee should be instructed to apply the brake and disconnect the battery cable. He/she should practice disconnecting the battery cable until this becomes a very familiar habit. In the case of a gas truck the ignition key should be turned off when the brakes are set. In any event the trainee should be instructed to advise both the supervisor and maintenance personnel of the malfunctioning of the truck.

A Vertical Runaway When the Hydraulic Lift Fails to Shut Down, and the Forks Continue to Rise

The trainee should be instructed in immediately dismounting from the vehicle and disconnecting the emergency battery lever or disconnecting the external battery cable connector.

Both of these disconnections should be practiced until they are a matter of habit. In the event that this type of malfunctioning occurs, the trainee should be required to notify supervisory and maintenance personnel as soon as possible.

Load Handling

The trainee should be shown how to adjust the distance between the forks, and how to adjust the forks so that they are given the widest spread to safely accommodate the load. The trainee should also be instructed in keeping the forks level, and how the forklift truck should approach the load slowly and at right angles to the load; that is, squarely. The trainee should be instructed and should practice the following maneuvers:

- Inserting the forks into the container or pallet opening until the load is positioned as far back on the heel of the forks as possible.

- Picking up loads by adjusting the lift control.

- Using the side shifter if the truck is so equipped.

- Backing out to a clear position, in the meantime tilting the load back to its limit, and adjusting the height of the forks to the carrying position.

- Checking to see that the loads are free of obstructions and in a stable condition before they are picked up by the forks. (The operator trainee should be given a series of loads, some stable and some not, and the trainee must decide which should be picked up and which ones should not be picked up. It should be pointed out to the trainee that unsafe loads should never be moved until the hazardous condition is corrected.)

- Carrying loads which are so large that the driver's vision is obscured. Turn the truck around and drive in reverse, permitting an unobstructed view in the direction of travel.

- Crossing railroad tracks or uneven paved surfaces with a loaded truck. When crossing railroad tracks or rough spots in the pavement, the operator should approach at an angle so that only one wheel crosses the rough spot at a time.

- On ramps at either the shipping or receiving docks. When the trainee is driving a loaded truck up a ramp he/she should practice driving with the load on the uphill side to keep the load from falling off the forks. When driving down a ramp, the trainee should be instructed and should practice driving backwards with the load on the uphill side.

- Unloading an on-highway motor carrier. The following safety practices should be observed: chocking the wheels of the truck, and securing the dockboard. If the dock platform has a safety stopping device, the unit should be hooked into the van body. Have the trainee inspect the floor of the truck for any rotten or broken deckboards. The danger of oil spills on dockboards or slippery dockboards should be pointed out, since a slippery dockboard may cause a serious accident. The operator trainee should, also, have the experience of checking for obstructions on the loading docks. As a safety practice, the operator trainee should check the entrance door on the vehicle and assure that he/she has at least two inches of lift-truck mast clearance before entering. Since wheels on the over-the-road carriers are chocked, the same practice must be observed for railroad cars, and their wheels should be blocked to prevent movement in either direction. Standard equipment, for this purpose, should be available on both the motor carrier truck docks and on the railroad car docks.

Parking

The trainee should practice parking the vehicle in approved locations in your facility. He/she should be instructed to set the brakes, lower the forks, placing them flat on the floor, neutralize the controls and turn off the electrical switch. If the vehicle is on a slope, blocking the wheels is a must.

Professionalism

Throughout the course, the training instructor should indicate that professionalism is required of each operator and that the individual should take pride in mastering the complexities of forklift truck vehicular operation. As indicated in the beginning of the training session, the instructor should have those qualities of leadership that will make it possible to instill in the trainees the degree of pride that it takes to become a truly skilled operator.

On-the-job Training

In most busy warehouses that do their own training, the on-the-job portion of operator training may last anywhere from several hours to several days. The operator trainee should be under fairly close supervision during this time. If the overall course objectives have been kept clearly in mind during the training session, operators should be relatively skilled in handling the lift-truck, although some of the operations they may perform slowly and with extreme caution. That is all to the good, especially if operators observe all of the defensive driving techniques and the safe operating procedures that they learned during the course of instruction. And it is well to observe, also, whether the operator has a professional outlook and desire to drive his/her truck safely and error-free.

Make sure your supervisors follow through so that you do come up with the safest and most efficient forklift truck operation that it is possible to obtain. Your training instructor should consider issuing an engraved diploma showing that the operator trainee has completed a course in forklift truck driver training. This should be followed up by issuing a temporary license after the classroom and the on-the-job/on-the-truck training is completed. The new operator should be carefully observed by his/her supervisor during the following month. After this period of observation, if there are no problems and the trainee has performed acceptably, then a permanent license should be given to the operator. Annually thereafter the operator's physical qualifications should be checked to make sure that the operator is still physically qualified to perform on a forklift truck. Also, some degree of formality in the training program is psychologically beneficial; therefore, a forklift truck driver's license should be issued every year thereafter on the basis of a short, written and performance test.

NOTE: Some companies have an annual forklift truck performance competition and this usually generates a great deal of enthusiasm and reinforces skills and safety practices.

You can make forklift truck driver training a successful program in your plant by doing the following things:

- Select qualified operators for training and licensing.
- Have only licensed operators operating mobile materials handling equipment.
- Revoke an operator's license if he/she no longer performs the duties of forklift operator in a safe and acceptable manner.

SAFETY ENGINEERING

How You Can Minimize the Accident Frequency and Severity Rates in Your Plant

Safety engineering is the study of the causes and prevention of accidental deaths and injuries wherever they may occur. One of the institutions closely associated with safety engineering is the National Safety Council from which information is collected by their more than 11,000 members of the council, from the large staff of technicians that works within the council, and from the U.S. government.

It is surprising that, in the industrialized countries of the world, accidents are responsible for more deaths than all of the infectious diseases combined, with the single exception of heart disease and cancer. According to the World Health Organization about 38% of all accidental deaths occur in motor vehicle accidents; however, on a world-wide basis, while motor vehicle accidents are the primary cause of accidental deaths, they are closely followed by those in the home and in industry.

While nonfatal injuries are far more numerous than deaths, the types of injuries fluctuate from year to year without any apparent trend. Motor vehicle accidents and accidents in the home are much more frequent than those accidents that take place in industrial settings; however, one of the main reasons for the lower number of industrial accidents is probably due to the emphasis industry places on safety, which is spurred by the realization on the part of management that industrial accidents are extremely costly in terms of both lost production and the higher rates that the company must pay for Workers' Compensation insurance.

Insurance companies have tended to collaborate with industry in developing structured accident prevention programs, and in developing methods of evaluating risks, and in assisting employers in establishing preventive measures. Safety engineering, industrial hygiene, and industrial medicine have been used conjointly to prevent injury to workers and to eliminate some of the high costs of accidents.

Some of the first measures in the field of safety engineering took place in providing guards and protective devices on various machines, installing floor gratings for better footing, and so forth. In like manner, industrial hygiene and medicine have focused on controlling environmental factors such as noise levels, which are measured in decibels, exposure to toxic gases and fumes, which are measured in parts per million, and other harmful employee exposures. There is an increasing emphasis lately on the part that personal factors play in causing accidents, such as stress and the role that mental and emotional adjustments have on the worker.

Notwithstanding the efforts of safety engineers, industrial hygienists, and medical personnel in this field of plant safety, the primary responsibility rests with the individual employer for:

- the application of safety engineering principles,
- employee education in safe methods of performing work, and
- the general enforcement of safety rules within the plant.

Unfortunately, in many cases, the employer delegates this responsibility to the lowest supervisory level of company management.

While the responsibility for safety is generally delegated in a downward direction, it still behooves the plant manager to have a working knowledge of the aspects that comprise the safety engineering world. As an example, statistical analyses of accidents are based on the frequency and severity rate. According to the American National Standards Institute (ANSI), the standard frequency rate has been established at the number of disabled injuries per one million labor-hours of exposure. ANSI has also defined the standard severity rate as the total time charged as a result of lost-time injuries per one million labor-hours of exposure. There are time charges for actual days lost and standardized charges for permanent disabilities and deaths. As an example, death or permanent total disability charges are arbitrarily set at 6000 days per occurrence. Permanent partial disabilities include charges that range from 35 to 4500 days.

In compiling statistics, it has been found that the frequency and severity rates vary widely from one industry segment to another. The lowest frequency and severity rates are found in the communications and insurance industries. At the other extreme are the mining, lumbering, and farming industries. It is suggested that not only do certain industries have inherent dangers, they also reflect such things as a lack of effectiveness of safety programs and safety education. In the hazardous industries of mining, lumbering, and farming, the workers usually are more or less independent and are widely spread over large areas where direct supervision is often difficult, if not impossible. Another contributing factor to the hazardous nature of these industries is the fact that permanent safeguarding of equipment is not widely used because the work environment or the locations are constantly changing. Solitary workers are left more or less to their own devices and has little to protect them from mining equipment, explosives, saws, axes, and the like.

How You Can Evaluate Your Safety Program

As the plant manager, you should determine periodically how effective your own plant safety program is above and beyond the indexes generated by the accident frequency and severity rates. There are three ways you can do this:

- Obtain the estimates of the total direct and indirect costs of accidents from your accounting department.
- Ask your accounting department to obtain the loss ratio, which is an index based upon the amount paid for insurance compensation in terms of what might be expected on the basis of industry averages.
- Have your safety department or your safety person apply statistical quality control to the accident record. The index you will obtain should indicate whether the frequency of accidents is becoming excessive or improving in relation to prior experience.

The three values thus obtained should serve to alert you and the plant safety director in which direction the trend of your safety program is progressing. In addition to the above, another indicator is the total cost of work injuries and accidents as the sum of insured and uninsured costs. Insured costs are defined as the amounts paid for compensation and medical insurance premiums. Uninsured costs are those costs attributed to lost-time accidents such as:

- injuries requiring medical attention, but with no work time lost;
- first-aid injuries; and,
- accidents that cause property damage and work stoppages.

A total evaluation of the effectiveness of your plant safety program should include a review of these areas:

- plant layout
- housekeeping
- maintenance
- employee training program
- medical facilities available
- protective equipment required
- fire-fighting organization and equipment
- the organization of your safety program

Another way you can affirm the effectiveness of your safety program is to determine how well your safety person (or director) gets along with the other department heads. Since change normally starts at the top and works its way down through the various levels of management to the employee, the education of the employee in the areas of safety and safety practices will directly reflect the attitudes manifested by plant management as well as the top management of the company; thus, all levels of management should demonstrate their full cooperation and consensus with the principles of safety and the safety program.

How You Can Identify the Critical Areas of the Plant

You or the person designated to act as the plant safety engineer should periodically review accident reports in order to improve safety conditions within the company. More important than the post-accident review, however, is the factor that concerns identifying the most accident-prone or critical areas of the plant. In safety engineering, this method of analysis is called the critical incident technique. In this methodology, the plant safety designee selects a random sample of workers from the several locations within the plant where the worker is exposed to various work hazards. The workers thus selected are interviewed and asked to describe incidents that could have become potential accidents. If the interviews are kept on an informal basis, it is possible that an attempt can be made to get the workers to describe safety errors that they have made or that they have committed that could have resulted in an accident. Under most conditions workers are not seemingly reluctant to discuss safety matters, inasmuch as this is being accomplished on company time. This methodology has a dual purpose since it makes the employee aware of the attention being given to the safety factors of employment and their environment, and thus serves to boost morale and, in addition, it is a much better source of accident prevention than any examination of company records could be.

Why You Should Control Environmental Conditions

Among the various groups that work in the area of plant safety, it has been known for a long time that certain environmental factors influence safety trends. Some of these conditions are extremes of heat and cold, humidity, noise, lack of ventilation, and vibration. When one or more of these conditions are present, the result is increased worker discomfort or fatigue, lower worker effectiveness, and, unfortunately, increases in the accident rate. OSHA has been patently effective in bringing these factors to the attention of plant managements in recent years despite the fact that every good plant safety program has always taken these factors into consideration. In Table 17-1, you will find values for the above variables that should be found acceptable to the employees and will promote improved working conditions. While it may not always be possible to achieve all of these ideal conditions, the plant management should make every attempt to approach them, since the benefits which will accrue to the company are definitely of value.

Table 17-1. Conditions for the work environment.

Factor	Desirable Conditions: Maximum/Minimum Values
Temperature	63-71°F (20-22°C) winter; 66-75°F (21-24°C) summer.
Humidity	25-50% relative humidity
Noise	Conversations to be carried on at a distance of 3 feet without extra effort: 80-85 decibels overall, and 50-60 decibels in the 1200-2400 Hertz band.
Ventilation	Sufficient added fresh air to remove odors; 20 cubic feet (0.6 cubic meters) per minute of fresh air.
Vibration	Reduced below threshold of perception; 0.002-inch (0.05mm) at 20 Hertz or more.

What You Can Do to Prevent Lifting and Back Injuries

While the manufacturing, maintenance, and service industries have become very much mechanized, there is still a vast amount of manual handling done in all of industry. As an example, many union contracts still have provisions that insist that men cannot be required to lift more than 50 pounds and women more than 35 pounds without a hoist, as exemplified in the United Auto Workers' contracts and later incorporated into the OSHA regulations. Despite this contractual provision, however, it often happens that loads or materials, cartons, and so on, are lifted where the weight limitations or restrictions are not fully observed, and it is not unusual for a man to be lifting 70 pounds and a woman more than the 35 pound loads that have been clearly delimited, and this without the benefit of any mechanical equipment such as a hoist. Nevertheless, if you should happen to be lifting only five or ten pounds out of a container, and you happen to be lifting in an improper position, in other words, if you are largely bent over and off-center, then severe strains are placed on the spine and back muscles that may occasionally result in injury, especially to the older worker. It is no surprise, therefore, that one of the most commonly reported accidental injuries is that to the spinal column and lower back. In addition, it can be safely stated that the manual handling of materials is the single largest cause of all fatal, permanent and temporary disabilities.

Your safety designee should educate the plant's personnel who are engaged in manual materials handling to observe the following criteria:

- In manual lifting, the most important vector of the force is the distance of the feet from the point at which the object is grasped.

- The lifting vector or force is greatest when the weight is lifted in the same vertical plane as the body, and decreases rapidly as the weight moves away from the plane of the body.

- The best height for lifting is at or slightly above the level of the middle fingertip of a person standing with arms hanging loosely at his/her sides: above this height, lifting power decreases very rapidly; below this height, more slowly. (Example, for a load on the floor, the human lifting force is about three-fourths to four-fifths of that force with the load at the best height.)

- Lifting with the back vertical and your legs bent affords a slightly stronger vertical pull than lifting with your back bent and your legs straight, and is thus less prone to induce a back injury.

For your general information, it has been found that the average male can move about 220 tons, or 200 metric tons, per eight-hour working shift through a horizontal distance of 3.3 feet, or approximately one meter; or 55 tons, that is, 50 metric tons, through a vertical distance of 3.3 feet, or one meter.

From a physiological standpoint when comparing male and female performance, it has been found that women demonstrate about 55% to 65% as much physical strength as do men in equivalent tasks.

Safety Areas that Should Be of Special Concern to You as Plant Manager

While your particular physical distribution center may not have any of the following specific problem areas, you are sure to find in this following list a number of areas for concern that should be considered in planning your safety program.

Robotic Applications

If the physical distribution center has attained the degree of mechanization enabling it to employ robots for such operations as pallet loading or de-stacking, or loading and unloading conveyors, then there are some safety measures that must be employed to safeguard humans in the area contiguous to the robot's operation. In Chapter 16, the swing clearance of moving robotic arms was given together with a diagram showing the swing arm area of coverage. From the standpoint of safety this area requires careful guarding by safety railings or, as a more thorough approach, placing the robot into an enclosure. In some plants, chain link fencing is used around the robotic area of operation. The robot arm moves so very rapidly and, moving as it does in silence, it is quite possible for a human employee or visitor to be hit unless the proper safeguards are provided, such as the enclosure mentioned above.

In order to protect maintenance workers, it is necessary that interlocks be available within the control panels so that the workers can safely work in the area and upon the mechanism without being caught unawares by sudden start-ups of the robot system. The robot manufacturers can provide safety precautions and certainly these safety measures should be given to the plant safety director or your designee so that the provisions for safety may be implemented properly.

How to Safeguard Electrical Components

Almost all accidents involving electricity are preventable. Electric shock is a function of the rate of current flow through the body; the higher the current, the greater the damage. As an example, a 60-cycle alternating current of 100 milliamperes (0.1 ampere) may result in a fatal injury if it passes through the vital organs of the body. If entrapped by an object, a person may still free him- or herself from the object if the current is in the range of 8 to 16 milliamperes, depending on a number of factors:

- The body's resistance to electrical current is chiefly supplied by the epidermis, or skin.
- Wet skin is 100 to 600 times less resistant to an electrical current than dry skin.
- The longer the length of time the current continues to flow through the body, the greater the severity of damage.
- In the case of high voltages, only short exposures can be survived.
- Electric currents may sometimes cause interference with breathing by contracting the chest muscles or paralyzing the respiratory nerve centers.
- The current may sometimes block the rhythm and muscular action of the heart, or it may destroy tissue, nerves, or muscles from heat due to the heavy current.
- It should be noted that burns from electrical flashing or arcing are extremely deep and very slow to heal.

  Accidents due to electrical hazards are mainly caused by switches and systems improperly selected for the task or without interlocks and fail-safe features. It should be noted, also, that circuit breakers and ground fault systems are important safety precautions that your electrical maintenance people should always provide or certify. The importance of ground fault systems is that they cut off the current flow if a machine is improperly grounded or if a short develops.

Where small quantities of hazardous materials are stored, every plant should have safety cabinets expressly designed for this purpose. Storing several cans of solvent on a shelf in the maintenance room is a bad practice. The maintenance personnel should be provided with safety cabinets that can store as much of their materials that are hazardous as possible. Safety cabinets are designed for several gallons of materials, and for two or more 55-gallon drums, and they should be used. Where larger quantities of hazardous materials are stored, special rooms should be provided where the electrical fixtures are all explosion-proof and where a drainage system will not permit liquid hazardous materials to run freely.

What You Must Do to Provide Safety for Chemical and Hazardous Materials

Your physical distribution center may have a number of products that contain chemicals in solid, gaseous, or liquid forms. The materials are classed as hazardous if they have a known toxicity and their physical properties are such that their flash points fall below 100°F. Some materials become hazardous when they are mixed with other chemicals, and they will react in a dangerous manner; also, some chemicals will decompose under heat and become unstable and hazardous. An excellent source of information for hazardous materials is the booklet published by the Department of Transportation entitled "Hazardous Materials, Emergency Response Guidebook," DOT P5800.3. Every warehouse and distribution center should have at least one copy of this manual in their possession. This book was developed under the supervision of the Office of Hazardous Materials Regulation, Materials Transportation Bureau, Research and Special Programs Administration of the U.S. Department of Transportation. R. M. Graziano, Agent, 1920 L Street NW, Washington DC 20036. Also, the Defense Logistics Agency of the Department of Defense, which is located in Richmond, Virginia, has established a data base composed of the various characteristics of industrial chemicals and hazardous materials. Included in the information are recommended safety practices for the receipt, storage, handling, and disposal of chemicals and hazardous materials. Computer printouts and microfiche describing these characteristics may be obtained from this agency at a very nominal cost.

If you are concerned about whether or not you are complying with safety procedures, you should consult the OSHA regulations, which are probably the best guide available on this subject.

What You Should Know About Radiation Hazards

The use of radioactive materials in manufacturing processes is constantly increasing, and if your physical distribution entity is a part of the manufacturing complex, then you should be aware of some of the potential hazards that exist with these substances.

The measurement of radiation is performed indirectly by means of ionization in which electrically charged atoms are produced by the passage of radiation through a medium. If your plant is large enough to have a combined manufacturing and warehousing operation, then you will no doubt have a safety engineer who is familiar with the potential hazards involved in handling radioactive substances. The plant's safety engineer, of course, is concerned with the alteration of human body cells by exposure to radioactive substances. He/she will have installed protective and preventive safety programs which would include radiation detection, measurement, shielding, and monitoring personnel exposure levels in order to limit personnel exposure to the minimum accepted levels.

As an example of some of the radioactive sources in manufacturing, consider for a minute the use of irradiated tools, which can measure the wear on cutting surfaces and on dies; gauges that can measure and control the thickness of layers of paint; radioactive isotopes which follow fluid flow in processing lines, in lubrication, and in the wear on the internal parts of combustion engines and fabricating machinery.

As with any new technology, a number of instruments have been developed to make surveys of radiation in plants, and it is recommended that, if you do not have a plant safety engineer, your materials handling or materials management technician be given intensive training in radiation safety.

Why You Should Be Concerned About Safety Equipment

Product liability law suits have engendered the necessity for designing into equipment fairly reliable safety devices, and in general these safety measures are far more reliable than the safety practices of human beings. While all this remains true, there is still the need for personal safety equipment in the plant. As an example, where there is construction work, hard-hats are required, safety goggles are demanded or mandated for factory workers, welding shields are used to surround the worker using a welding torch, and the like. While most factory workers are required to wear safety shoes with steel toe parts, it is also true that in conforming to safety regulations, certain employees in the physical distribution center should also be required to wear them.

The plant's safety director or safety program designee should become knowledgeable of all local, state, and federal laws that require specific items of protective equipment to be used within the plant and its environs.

18

Industrial Powered Trucks

SELECTING MOBILE MATERIALS HANDLING EQUIPMENT

One of the major focuses of the *Managing Warehouse and Distribution Operations* is to apply a systems approach to materials handling in a warehouse or physical distribution center. This approach can be served best in the area of equipment selection. Rising labor costs can justify using special, customized or even general-purpose equipment in specific applications because the cost per labor hour is often a great deal higher than the cost per operating hour of the equipment to be selected. There are many benefits to be obtained when the proper equipment is selected for a task:

- higher productivity for the operation or the process,
- a good working climate with no cause for labor unrest or complaint,
- a higher rate of return on the investment,
- minimized labor and equipment down time,
- low maintenance costs.

NOTE: Since large sums of money are involved in equipment selection, there is always the need to take a cautious and conservative approach in equipment purchases. Materials handling equipment can be a vital element of the materials handling function in a plant, or it can be upsetting and a focal point of labor complaint. For this reason, it is absolutely essential that you select one of your technicians to become as expert as possible in the area of equipment. You will find that some people have a natural aptitude for evaluating materials handling equipment, and you should try to promote this expertise as much as possible.

If you do not have the in-house expertise and your needs are immediate, consider hiring a consultant to help solve your materials handling problems. One of the consultant's tasks would be to develop a cadre of employees of your plant who can assume responsibility for selecting equipment and justifying its cost—that is, calculating the ROI for each equipment acquisitions to be made.

Let us assume that you have appointed a technician to serve as your materials handling equipment specialist. One of the first tasks for this technician would be to obtain data that

235

will enable him or her to make certain basic decisions as to the type, size, and the quantity of equipment required in a department-by-department analysis. There is a good deal of basic data to be obtained:

- the volume of material to be handled
- how far the material has to be moved
- the manner in which the material is packaged or not packaged
- where and how it is to be stored in the plant
- whether or not the volumes to be handled vary from day to day, or by day, week, or month.

Additional factors that can influence equipment selection are such physical characteristics as:

- the type of terrain to be traversed
- the load-bearing characteristics of the soil, of the building, and the storage areas in general.

Many pieces of mobile materials handling equipment are designed primarily for use on concrete or woodblock floors. The materials handling technician in charge of selecting equipment must know, for example, if a piece of equipment will have to negotiate muddy yards or steep ramps. The frame of an industrial truck may be so low to the ground, or it may be so underpowered, that its gradability (the measure of how steep an incline it can climb) is limited.

WHAT TO LOOK FOR IN AN INDUSTRIAL POWERED TRUCK

There are three general groupings of industrial powered trucks:

- electric powered
- internal combustion engine powered (gas or diesel)
- gas- or diesel-driven electric generator type. Gasoline powered trucks can be further broken down into those that are powered by straight (leaded) gas and those using liquid propane (LP) gas.

Your equipment specialist has a wide variety of choices when selecting industrial powered trucks: they can be purchased new or used, leased, or obtained on a lease-purchase basis. Sometimes it is better to lease a particular piece of equipment in order to determine whether it is suitable for the particular task at hand. On the other hand, you can enter into a lease-purchase agreement and obtain the best of both worlds.

Keep in mind that gas, internal combustion engine driven trucks have a higher trade-in value than electric trucks of equal capacity, because of the higher demand for the used gas truck, because it requires neither a battery charger nor the installation of heavy-voltage electric lines to supply the charger. The battery in a used electric truck may be the deciding factor, because the average life of an electric industrial battery is from 5 to 7 years, and a battery replacement can cost $1500 or more. Electric trucks are not usually traded in at an early age, and most electric trucks last through several battery replacements, indicating that the truck may be 10 to 15 years old at the very least.

The apparent popularity of gasoline trucks is that the small operator usually likes the lower initial cost, and the truck can be used almost anywhere that a forklift truck may be used. In the industrial truck industry, most forklift trucks are sold to a marketplace where only two to eight trucks are employed in the business; therefore, the emphasis is on low initial cost because the operators of these businesses need cash as well as equipment.

Because of the increased emphasis on the quality of work in the workplace, the number of electric trucks employed has continued to increase over the past few decades, and it is estimated that over 30% of the forktrucks presently in use are now electrically powered. This upward trend is due to several factors:

- somewhat lower overall maintenance cost
- lack of smoke, fumes, or toxic emissions in internal combustion truck exhaust
- lower fuel costs.

Solid, Cushioned, and Semi-pneumatic Tires

In getting to know industrial powered trucks, another categorical consideration is tire type, which, in general, depends on where the truck is used. Powered trucks that are used indoors will have solid or cushioned tires and trucks that are used outdoors will have pneumatic tires.

Solid or cushioned tires are made of rubber or polyurethane. The rubber tire is black in color and the polyurethane tire may be identified by its dark amber color. Polyurethane tires are relatively tough and have excellent wear characteristics when used at speeds under seven miles per hour; however, because of the tremendous heat build-up during rotational flexing, they are never used for high-speed yard work but are exceptionally good for indoor warehouse or production activities. Solid, industrial truck tires are used primarily in warehouse or production work involving high stacking because they give increased stability to the truck during the high lifting operation. If pneumatic tires were used during the high lift, then the overturning moment would be generated that would send the load tumbling.

Cushioned tires are similar to solid tires, and the terms are sometimes used interchangeably. Semi-pneumatic tires have a hollow core which is filled with air or foam. Semi-pneumatic tires are used where better riding characteristics are desired; for example, wherever high-speed operations are required, such as in loading dock operations.

Solid tires can be either molded directly onto a rim, or molded on a steel sleeve that in turn is pressed onto the truck wheel under high pressure. Some companies have their own tire-pressing device; however, this is usually a job for a contractor.

Pneumatic truck tires, either the tube type or tubeless, are used for outdoor yard work. Trucks equipped with pneumatics do not allow for very high stacking capabilities because of their lack of stability under heavy loads. However, pneumatics do possess a very high degree of flotation, which means they can spread the loads they are carrying over a very much larger footprint area. They are especially effective in muddy yards, in sandy soils, and over crushed rock terrain. At construction sites, the industrial trucks used have especially large, oversized, pneumatic tires because of the rough terrain.

TYPES OF TRUCKS

Counterbalanced Trucks

The most commonly used type of industrial powered forklift is the counterbalanced forklift truck. (See Figure 18-1).

Photo courtesy Hyster Company, Danville, IL

Fig. 18-1: Counterbalanced forklift truck.

Since this truck is so universally used in industry, it is important to know how the various forces work on this truck when it is operating under a load. Figure 18-2 illustrates how the truck actually distributes the various vectors of forces at work.

To determine which types of counterbalanced forklift truck to use, it is usually necessary to consider the following characteristics: the capacity, the mast height, fork size, power plant, free lift, or whether the vehicle is to be operated in a standing-up or sitting-down position.

Capacities

To determine what capacity the forklift truck should have, decide the size of the loads to be lifted, stacked, or transported. For example, if the loads average approximately 1500 pounds, with no loads greater than 2000 pounds, select a 2000-lb. or 2500-lb. capacity lift

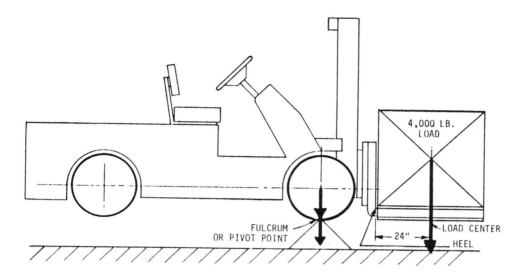

Fig. 18-2: Forces acting upon a loaded, counterbalanced, forklift truck.

truck. Because almost all counterbalanced lift trucks are designed for an approximately 25% overload, in the above example it would be safe to use a 2000-lb. truck if an occasional overload was only 500 pounds. Your forklift truck will last a lot longer if it is sized upwards in its basic capacity; that is, a 2500-lb. or a 3000-lb. forklift truck will last a great deal longer carrying 1500-lb. loads with an occasional 2000-lb. load rather than a 2000-lb. truck which would be working close to its design limits most of the time.

Mast Height

Mast heights and styles vary depending on how high the loads are to be stacked in your warehouse. Most industrial powered truck manufacturers have their own company standards, although there are certain industry standards which enable you to obtain 72-inch, 83-inch, 95-inch, 107-inch, 114-inch, 127-inch, mast heights, and so forth, from a single manufacturer. It is much better to settle for a standard mast height which will be within a few inches of what you need, rather than to go to the next higher standard size, or to give the manufacturer a special mast height. Remember: whenever you order the mast height that varies from the particular manufacturer's standard, you will pay extra and wait longer for delivery.

Fork Size

Industrial powered fork-truck fork lengths are very important in your handling processes. It is fortunate, however, that the forks can usually be had in 2-inch increments from 36 inches to up to 6 feet in length and with a cross-sectional area suited to the weight of the load. The longer the fork length, the heavier the heel thickness will be. The heel of the fork is the point at which the blade is attached to the upright portion of the fork. These are usually L-shaped, and the heel is in the notch of the L. You can also specify the shape and the taper of the fork point, such that it could be either a chisel point or blunt. One of the best-known manufacturers of forklift truck forks is the Dyson Company, and their forks are made in such large quantities that they are surprisingly inexpensive.

When choosing forklift fork sizes, it is always better to get forks that are slightly longer rather than shorter than your requirements, because the longer forks can handle many variations in load sizes, whereas shorter forks have decided limitations.

Power Plants

With American-label industrial trucks, your choices of power plants—gas, diesel, or electric—will vary according to manufacturer. But in general, each manufacturer can give you the engine brand that you request. If the manufacturer's standard is a Ford and you ask for a Chrysler engine, you are going to have to wait a little longer. Most fork trucks, especially of the smaller capacities, have Continental or GM engines.

With gas engines, the choices are generally Ford, Chrysler, Continental, or GM. There are a number of European and Japanese engine manufacturers who have entered the picture, and their engine production is usually so large that you should consider the engine that your plant maintenance people are most familiar with as a power plant choice.

There is a difference in power plant choices with electric trucks, and, generally speaking, the differences rest with the manufacturer. General Electric is one of the largest of the control manufacturers for electric trucks in the country.

Lift and Free-lift

Forklift truck masts are usually telescopic in that they are double-, triple-, or quadruple-staged in which one section slides over another to obtain the desired lifting height. The single-stage masts for the smaller lift trucks are also quite popular. Because the multiple-stage mast is made in sections, they must either slide one within the other or roll one within the other, with small roller bearing rollers. Free lift in the fork truck mast means that the movement of the forks from the ground up can be made without the movement of any of the other sections. In other words, the forktruck forks will elevate without any of the other sections or stages of the mast moving. This is extremely important when the fork truck is working in a covered van or truck, or in railcar loading, where, without sufficient free lift for the forks, the operator would puncture a hole in the roof of the carrier with the mast every time he tried to lift a load inside the carrier.

When drawing up the specifications for your forklift truck, you should determine the average door height of the carriers you will be unloading. This gives you a collapsed-mast height and, as mentioned, the free lift is very important in this situation. To obtain some idea of what the mast height should be, see Figure 3-1 for motor truck and railroad freight car door height dimensions.

Stand-up and Sit-down Trucks

Narrow-aisle, straddle trucks are with few exceptions all stand-up trucks. Where the lower-weight capacity trucks are concerned these are always stand-up trucks.

Straddle, Outrigger, and Narrow-aisle Trucks

Almost all narrow-aisle trucks are either straddle, sideloaders, or right-angle-turn trucks. In addition, most straddle forklift trucks are standup rider types.

The outriggers, which give the forktrucks stability, straddle the pallet load: the load on the forks rests between the two outriggers as it is lowered.

When the forktruck is used to place loaded pallets into a storage rack, it is necessary to have a shelf beam that is somewhat raised above the level of the floor in order for the outriggers to slide under the shelf beam to deposit the pallet load as the forks are lowered onto the beam to deposit a load. This is one disadvantage of the standup straddle truck with outriggers: you waste approximately six or more inches in overall height by having the shelf beam slightly elevated above the floor level. Nevertheless, the advantage of this type of straddle truck is that it saves aisle space because of its very short turning radius, as shown in Figure 18-3.

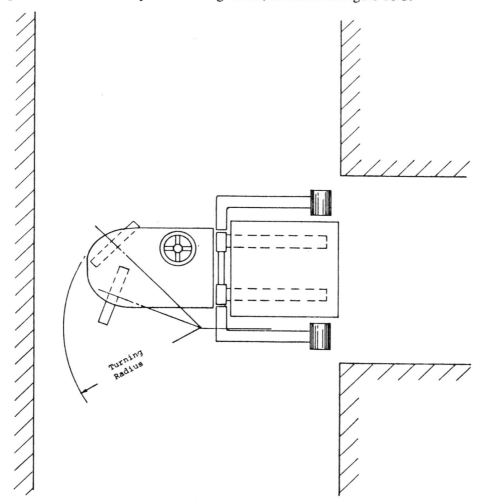

Fig. 18-3: Plan view of storage area showing the short turning radius of a straddle truck.

Walkie Trucks

There are essentially two types of walkie trucks: one is battery-powered and the other is purely mechanical (i.e., it has to be manually propelled).

One of the difficulties in using the strictly mechanical walkie truck is that it takes a lot of effort on the part of the operator to move a heavy load up an incline as, for example, loading out a carrier using an elevated dock plate. Battery-powered walkie trucks give you a choice of either low lift or high lift. The lifting walkies can be counterbalanced by a combination of the weight of the batteries and the distance of the load to the center of gravity and by outriggers in high-lift units. In the low-lift units, the load wheels and the forks never leave the ground, and the wheels are raised and lowered by means of a cam linkage in the lifting mechanism. Because the walkie truck operator guides the walkie truck by means of a swiveling handle, the operator controls are in this handle. A warning horn button and a safety or panic button should be included in the handle controls. The panic button should be of the reversal type; in other words, when the operator strikes the button or when the button is pressed into any part of the operator's body, the truck will reverse its direction automatically.

Low-profile Trucks

The so-called low-profile forklift trucks were developed primarily because of the low overhead height of some carrier doorways. These are usually over-the-road motor trucks in which the distance from the truck bed to the top of the door frame measures only 80 to 87 inches. A driver seated on a counterbalanced forktruck who sticks his head outside the limits of the truck configuration is susceptible to head injuries as well as decapitation.

Another obstacle encountered by forktrucks entering an over-the-road carrier is the dock plate used to adjust the carrier bed to the dock height: the truck must climb over the crown of the dock plate in order to enter the carrier. The problem has been to achieve better gradability and a low mast height, therefore several of the forklift truck manufacturers have developed the low-profile forktrucks in which they have lowered the truck seats and the overall mast heights.

NOTE: If you are the plant manager in a distribution center which handles all types of over-the-road carriers, you should have at least one low-profile truck and, if possible, another similar truck as backup, in instances where low door height carriers must be unloaded or loaded.

Forktrucks for Right-angle Stacking

The Drexel Company introduced the first right-angle stacking truck two decades ago. Since then a number of other manufacturers have limited and improved upon this overall truck design. The Towmotor Company developed a 590 series, with an outrigger which permitted the truck to pivot around in a relatively narrow aisle. However, this truck was not a true right-angle stacker, because the frame of the truck did not permit articulation of the mast. The Clark and Hyster companies and several other forktruck manufacturers have come out with swiveling masts which permit the forktruck body to stay parallel to the aisle while just the front end of the vehicle swivels around into the stacking position.

There are many space-saving advantages in using right-angle stacking trucks.

- the aisles in the storage bays can be much narrower, often just a few inches on each side of the load and the truck body itself.

- they can stack relatively high, which means that the operator of the physical distribution center can take full advantage of ceiling heights up to 30 or more feet. When stacking this high, it is necessary to use a **height selector** which is automatic in operation. With this device, a reasonably skilled operator can safely place material in storage and remove it from relatively high storage racks.

CAUTION: The forklift operator must be especially trained for the work on a right-angle stacking truck. It usually takes several weeks for an operator to achieve the maximum proficiency with this vehicle. Spatial or depth perception is extremely important in this job, and not every forklift driver can become proficient with this truck because of this requirement. An ordinary driver of a counterbalanced lift-truck will find it extremely nerve- racking to be right-angle stacking at relatively high levels in storage bays. For this reason, test the depth and spatial perception of any operator who is going to be in training with this truck.

Sideloader Trucks

Although sideloader trucks are more expensive than the usual counterbalanced forklift truck for equal capacities, the sideloader truck is the only vehicle that can stack material 20 feet or more in height, and can also transport materials down aisles that are 6 feet or less in width. There are some sideloaders, also, that are manufactured to transport and stack loads that are 20 feet or more in length, such as: pipe, barstock, sheet steel, etc. The load-carrying capacity of these trucks can be anywhere from 2,000 to 10,000 pounds or more. The exceptional mobility of the sideloader is its capability of transporting materials from storage racks directly to the point of use in a production operation, and vice versa.

One problem with sideloading trucks is that they usually stack at right angles to the aisle in one direction so that if you want to store on both sides of the aisle, the truck must move out of the aisle, make a 180-degree turnaround and come back into the aisle to handle the other side of the stacks.

NOTE: To prevent damage to the storage rack legs where you have a sideloader operation, some companies put guardrails on both sides of the aisle so that the truck can shoot down the aisle with the truck self-steering. This not only prevents damage to the rack legs, but leaves the operator's hands free to do other work.

Four-directional Trucks

The four-directional truck was first developed for shipboard use by the U.S. Navy. Because of its amazing versatility, it has found application in specific industrial situations where its increased maneuverability makes handling in tight spaces easier. As the name of the truck implies, it can proceed in a straight-ahead direction then, by turning its wheels 90 degrees to the body line of the truck, it can traverse at right angles.

Rotating Mast Trucks

A rotating mast truck is a variation of the right-angle stacking truck. Like all special trucks, the price of the truck increases with the complexity of the truck. Another problem of these trucks is the increased maintenance cost, which is relative to the complexity of the vehicle. Because not too many of these truck are produced, the spare parts costs are correspondingly high.

Container Handling Trucks

Sea containers are aluminum boxes with a cross-section of 8 feet × 8 feet, and several different lengths such as 20 feet, 27 feet, 35 feet, or 40 feet, and so on. To handle these sea containers, some manufacturers have developed mobile industrial powered trucks and straddle cranes. The Clark Company is the leader in the field of straddle carriers, followed by Drott. The Piggy-Packer, the Taylor, and the Towmotor are the predominant pieces of converted forklift equipment, with capacities of 50- to 60-thousand pounds. The largest of the sea containers—which are the 8 foot × 8 foot × 40 foot variety—handle approximately 30 ton, and that is why the larger of the industrial trucks have been adapted to meet this handling challenge. If handling sea containers is only an occasional part of your distribution center's activities, you should use a forklift truck with a container-handling attachment. The conversion from heavy-duty forklift truck to container-handling truck is relatively easy: the operator needs only to lock into the container-handling attachment and hook up some hydraulic and electric lines to the truck.

LIFT TRUCKS

Figure 18-2 shows the forces acting on a loaded counterbalanced forklift truck. This sketch shows how the front wheels (or load wheels, as they are called,) serve as the fulcrum or pivot point of the loaded truck. Like the pivot on the balance beam of a scale, it divides the weight of the loaded truck between the front part where the forks are located to the after section of the truck which has all the mechanisms and counterbalanced weight of the truck. The load center of the truck is a point that is established from the heel of the forklift fork. As shown in this illustration, it happens to be 24 inches from the heel. (The length of all forktruck forks is measured from the heel of the fork.) If the load center should happen to shift outwardly, as in Figure 18-4, the rated capacity of the truck will be reduced. The farther out from the center of gravity of the load, the greater will be the reduction in truck capacity.

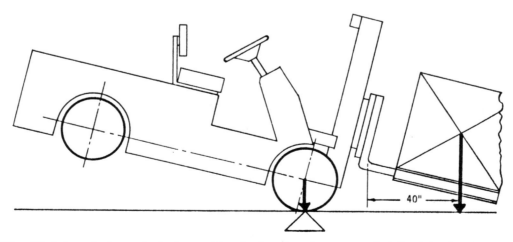

Fig. 18-4: Loaded counterbalanced truck showing the outward shift of the load center when its rated capacity is exceeded.

Gradability

Gradability is a measure of how steep an incline a materials handling truck can climb. In Figure 18-5 the truck attains an increase in height of Y in the horizontal distance of X. The percentage of grade is the ratio of rise over horizontal distance.

The equation is:

$$Percentage\ of\ grade = \frac{Y}{X}$$

If, for example, $X = 250$ ft and $Y = 10$ ft, the percentage of grade is 4%. The equation is as follows:

$$\frac{10}{250} = .04 = 4\%\ grade$$

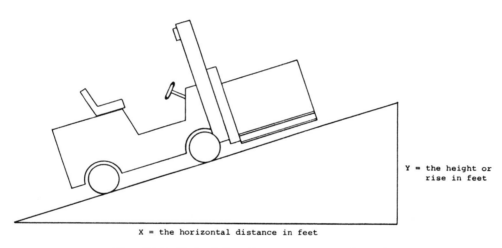

Y = the height or
rise in feet

X = the horizontal distance in feet

Fig. 18-5: Calculating the percentage of grade.

LIFT TRUCK ATTACHMENTS

The Towmotor Company developed the forklift truck shortly after the automobile came into prominence in the United States. The forklift truck was developed from an automobile chassis, with a mast and forks placed on the front end of the truck. From that time various attachments, such as booms, hooks, and scoops, were added. In today's world of forklift truck achievement, attachments range from simple mechanical carton lifters to right-angle fork movements and other complex devices.

The Basiloid carton clamp and a few other mechanical devices affect the load-carrying capacity of the lift-truck only slightly. These are the exceptions, however, because with the addition of a fairly heavy piece of machinery on the front end of a forklift truck (for example, carton load rotators, barrel lifters, paper-roll clamps), the center of gravity of the truck is affected so that the load-carrying capacity of the lift-truck falls off sharply. Attachments that are placed on the mast or carriage of the forklift truck tend to extend the CG outward several inches or more. As shown in Figure 18-6 this substantially decreases the rated capacity of the truck. Supplier attachment manufacturers can tell you to what extent your lift-trucks will be downrated because of this loss of CG. It is unfortunate that even a small change in the CG can mean a loss in capacity of the lift-truck which will make it unsuitable for certain types of work. As shown in Figure 18-6 a telescopic fork extender has been added to the truck and the resultant loss in CG is shown as the composite CG-3 is shifted forward.

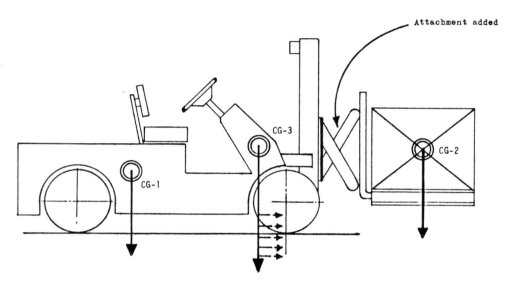

Fig. 18-6: The composite CG is shifted forward by adding an attachment.

Side-shifter Attachments

One of the most popular and useful of all forklift truck attachments is the side-shifter. Many companies that buy lift trucks require that each of their fork-trucks be equipped with this attachment because it saves a great deal of time and largely eliminates damage that occurs when the load is being placed into storage. This is especially true when the forklift truck driver has elevated the load and is attempting to place it into a storage rack. Even the most mediocre of forklift truck drivers can become a competent professional when his or her truck is equipped with the side-shifting mechanism. The side-shifter can move a load from 4 to 6 inches on either side of center. This capability saves a lot of damage to the storage racks and the merchandise itself. An illustration of a side-shifter attachment is shown in Figure 18-7.

Like most attachments that are placed in front of the mast of a forklift truck, the side-shifter movement is accomplished by means of a hydraulic cylinder. Sometimes there is more than one hydraulic cylinder on each attachment. Because the side-shifter is such a popular attachment, several of the forklift truck manufacturers make their own side-shifters; however, side-shifters as well as a number of other forklift truck attachments are manufactured by specialists in this field, such as: Cascade Company, Portland (OR), Long Reach Company (TX), Little Giant, Peoria (IL), and HMC, St. Louis (MO).

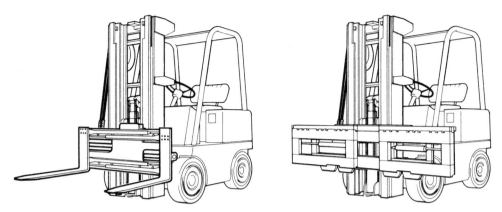

Fig. 18-7: Side-shifter attachment.

Rotator Attachments

Rotators are used in some industrial applications, for example, where a box with fork pockets is dumped by rotating the box to empty the contents into a bin. The rotator is attached between the truck and the fork carriage either by a large worm gear, or by a chain drive on two sprockets.

Rotator attachments of this type are very sturdily built and will last for years of arduous service. Therefore, when choosing either of these attachment types, you should choose the attachment which will lose the minimum of load center for your particular application; it may not matter too much if you do lose some load center, depending on your particular application. In most physical distribution facilities, rotators are usually used where stacked merchandise must be turned over to avoid a shelf-life loss; for example, a chain drive rotator provides a closer fit to the carriage of the forktruck, than a large gear and worm drive rotator, therefore, it does have an added advantage of permitting heavier loads to be carried without too much of the load center being sacrificed. (See Figure 18-8.)

Fig. 18-8: Load rotator.

Slipsheet Attachment

A slipsheet attachment is usually called a push-pull and is illustrated in Figure 18-9. There is a broad platen at the base of the attachment and a mechanism to grab the lip of a piece of corrugated or fiberboard sheet which is placed under the load. The push-pull attachment extends to grab the lip of the corrugated or fiberboard material and it will then retract, pulling the load up over the platen of the attachment which serves as the forks of the lift-truck. In this application, the push-pull attachment cannot be used to get under a pallet as forklift forks normally would be used. The push-pull attachment must be used with the slipsheet or the Bel-O-Pak type of pallet, which has a lip on it just as the slipsheet would have. The advantage of using a slipsheet instead of a pallet and the Bel-O-Pak slipsheet combination is that the tare weight and the cube of the wood pallet are eliminated, and greater storage density can be achieved with a resultant savings.

Courtesy Cascade Corporation, Portland, OR
Fig. 18-9: Slipsheet, push-pull attachment.

Carton Clamps

Carton clamps are used to stack, destack, and transport cartons without the use of a pallet. Two broad, flat arms squeeze a pallet-sized load of cartons and lift them without crushing the contents. One of the problems with using carton clamps is that the size and fragility of the load must be taken into account, because there is the possibility of damaging the contents of the containers by crushing.

Nevertheless, there are decided advantages in being able to handle cartoned materials without the use of pallets. One advantage if that the use of pallets creates hazards through nail punctures. In addition, you can obtain a decided space savings by eliminating the several cubic feet taken up by each pallet. There is another cost savings by eliminating pallets in the handling of materials because the tare weight of the pallet and the returnable nature of the pallet add expense to shipping costs. The slipsheet and the Bel-O-Pak combination slipsheet and pallet were developed for these reasons. Figure 18-10 Is an illustration of carton clamps.

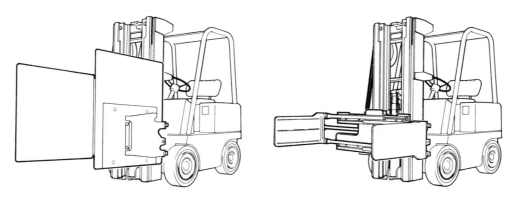

Courtesy Cascade Corporation, Portland, OR
Fig. 18-10: Carton clamps.

Edge Lifters

There are several simple mechanical attachments on the market that require no electrical or hydraulic hookups. For example, the Basiloid carton clamp is one such device, and it is categorized as an edge lifter. To use the Basiloid carton clamp, however, the manufacturer of the carton must provide a lip around the top edge of the carton so that the edge lifter can extend under this lip to lift the cartoned material. These materials usually consist of appliances in which the Basiloid carton lifter is extremely effective.

Other Attachments

Variations of the above attachments can be found in many different industrial and distribution center applications. Most attachments work primarily on the basis of hydraulic action. Because the forklift truck has a power plant (i.e., the engine or the motor and the hydraulic pumping system), all that remains to actuate most attachments is to hook the attachment device or mechanism on the carriage of the forklift truck mast and connect it into one of the valve blocks of the fork-truck's hydraulic system. In most fork-trucks, there is usually a three-way hydraulic valve provided expressly for this purpose. For this reason, whenever you purchase or lease a forklift truck, obtain the type of valve block needed for the specific attachment that you expect to mount on the carriage.

There are some additional attachments other than the Basiloid carton clamp that require no hydraulic hookup. Booms can be mounted on the mast for rigging operations. Prongs or some variation of prongs can be used in rug or carpet handling. There are other variations of prongs used in moving concrete blocks: a series of tines are used in place of forks to stack and load concrete and cinder blocks. In some applications, the block tines for concrete block handling are provided with a side-shifter mechanism to make it easier to handle, load, and stack this material. This type of application increases the efficiency of the operation and eliminates much of the unnecessary maneuvering and nonproductive movement of the fork-truck.

INDUSTRIAL TRUCK BATTERIES, CHARGERS, CABLES, AND CONNECTORS

Battery Construction

Contrary to popular belief, a storage battery does not actually store electrical energy; it stores chemical energy which is, in turn, converted into electrical energy while the battery is discharging. In the recharging process, the electrical energy supplied to the battery is spent in changing the active materials back into their original state, thus restoring the original chemical energy necessary for another discharge of electricity. These exchanges of energy are made possible by the mechanical design of the cell itself. The construction of the storage battery is that of an electrochemical apparatus that accepts electrical energy delivered to it by any suitable electrical charging apparatus, thus converting this electrical energy into chemical energy, which is gradually accumulated while being charged. A battery is composed of a number of cells. Figure 18-11, shows a battery jar with one of the cell units exploded to indicate the materials of which it is composed. The number of cells in a battery depends on the voltage requirements.

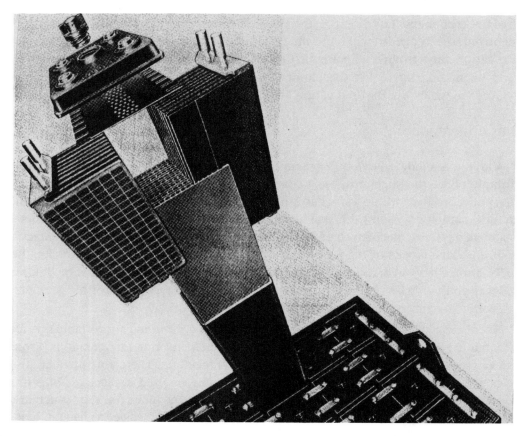

Fig. 18-11: A rubber or plastic battery jar with an exploded view of a cell to show the positive and negative groups with their posts, separators, and cover.

Figure 18-12 shows the composition of a simple cell which is essentially a container, usually a hard rubber or plastic jar, that contains the electrolyte into which are placed two electrodes (a negative plate also called a cathode and a positive plate, an anode) that are of dissimilar composition and are separated electrically from each other with a dielectric. The electrolyte in a lead-acid cell is composed of sulfuric acid and water.

The capacity of a battery, determined by the work effort or energy to be expended, is expressed in ampere hours, that is, the number of amperes required for the duration in hours that the battery is to be utilized. The ampere hour capacity of the battery determines the

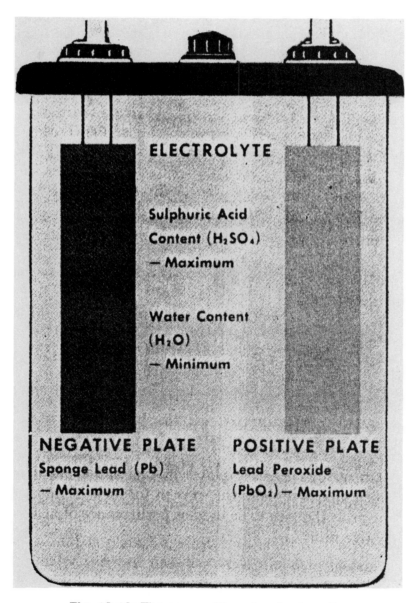

ELECTROLYTE

Sulphuric Acid
Content (H_2SO_4)
— Maximum

Water Content
(H_2O)
— Minimum

NEGATIVE PLATE
Sponge Lead (Pb)
— Maximum

POSITIVE PLATE
Lead Peroxide
(PbO_2) — Maximum

Fig. 18-12: The composition of a simple cell.

physical size and the number of positive and negative plates to be used. Since there is a wide variation in job requirements for the various applications on which the mobile industrial powered equipment is to be used, there are many different sizes and types of battery cells that are available.

After a battery is placed into a fork-truck and set in motion, the battery is said to be on discharge. It is during this period of discharge that the chemical energy in the battery is being converted into the electrical energy of the motive force that is being used to propel the vehicle.

NOTE: The basic principle of construction of lead-acid batteries doesn't vary very much among individual manufacturers, despite the assurance that each one makes. Generally speaking, the performance and longevity of the battery of a specific ampere hour capacity will be only as good as the weight of the battery, that is, the heavier the battery, usually the heavier the plate construction. The more lead in a battery, the longer it will last and keep supplying the maximum of its rated capacity.

For a full discussion of the lead-acid industrial battery, see Appendix C.

Calculating Battery Capacitance Requirements

In selecting a battery, the correct ampere hour capacity is of primary importance, because a battery that is under capacity will run down before the end of its working shift. By the same reasoning, if the battery has an over capacity, it would cost considerably more than necessary. Industrial truck manufacturers or battery representatives can help you select a battery of the proper capacity for your equipment and application. However, as plant manager, you should know how to calculate battery capacity requirements against your operating conditions.

The *Handbook of Material Handling,* prepared by the Electric Industrial Truck Association, has a procedure that you can follow for this calculation. Figure 18-13 shows the requirements of power in watt hours necessary to move specific weights over given distances on a level concrete surface.

By using this chart together with other constants given in the *Handbook of Material Handling,* we can arrive at a power figure requirement that will cover not only level concrete transportation, but also such items as grade, lift, and tilt.

As an example, we'll take a battery-operated truck that has a combined weight of battery and operator of approximately 3650 pounds, or 1.825 tons. With a load of 2000 pounds, or one ton, and an average lift of three feet, the weight totals 5650 pounds, or 2.825 tons. The truck and load will travel a distance of 110 feet, of which 80 feet is on level concrete, and the balance of 30 feet is an upgrade of 10%. We deposit the load and then return the unloaded truck back over the same route, which now means a downgrade for 30 feet and the same 80 feet over our level concrete path to the starting point. We want our computations to show the watt hours required for:

- the total run with the load.
- the extra power for 30 feet of loaded travel up a 10% grade.
- a return run unloaded with a deduction for the down grade side.
- lifting.
- tilting.

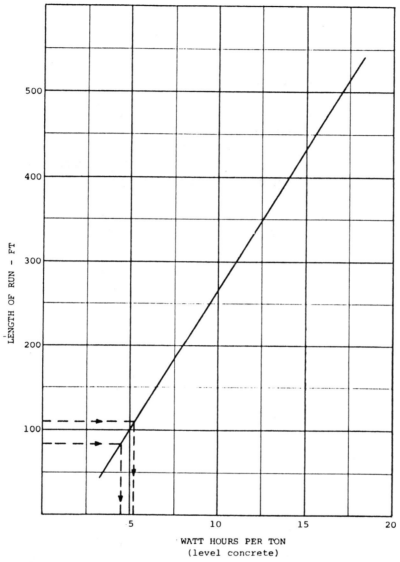

Fig. 18-13: Graph of watt hours per ton required to operate industrial powered trucks over level concrete.

Using the power chart in Figure 18-13, we first locate the total distance to be traveled (110 feet) on the left-hand side of the chart and extend a line until it intersects the standard line. Then by dropping the line straight down to the bottom of the chart, we have determined that it takes 5.4 watt hours to move one ton over a distance of 110 feet on a level concrete surface.

Because our loaded truck weighs 2.825 tons, we multiply this by 5.4 watt hours needed to move one ton. This gives us the number of watt hours required to move 2.825 tons 110 feet. Multiplying 2.825 by 5.4 we have 15.26 watt hours.

Using the Electric Industrial Truck Association (EITA) data, we can find the extra power needed to traverse the 30 feet of 10% upgrade, as follows:

The extra power required for the upgrade
= tons × length of grade × percent of grade
× a constant of .013.

Substituting our figures into the equation:

$$2.825 \times 30 \times 10 \times .013 = 11.02$$

The result is 11.02 watt hours of extra power required for the upgrade.

The total distance for the return trip is 110 feet. We deduct 30 feet for the downgrade and we have the level distance of 80 feet we will use for the calculation. Referring again to the standard chart, we find that it takes 4.4 watt hours to move one ton over a distance of 80 feet on a level concrete surface.

Because the operator and truck are now traveling unloaded, the total weight is 1.825 tons. The calculation for the number of watt hours required here to move 1.825 tons 80 feet is 1.825 × 4.4, or 8.03 watt hours. The EITA formula for calculating the watt hours for lifting is as follows:

watt hours per lift = load in tons

X feet of lift × a constant of 2.

Substituting our figures in the above equation:

1 ton × 3 feet × 2 = 6 watt hours.

Calculating the tilting watt hour requirements, the EITA formula is as follows:

watt hours per tilt = load in tons × a constant

This gives:

1 ton × 1 = 1 watt hour.

The addition of the above items is as follows:

Run with load	15.26 watt hours
Extra power for upgrade	11.02 watt hours
Empty return, no grade	8.03 watt hours
Lifting	6.00 watt hours
Tilting	1.00 watt hours
Total =	41.31 watt hours/round trip

If we assume that the truck makes 250 round trips daily, we can obtain the daily watt hour requirements by multiplying 41.3 watt hours by the number of round trips, which is 250, giving us a total of 10,325 watt hours.

Assuming that the truck is a 32-volt forklift truck powered unit, we can use the formula

$$ampere\ hours = \frac{watt\ hours}{volts}$$

This gives:

$$\frac{10,325\ watt\ hours}{32\ volts} = 322.7\ ampere\ hours$$

Therefore, a battery rated at 323 ampere hours, or the nearest figure for a standard-size industrial battery above 323 ampere hours would be the minimum size battery for this duty cycle.

Determining Battery Condition

Determining the condition of an industrial battery requires three forms:

- records
- test discharge
- internal inspection

Records

Good record keeping provides a day-to-day case history of the industrial truck battery. The forms used should indicate the following information:

- the date
- the battery number
- the number of the truck the battery was removed from
- the specific gravity of the battery when it was placed on charge (this can be taken from the pilot cell reading)
- the temperature (of the pilot cell)
- the time it was placed on charge
- the time it was taken off charge
- the specific gravity of the battery when it was taken off charge

The reason historical records for the industrial truck battery are necessary is simply that by comparing specific gravity of the battery (corrected for temperature), and the "time on charge data" with the previous day's reading, any abnormal battery function or abuse will be indicated and corrective steps can be taken immediately. Another reason for the historical records is that by examining the trend of the current or most recent entries, the records will show when a battery is deteriorating and should be replaced by a new one.

Every six months, the fully charged specific gravity and voltage readings should be taken of each cell and compared with those of the preceding six-month interval. These readings should be taken at the end of an equalizing charge. Such comparison should reveal any serious differences in battery condition as well as any differences between the cells, and steps can be taken to replace or repair the battery.

NOTE: If your company has a fairly large number of industrial trucks and requires a large number of truck batteries as well, then it would pay to repair and replace cells in the battery. This can be done in-house or by contracting service to a local company.

Test Discharge

To determine whether a battery is delivering its rated capacity, a test discharge may be made. The test consists of discharging a fully charged battery at a constant ampere hour rate until the battery voltage drops below the accepted discharge-termination value of 1.75 volts per cell. The time it takes for the voltage to drop below 1.75 volts per cell will indicate whether the battery is delivering rated capacity.

To simplify test discharging and standardize the method, industrial electric batteries are generally discharged at the "six-hour rate" indicated for the particular battery under test. Prior to testing, a battery should be given an equalizing charge, and the fully charged specific gravity should be adjusted to normal. During the testing period, individual cell voltages and overall battery voltages should be recorded at intervals: first interval, fifteen minutes after the test is started; and then hourly until the voltage of any one cell reaches 1.80 volts. From then on, at 15-minute intervals the recording should continue at this frequency. After this, the cell voltages should be under constant observation and the time recorded for each cell voltage as it dips below 1.75 volts. The test discharge is terminated when the majority of the cell voltages reach 1.75 volts; however, the test should be stopped before any single cell goes into reversal.

The specific gravity of each cell of the battery should be recorded immediately after terminating the discharge. These readings will show whether the battery is uniformly charged, or if one or more cells are low in capacity. If the battery is uniform in value and has delivered 80% or more of rated capacity, it is ready to be returned to service.

Internal Inspection

Should the test discharge indicate that the battery was not capable of delivering more than 80% of rated capacity, and all the cells happen to be uniform in value, then an internal inspection should be made of at least one of the cells.

Sometimes an internal short circuit may be the cause of failure; however, this can be repaired. As an example, the positive plates, which normally wear out first, should be examined. If it is found that they are falling apart or that the grids, that is, the lead framework supporting the lead peroxide, the "active material," have many frame fractures, then a replacement battery would be required.

NOTE: If the positive plates are in good condition and the cells contain very little sedimentation, then the battery may have become sulfated.

A *sulfated battery* is one that has been left standing in a discharge condition or is undercharged so that abnormal quantities of lead sulfate have formed on the plates. When sulfation occurs, the chemical reactions within the battery are affected and a severe loss of capacity usually results. Some of the causes of sulfation are:

- undercharging (which does not thoroughly mix the electrolyte)
- neglecting the equalizing charge procedure
- standing in a partially, or completely, discharged condition.

Make sure your battery maintenance personnel understand that permitting a battery to remain in a partially discharged condition allows the sulfate deposited on the plates to harden and close the pores in the plates, which would ordinarily permit the flow of electrolyte. Batteries should be charged as soon as possible after they have been discharged, and they should never be allowed to stand in a completely discharged condition when temperatures are below freezing or stand in a completely discharged condition for more than 24 hours at a time.

Battery maintenance personnel should pay particular attention to the following critical areas and warning signs in order to keep your batteries productive and economical to operate:

- *Low Electrolyte*—Just as in your ordinary automobile battery, if the level of the electrolyte is permitted to fall below the tops of the plates, the exposed surfaces will harden and become sulfated.

- *Adding Acid*—The periodic addition of acid to improve the specific gravity of the electrolyte will only aggravate the condition of sulfation if it exists.

- *High Specific Gravity*—As a general rule, the higher the fully charged specific gravity of a cell, the more likely is the possibility that sulfation will occur and the more difficult it is to reduce. Any battery that has cells which exceed the specific gravity by more than 0.015 above the average, the chances of sulfation in these particular cells will be greatly increased.

- *High Temperature*—High summertime temperatures or working in a high-temperature environment will normally accelerate sulfation, especially when the battery is standing idle and is partially discharged.

Another good indication of sulfation is when all of the cells of a battery give low specific gravity readings and low voltage readings as well; in addition, the cells of such a battery will not become fully charged after a normal charging period. An internal inspection of the battery will disclose negative plates with a slate-like feeling, sulfated negative plate material will be hard and gritty and have a sandy feeling when it is rubbed between the thumb and forefinger. This internal inspection should be made only after a normal charge has been placed on the battery, because a discharged plate is always somewhat sulfated. A good, fully charged, negative plate is spongy and springy to the touch and has a metallic sheen when stroked with a fingernail or a knife; a sulfated positive plate has a lighter brown color than a normal plate.

CAUTION: In normal battery operation, it is often difficult to determine the early stages of sulfation. Only by giving periodic equalizing charges and comparing individual cell specific gravity and voltage readings can sulfation be detected.

Your maintenance personnel can undertake the following steps to restore a sulfated battery to fairly good operating conditions:

- Carefully clean the battery.

- Add water to each cell to bring the electrolyte level to the proper height.

- Place the battery on charge at the prescribed finishing rate until full ampere hour capacity has been induced based on the eight-hour rate. If, at any time during the charging procedure, the temperature of the battery exceeds 110 degrees Fahrenheit, the charging rate should be reduced to maintain the temperature at or below this point. If any cell should give readings lower than the average cell voltage of the battery by an amount equal to 0.20 volts, then pull and repair the cell before continuing with the procedure.

- After the full ampere hour capacity has been given to the battery, continue the charge at the finishing rate until the specific gravity shows no change for a four-hour period, when the readings are taken hourly. Record the voltage and specific gravity readings and correct the specific gravity readings for temperature. These readings will indicate the state of charge of the battery. Place the battery on discharge at the six-hour rate as previously described under "Test Discharge."

- If the battery gives rated capacity, no further treatment is required other than the normal recharging and equalization of specific gravities.

- If, however, the battery does not deliver near rated capacity, then continue the discharge without adjusting the discharge rate until one or more cells reach 1.0 volt.

- Recharge the battery at the finishing rate, and continue charging until there is no further rise in the specific gravity over a four-hour period with readings that are taken hourly.

- Discharge the battery again at the six-hour rate, and if the battery gives full rated capacity, recharge it and put it into service.

- If the above procedure does not result in at least 80% of capacity, perform it one further time.

- If the battery has not responded to the above treatment, then it is sulfated to the point where it is no longer practical to attempt further treatment, and the battery should be replaced.

The equalizing charge is a proven method for sustaining the life of a battery. This low-rate charge which restores all of the cells in a battery to a fully charged condition should be given at least once a month, but no more often than once a week, depending on the duty cycle of the battery. When forklift truck batteries, for example, are used on the heavy-duty cycle (that is, where the batteries are discharged to a major point one or more times a day depending on the number of shifts worked), then the equalizing charge should be given weekly. If the batteries are used only on a light duty cycle, requiring charging once every two or three days, then the equalizing charge should be given only once a month. Because there are many cells in a battery, it is quite usual to use the center cell in the battery as the pilot cell for the equalizing charge.

Battery Chargers

The original charging devices for industrial electric batteries were the motor generator sets. There has been a gradual shift from motor generators to what is now known as the silicon-controlled rectifier (SCR) type of charging machine. This is not to say that motor generators were unreliable, because with proper maintenance (such as brush replacement, armature truing, and the like), they sometimes lasted from 20 to 30 years, and even longer; however, they are not as efficient in the use of electricity as the SCR units. Manufacturers of extremely reliable SCR units today are KW, Westinghouse, Gould, and Exide.

Cables

The wire for cables should be selected with the largest gauge possible for the type and size battery to reduce charging resistance. It does not pay to skimp on this provision, because the lower the charging resistance, the less energy will be required to charge the battery.

NOTE: Battery cable wiring and the wiring for battery chargers should use the wire that is of the heaviest gauge possible to do a satisfactory job.

Connectors: Charging Plugs and Receptacles

The industrial battery requires a plug and receptacle to be used for connecting it to the machine that it drives and to its charging equipment. These devices or connectors are known as charging plugs and receptacles. They are made in several sizes in five or more types, designed to be easily disconnected and quickly connected.

These devices are locked together as a unit when they are in use or on the charging machine. They consist of two separate parts, the plug, which is the male half, and the receptacle, which is the female half. One half is shipped with the battery, and the other is shipped with the forklift truck machine or other mobile piece of equipment. Battery charging equipment usually has leads furnished with either a receptacle or a plug; it is fairly obvious that the purchaser of battery-powered equipment must make certain that the same type and size of charging plugs and receptacles are supplied with each of the parts of the truck battery charger. The purchaser of an industrial truck and battery should also be specific about what units the plugs and receptacles should be attached to—for example, the receptacle is usually attached to the battery unit and the plugs are assembled with the truck and the charging equipment.

CAUTION: Although the plugs and receptacles are of rugged design, they are not indestructible and can be damaged by misuse, for example, if a forktruck drives over a receptacle. Keep foreign materials such as water, grease, oil, or dirt out of the receptacle.

CAUTION: When your maintenance personnel are repairing a damaged or dirty plug or receptacle connected to a battery, they must not forget that the leads that terminate in the receptacle are live or "hot" with the total voltage in the battery existing across the terminals. As an example, one lead is secured to the positive post on the battery and the other to the negative. The terminal lugs enclosed within the receptacle are held apart with very little danger of short-circuiting, but before the terminal lugs are removed from the receptacle, the battery circuit must be opened or broken. If this is not done and the terminal lugs are accidentally touched together, a short-circuit and arcing will occur that can severely injure personnel and equipment. The arc strength will depend on the size of the battery, of course, but the power carried can reach 10,000 amperes and exceed the current carrying capacity of the leads.

CAUTION: The short-circuit rate is approximately equal to three times the one-minute discharge rate of the battery.

If it is necessary to open the circuit of the battery, either disconnect one lead from the battery post or sever one of the cell connectors. The terminal lugs are held in the plug or receptacle by a bolt or screw that, when loosened, will permit the lugs to be withdrawn for cleaning or replacement. When proceeding to repair a broken or damaged terminal lug, it should be cut off from the cable and the proper length of wire to fit the terminal should be bared, cleaned, and tinned. Occasionally, some terminal lugs may have short or shallow recesses into which the wire must be soldered, and it is extremely important to clean and tin the wire to obtain a secure bond to ease the flow of electricity.

CAUTION: When you reassemble the terminal lugs in the receptacle or the plug, make sure that you place the negative wire on the negative side and the positive lead on the positive side. If the leads are reversed in reassembling, the battery will be placed on charge in reverse and will be badly damaged.

CAUTION: During the changing or repair of either plugs or receptacles connected to the charging equipment, the power should be shut off completely so that there is no voltage across the terminal lugs and no chance of a disastrous short-circuit.

19

How Equipment Maintenance Contributes to Profitability

PREVENTIVE MAINTENANCE FOR MATERIALS HANDLING EQUIPMENT

In many ways a good equipment maintenance program that emphasizes preventive maintenance can contribute to the profitability of your company. Scheduled preventive maintenance does a number of things to increase profitability. First, it is a good morale builder, because one of the problems that poorly run companies experience is the constant breakdown of equipment and the contributing demoralization of the work force. Second, good preventive maintenance ties in directly with your plant's safety program, because well-maintained equipment is safe to operate. Third, it sends a message to your employees that the company's management is businesslike and will not tolerate shoddy performance. In the short run, preventive maintenance will cost money; however, over the long haul, it will save many-fold over the initial cost of setting up a good maintenance program.

NOTE: There are a number of companies whose sole business it is to set up operating schedules for preventive maintenance and who have computerized the information required.

SHOULD YOUR MAINTENANCE PROGRAM BE IN-HOUSE OR UNDER CONTRACT?

There are several ways you can approach the establishment of a satisfactory maintenance program. You can set up an in-house maintenance program using the regular plant maintenance work force; however, if you do not have the expertise or the mechanical skills on your staff, then you are probably going to have to rely on contract maintenance service. Contract maintenance services, which can be provided at a guaranteed rate may be the solution to establishing your plant's materials handling equipment preventive maintenance program.

Before you select either the in-house or maintenance contract program, you should evaluate the factors which would establish your course of action. For example, any good evaluation would demand that you base your conclusions on cost and reliability.

An in-house maintenance program can, under certain conditions, provide immediate service, because it is there at hand. This factor creates a false sense of security since immediate service alone is not a criterion for a maintenance program. In-house maintenance programs at some plants tend to become the quick "band-aid" rather than ongoing "preventive medicine." However, establishing a contract maintenance program can give you the same benefits as having maintenance performed in your plant on an as- and when-required basis.

Any good maintenance program for materials handling equipment requires a systems approach in which the following components are addressed:

- periodic lubrication and routine service
- periodic inspection and engine or motor tune-up
- minor repairs, including replacement of parts and the like
- major overhauls, including engine and motor replacement and the like

A good way to compare the reliability of service levels of the in-house versus the contract service method of establishing preventive maintenance can be determined by using a checklist somewhat in the format of Table 19-1.

Table 19-1: Comparative Benefits of In-house and Contract Maintenance Programs

Item	In-House Maintenance	Contract Maintenance
Routine Service	This can be satisfactory if the schedule is adhered to in a very strict manner.	The contractor should be a specialist in this area, and will follow a very strict schedule.
Periodic Inspections	This will be satisfactory if your plant mechanics have all the necessary skills.	The contractor should be a specialist in this area, and will follow a very strict schedule.
Minor Repairs	Minor repairs can usually be made in a satisfactory manner if performed on time and according to schedule; however, this may compete with other maintenance activities and tasks in this department, so that it may become a question of dead-lining the equipment until the plant maintenance group can get around to performing the repair. That means that another piece of materials handling equipment will be out of action until the maintenance group can get around to performing the job.	If the maintenance contractor does not have an on-the-job, that is, in-your-plant type of service with mechanics in residence, then a special call would be needed to have the repair performed. Any contract maintenance work would have this characteristic spelled out in the contract to the point where a specific time lapse would be given for any minor repair, that is, within twelve hours of being called, or the like.

Major Overhauls

Major overhaul work competes with many other maintenance needs and other users of the maintenance facilities. Unless replacements are leased, down-time for the equipment can accrue, unless, of course, you have a few pieces of standby equipment in your operating fleet at the plant.

The contractor can provide replacement equipment while he is performing the major overhaul, and this should be spelled out in any contract maintenance provision.

Table 19-1 indicates that, for the smaller plant, the contract maintenance approach meets much of the reliability requirements more directly. For the smaller plant, then, the in-house maintenance approach has many qualifications which may be disregarded if certain circumstances of operation are met, as we shall discuss below.

Determining Whether In-house Maintenance Personnel Are Qualified

Large physical distribution centers have the best opportunity to provide in-house maintenance service equal to contractual service simply because they have the specialists on hand to service materials handling equipment only. With this qualification the comparison of the in-house versus contract maintenance develops into a cost comparison only. In the smaller warehouse, materials handling equipment is maintained alongside all the other mobile equipment; thus, regular vehicular mechanics do the work and they are not always familiar with a particular piece of materials handling equipment. Also, special tools, parts, and the like may not always be available for the maintenance of materials handling equipment.

The qualifications and competence of the mechanics who are performing maintenance work in a plant are, in large measure, a contributing factor in the reliability of the maintenance performed, and no matter how well-conceived the overall program of maintenance may be, that is, with the proper schedules and the like, it is the qualifications of the mechanics who are to perform the work that make for a good preventive maintenance program.

If the plant already has an in-house maintenance work force, it is certainly just a matter of time before the maintenance crew develops a reputation for good work, or for bad work, for that matter. If the maintenance department is doing a creditable job of maintaining the equipment in good operating condition, then you may not wish to consider contract maintenance except perhaps in comparing the cost of doing this business in-house versus having a contractor do it.

Obtaining Suitable Facilities to Perform Your Maintenance

The larger physical distribution operations usually have space set aside for the maintenance facilities and have specialists devoted to maintaining the equipment on board. In the smaller companies, sometimes the facilities are not properly oriented in this direction. When this is so, then the question of contract versus in-house maintenance develops two areas for consideration. One is cost, and the other is the quality of service to be performed.

How to Reduce the Cost of Maintenance

Stocking spare parts for the maintenance of a mobile materials handling fleet can be extremely vexing if there are a number of different categories of handling equipment and the manufacturer's equipment has not been standardized on one company. In other words, you are going to have a number of parts that will be quite similar, but not the same part, for different manufacturers. And, therein lies the problem. Even standardization on a manufacturer's line sometimes can be troublesome, also, in particular when the model changes come out and different pieces of equipment have spares that do not fit into a standard category. Therefore, regardless of the size of the company, a mixed fleet of materials handling equipment will always have parts problems. This is another reason why you might find it will be less expensive to have a contractor maintain your equipment and place the responsibility for spare parts supply directly on his/her head.

Contract maintenance organizations may have the same difficulties with parts that you have, but it is a problem that they must resolve satisfactorily before they can offer their services to any physical distribution center.

It goes without saying that contract maintenance companies could not stay in business if they were not competitive. Thus, it is a suggestion for you as a plant manager to have your supervisory staff check out how well other companies that are serviced by the contractor have fared in their hands.

Checking the Reliability of the Contractor

In the main, larger companies may be better equipped than smaller ones to support a satisfactory in-house maintenance program for materials handling equipment, but this should not rule out the possibility of their considering contract maintenance under various conditions.

The question of reliability remains the criterion to be applied to either contract maintenance or to in-house programs which, in the final denominator, points out the availability of equipment for use in the plant, i.e., what is the percent of up-time that can be maintained?

Some service contracts might be able to guarantee a specific level of maintenance service, but they may not be able to guarantee a required level of equipment availability. There are numerous factors which might make an availability guarantee, or up-time, extremely difficult for the service contractor. For example:

- the operating environment is dirty,
- the warehouse housekeeping is poor,
- the equipment involved is overaged,
- the degree of training of the plant operators is poor, and,
- the safety with which the operators perform their tasks leaves a lot to be desired.

If this sounds like a worst-case scenario, then you, as a plant manager, should be the judge of the conditions that will hamper or make the service contract survive with a reasonable assurance that the availability of equipment within your plant will be up to your standards.

The following questions are suggested as a checklist in the consideration of using maintenance contract services:

- Does the service contractor guarantee the meeting of minimum requirements?

- Will the service contractor be able to meet the varying environmental conditions in which the equipment in your plant must operate?

- Will the service contractor provide an adequate inspection program in which problems in your operating fleet can be discovered in time to avoid unnecessary work stoppage or down-time of the equipment?

- Will the service contractor make provisions to insure that parts shortages will not result in unnecessary down-time; for example, will it provide replacement materials handling units as a temporary measure?

- Does the service contractor have a list of other plants using its contract maintenance service, and are they satisfied with the work that this company has performed or is performing?

- Will this service contract comprise a total maintenance program? If it does, how flexible is the service contractor in providing for unplanned or unscheduled problems? Does the contractor charge premium prices for work of this nature, or does he/she include this in the overall contract price?

What You Need for a Good In-house Maintenance Program

These are the criteria you need for obtaining a good preventive maintenance program:

- Can your regular maintenance work force support a program required to adequately maintain your mobile materials handling fleet?

- Will you be able to provide the proper facilities for the maintenance program, and can tasks be adequately performed if space and facilities can be provided at some later time?

- Do you know whether your equipment mechanics are competent to handle the equipment you have on hand? If they are not, can they be given factory training, and the like?

- Do your mechanics work full-time on your equipment, or are they constantly being interrupted to perform other plant maintenance work?

- If your mobile materials handling equipment fleet is a mixed bag with unusual parts requirements with obsolete or over-age equipment, can your resident mechanics and the purchasing department handle these problems adequately?

- Can your in-house maintenance program meet the minimum levels of availability for the materials handling equipment that you have?

If you cannot develop a clear and decisive picture between the way in-house maintenance would be performed in comparison with contract maintenance, then you must consider the factor of cost as well as reliability.

What Does Maintenance Actually Cost You?

To get a handle on the cost of maintaining materials handling equipment in your plant, you have to get cost data from the accounting department. Since in any plant there is normally a large capital investment in materials handling equipment, and usually each piece of equipment represents a fairly large capital investment, its subsequent repair and maintenance will have a decided effect on the total cost of maintaining the fleet of equipment. To get a better picture of costs, the analysis should be structured on two levels:

- repair costs per fleet unit
- total cost of ownership and operation of the mobile materials handling fleet.

In any good materials handling equipment maintenance program, each unit of equipment should have its individual cost records which would summarize the monthly use of labor and the cost of materials; that is, spare parts, lubrication, etc., used in maintaining these vehicles. When such data is kept, the analysis of the monthly as well as the year-to-date or purchase-to-date data (of costs) can help spot the pieces of equipment that are giving the most trouble. Including operating hours will provide a measure against which to compare higher labor costs and parts for the vehicles in the system, since the fact of costs alone may not indicate the questions like usage and abuse of equipment. In analyzing this cost data, excessive material cost which occurs at irregular intervals may be an indication that the planned maintenance approach is being replaced by a "fire-fighting" or the "breakdown maintenance" approach, that is, the vehicles being maintained only when they break down.

Repair costs for specific units of equipment can help provide indications concerning the existence of specific problems:

- Largely varying costs for the same model and year of equipment can denote a potential or possible equipment abuse problems, which could result in higher maintenance costs.

- Varying costs for similar equipment used in or about the same fashion or with similar operations may indicate the existence of an unsatisfactory piece of equipment.

- Maintenance costs for specific pieces of equipment that become progressively higher can indicate the need for a major overhaul or a unit replacement.

Cost data can describe a picture of what the in-house maintenance costs really are; however, they must still be compared with the guaranteed costs for contract maintenance service. If it is found that the contract maintenance costs would be lower, it would still require that a certain amount of cost data be forthcoming, with equipment records being maintained by the contractor, so that it is possible to keep a running indication of the satisfactory performance of the service program as performed by the contractor. In any case, having in-house maintenance costs described for each unit of equipment will be extremely helpful in making a cost comparison as to the value of the contractual service work. Analyzing the costs for each unit of equipment will be very helpful in forming a basis for comparing contract services with in-house maintenance.

Regardless of whether or not you have contract maintenance services in your plant, the continuing collection of maintenance cost data per operating hour will help in determining the effectiveness of the maintenance services in your plant and, if you do have contract services, then the continuing monitoring of these costs will be extremely helpful when the time comes to renew the service contract.

How You Can Use the Systems Approach to Maintenance to Save Money

To apply the systems approach to maintenance problems means that every element of cost must be included in your analysis. In viewing the economics of ownership, the following items are all part of the total system:

- capital investment
- depreciation
- maintenance costs
- down-time costs
- the availability of equipment
- the cost of equipment obsolescence

The last three factors are subjective evaluations; for example, down-time, availability, and obsolescence are very difficult to assign numbers to; however, they are cogent parts of the total ownership cost. Also, to the last three elements we should add the trade-in, or scrap value of the equipment which is the residual value, and for large pieces of materials handling equipment can represent a fairly substantial amount of money, especially due to the inflated prices of new equipment.

Capital investment, depreciation, and maintenance costs are readily obtainable accounting figures. It is when we attempt to assign values to down-time, availability, and equipment obsolescence that problems arise.

If down-time means a work stoppage, then arbitrarily multiplying work crew size by hourly rates plus fringe benefits can establish a useable accounting figure. The availability of equipment and equipment obsolescence are more nebulous in that they may tend to get very subjective depending on the age and experience of the analyst. Nevertheless, both of these elements may be assigned values arbitrarily based upon hypothetical solutions to the problem. For example, the obsolescence factor for forklift trucks may be approached from the difference in travel and lifting speeds of the old piece of equipment versus the new, and the percentage difference applied to productive output. In the same way, equipment availability can be deduced and a number assigned based upon the "what if" question: if the additional equipment were available how much additional output would be produced?

When the above estimated values are introduced into the cost of ownership they are no less valid than the actual cost data represented by statements and invoices, because they tend to view ownership's hidden costs in a realistic light. Which brings us to the subject of "life-cycle costing." When evaluating one piece of similar equipment with another for the purpose of buying the equipment it is not enough to compare the initial cost and performance, but it is necessary to enter into the cost of ownership all of the costs that will be incurred over the life of the equipment; for example, spare parts costs and maintenance, then subtract any trade-in, or residual value, and the like. Past experience with each manufacturer's product and the keeping of accurate maintenance costs will enable your equipment personnel to compile a data file which will be invaluable in making management decisions on whether or not to maintain an in-house maintenance force for equipment servicing or to use contractual services.

By pursuing all of the above factors relentlessly, your supervisory staff can be made aware of the subtleties of owning and operating equipment, so that you have gained another advantage in having them focus on maintenance concerns.

20

How to Justify Equipment Replacement

HOLDING THE LINE ON EQUIPMENT MAINTENANCE COSTS

Chapter 19 described the subject of life cycle costing, a concept that fits in well with our view of the systems approach to managing a physical distribution center. In most warehouses and distribution centers the lift-truck is probably the single most important piece of equipment, unless of course the distribution center is a very large one and you have automatic storage and retrieval systems, a large conveyor installation, and the like. Outside of these larger installations, however, the forklift truck has a considerable impact on how well the activities of the warehouse are conducted. Maintenance costs have a very large effect on the total economic life, or life-cycle cost, of a forklift truck.

There is always a critical shortage of qualified mechanics to service lift-trucks, due in large part to the many technological advances that have been made in the designs of both gas and electric lift-trucks. Many general plant mechanics are not totally qualified to handle all of the repairs required to keep a lift-truck in good operating condition. Several of the larger lift-truck manufacturers have tried to overcome this difficulty by establishing mechanic training centers in order to develop the necessary skills in their service personnel. Furthermore, test equipment has also been developed that will permit a general mechanic to more easily troubleshoot and repair the lift-truck.

In the past, a higher caliber of maintenance capability was necessary to service the electric-powered and diesel engined trucks than their gas-powered counterparts. The differences among servicing requirements for gas, electric, or diesel trucks have narrowed due to the introduction of electronic controls and plug-in circuit board components, which have made servicing considerably less difficult. Paralleling this technology, gasoline engine trucks have become more complicated due to the introduction of high performance, automatic transmissions and electronic ignition components.

Maximum forklift truck up-time (i.e., availability) and performance at a minimum total cost are not easily attained with maintenance personnel who are not especially skilled in this type of vehicular repair. Unfortunately, as the skill requirements for servicing lift-trucks increase, the cost of labor also increases.

NOTE: In general, the maintenance costs for gasoline engine lift-trucks are higher than for electric vehicles of the same capacity.

It has been estimated that the maintenance costs for gasoline forklift trucks consist of 60% labor and 40% parts. However, maintenance costs for electric forklift trucks, with their more expensive components which can be installed quickly, are generally closer to 50% labor and 50% parts. Therefore, as labor rates increase, the electric lift-truck with its lower maintenance requirements should provide an increasing cost advantage over the gasoline lift-trucks over its life-cycle.

The environment in which a lift-truck fleet operates can have a decided effect on maintenance and down-time costs and can have a decided bearing on the proper equipment to use. A corrosive environment, one which is dirty and dusty, will increase maintenance costs for internal combustion engine trucks. Thus, as the cost of maintenance increases per operating hour, the higher acquisition cost of electric lift-trucks is offset more rapidly. When the gas or internal combustion engine carburetors draw in polluted air the throttles are caused to stick and, as dirty air is drawn into the combustion chambers, the blow-by forces grit and abrasive particles into the lower end of the engine, causing excessive wear on bearings and rings.

Fortunately, electric driven motors for lift-trucks can be effectively sealed against dirt and other forms of pollution. By contrast, in dusty or dirty environments, the radiator of the gasoline lift-truck will become clogged, and the engine will overheat. When all these factors are combined, the total effect is a sharp rise in maintenance costs.

The increasing cost of fuel may be the single most important factor affecting the decision of whether to use gas or electric lift-trucks. A decade or more ago, the difference in cost of the power consumed between the gas versus electric lift-truck was considered insignificant. In today's economy, however, this is no longer the case. Another factor that weighs the decision heavily in favor of electric is the environmental awareness of the deleterious, polluting effects of using gasoline internal combustion engines in enclosed spaces. The shift has been to liquid propane or electric with the electric trucks taking precedence, despite their higher cost.

THE THREE MAIN METHODS FOR JUSTIFYING EQUIPMENT REPLACEMENT

There are many ways that companies justify the replacement of mobile materials handling equipment. Usually the smaller the company, the less formalized is the method for replacement. Where large fleets of materials handling equipment are involved, the formulations used to justify equipment replacement become quite complex. Needless to say, the complexity consists, in large part, in obtaining historical data of the operation of a piece of materials handling equipment. Job assignment, utilization hours, and the life cost per hour of equipment use, and the like, have all been used to justify replacing various pieces of equipment.

In some of the smaller plants, the older piece of equipment is usually either kept as a standby vehicle or it is placed into functions which require only a few hours of operation per day, and the newer vehicle is placed on more arduous jobs.

There are three main methods of justifying equipment replacement. In the first two methods the replacement of the vehicle is made only after incurring expense to repair the equipment: this is the cost which drives the price per hour of operation up beyond the economical range. Method three anticipates increased repair costs and recommends replacement before these expenses are incurred.

Method #1: Calculate the Average Cost per Hour of Operation

Since each piece of equipment has its own identification number, the method of computing costs against each of the numbered vehicles is to tabulate the total hours the vehicle has been utilized and the repair, maintenance and fuel or power costs for the vehicle. This gives you an average cost per hour of operation which can be compared to the repair and maintenance costs that have been tabulated for the whole fleet of vehicles. A vehicle whose expenses are much higher than the average for the fleet should be replaced. The estimate of the savings to be derived from replacing such older vehicles, would be the justification of replacement.

Method #2: Calculate the Increased Operating Cost per Hour

Equipment replacement can be justified in another manner by using the increased cost per hour of operation. By carefully tabulating all of the costs incurred by each piece of equipment and making a chart for each vehicle, the curve that is formed by the cumulative costs per thousand hours of operation will indicate the manner in which, as the truck ages, it will increase in hourly operating costs per thousand hours. In this method, equipment replacement is justified when cumulative costs show a sharp increase over the prior thousand hours' cost.

Method #3: Calculate the Lowest Total Cost Point

The lowest total cost point, or the LTCP concept, is based on the fact that a cost curve can be made for each piece of equipment as shown in illustration Figure 20-1.

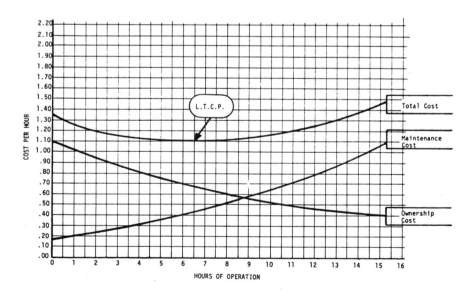

Fig. 20-1: The LTCP, or the lowest total cost point is illustrated in the graph as the sum of the maintenance and ownership costs.

This total cost curve is derived by charting the sum of the cumulative maintenance cost per hour and the cumulative ownership cost per hour of operation. By projecting the total cost curve into the future, it is possible, by extrapolation, to plan on equipment replacement before major repairs become necessary. The curve for the ownership cost is derived by decreasing the purchase cost at a quarterly declining rate. In order to keep the computations as simple as possible, the rate does not consider trade-in value, taxes, or freight charges against the vehicle. In this manner, the ownership cost curve indicates how much of the total cost of the unit has been used up at the end of any particular quarter. The rate used depends on the type of vehicle or unit, its capacity, and manufacturer, and is derived from records of equipment that have previously been replaced. The cost curve for maintenance indicates the total number of dollars spent in maintaining the unit in operating condition. All normal wear and tear items are included in maintenance costs except those repairs which are caused by the operator's abuse.

The total cost curve for a particular unit is obtained by adding the maintenance cost curve to the ownership cost curve. The point we are seeking is that period in which the unit will be operating at its lowest total cost. Eventually, the cost curve will begin to rise, and it is at this time that the unit will be ready for replacement.

The benefits in using the LTCP method for equipment replacement are described in the following paragraphs.

Consistency: The LTCP Method Provides a Consistent Way of Determining When to Trade In Equipment

It eliminates the very subjective approaches that are sometimes made by plants in replacing equipment, since it provides definite guidelines and formalizes the entire procedure on a sound economic basis.

Eliminates Costly Major Overhauls

When the LTCP is charted, you can predict trends in equipment behavior and make forecasts, thus enabling you to extrapolate to forecast equipment requirements. For example, if the unit is nearing the LTCP, then it would not be advisable to spend large sums for major overhauls. On the other hand, if the LTCP is not forecast to be imminent, then you might decide to go ahead with an equipment rebuild instead of waiting for the replacement of the unit.

It Minimizes General Maintenance

When the LTCP method is used, the quarterly reports on maintenance and utilization enable you to single out high maintenance cost units. The LTCP charts provide an opportunity to look at the equipment in retrospect and examine specifications, the operating conditions, and to ascertain the reasons why the cost for a particular unit is either out of line or is a unit working in a hostile environment.

Equipment Justification

Using the LTCP method is one way of helping you prepare requests for capital funds, since it gives more credibility to the justification of equipment.

Budgeting

The LTCP method enables you to forecast equipment requirements in a manner that tells you when you will have to replace equipment. The knowledge of when the equipment will be required and the necessary funding that take place require time, and the LTCP gives you time to place the request in your budget, get approvals, and have the equipment placed in the manufacturer's schedule for construction, thus reducing sometimes delayed delivery times and higher prices. The advance notice that LTCP can give management serves as a much-needed forecast for equipment dollars.

TWO WAYS TO DETERMINE RETURN ON INVESTMENT (ROI) TO GOOD ADVANTAGE

The discretionary levels at each company vary considerably in terms of how much a plant manager can spend without having to obtain approvals from a higher level in the company. As an example, if the parent company or the board of directors has established a capital expenditure limit of, five thousand dollars for a division manager's approval, then any expenditure below this sum will usually require only a one-page summary of benefits or advantages that may be obtainable upon the expenditure of funds. The company, on the other hand, may have further requirements of the plant manager when amounts extend beyond the $5,000 limitation, which may require more elaborate justifications and supportive data. If you wish to spend hundreds of thousands or millions of dollars, then you may need a staff of ten or more people working full-time for six to eighteen months to prepare the supporting data and proposal to justify this expenditure. A new warehouse with an automatic storage and retrieval system with computerized controls and a front-end conveyor installation may cost 15 to 20 million dollars. When sums this large are involved, there is a decided degree of formality that enters into the picture.

The following criteria usually govern this type of activity:

- Cost justification is required because the company management needs to establish the proper priorities for the allocation of all of its funds;
- If the money cannot be taken out of reserves set aside for this purpose, then the capital must be obtainable by either borrowing or other means;
- The ROI must satisfy any questions that the stockholders of the company might have; and,
- The company management must make a decision based on the satisfactory return that can be obtained on the cost of the money to be invested with, of course, the smallest possible margin of error.

Since there are many ways of determining return on investment, this section outlines two of the most commonly used methods to justify major capital projects.

Estimating Annual Return on Investment

The yearly savings divided by the investment gives the simplified annual return on investment. The equation is:

$$Annual\ return = \frac{Yearly\ savings}{Investment}$$

If we substitute figures for the above equation, we would have

$$Annual\ return = \frac{\$2,500}{\$10,000} = 25\%$$

or, a 25% per year return in this example. (This equation does not take into consideration the cost of the money.)

Determining the Discounted Cash Flow (DCF)

This widely accepted method is somewhat more sophisticated than the Annual Return method. The equation for this method is:

$$\text{Savings} - \text{depreciation} \times \text{tax rate} + \text{depreciation} = \text{cash flow (DCF)}$$

Using the Rate of Return, Payback Period, and Present Value of Money Concepts

Since there are always many requests for capital investment from the various departments of a plant, as a plant manager you ordinarily would choose the investment that will result in the largest return as one of the first projects to become involved with, unless of course there are other exigencies or reasons that would give a project priority.

Estimating Rate of Return

As a plant manager, suppose you had to select one of two investments for the purposes of improving both plant operations and the profit for your particular enterprise, as follows:

- Investment A: A conveyor proposal having to do with increasing the bin order picking productivity can be purchased for $10,000 and will have the result of saving $10,000 per year for the next seven years.

- Investment B: A gravity flow bin order picking system can be purchased for $20,000 and will save $15,000 per year for the next seven years.

When deciding between investment A or investment B, you see that investment A will return 100 percent per year and investment B will return only 75 percent per year or:

$$\text{Savings} - \text{Cost} = \text{Return}$$

The amount for investment B is $20,000; however, if we take $10,000 (equivalent to the cost of investment A) from investment B and say that it will return 100% in the first year, we can say that the additional $10,000 will return $5,000, or 50% in the first year. Therefore, if you cannot make an alternate investment, that is, an additional investment with the second $10,000 increment that will return the same amount, 50% in the first year, then the second investment, B, would be the more logical investment of capital. Although this example has been oversimplified, there are many factors to evaluate when considering the investment of capital. This simple example illustrates that the **rate of return** may vary considerably according to the method of selecting the investment; however, there are additional considerations that must be evaluated, also.

Calculating the Payback Period

One of the other considerations mentioned above, when considering capital investment, is the payback period, which is the length of time required for the return to equal the investment.

For example, if you are going to invest $100,000 in new equipment, and your staff has projected that the annual return on this investment will be equivalent to $10,000, you can apply a payback period to see exactly how effective this return will be. Assuming your company pays a tax rate of 40%, which we can round off to fifty percent for easier calculation and for the sake of a conservative estimate, then your payback period before taxes is the equivalent of ten years. That is to say, $100,000 $10,000.

If the payback period is figured after taxes, then the payback period is twenty years, or $100,000 ÷ $5,000.

CAUTION: When comparing different investment possibilities it is important to use the same rules for each investment; otherwise your comparison will be biased because of the disparate factors involved. If you use a payback period after taxes for one investment, then when considering another investment opportunity, you must use the same basis for consideration.

The following examples compare three different investments competing for company dollars, investments X, Y, and Z.

Investment X

In investment X you propose buying a piece of conveyor equipment costing $20,000 with a life expectancy of ten years. The gross savings in the first year will be approximately $38,000, but there will be no further savings after that year.

If you perform the following calculation, you obtain:

1. Gross savings	$38,000
2. Less depreciation	2,000
3. Savings before taxes	36,000
4. Taxes @ 50%	18,000
5. Net savings	18,000
6. Add back depreciation	2,000
7. Cash flow	$20,000
8. Payback period = one year	

Therefore, as shown above, you can invest $20,000 in investment X for a piece of equipment and obtain a $20,000 return in the year; thereafter, there are no further returns. In item 6, above, the depreciation was added back to the savings to arrive at a **cash flow** amount; therefore, it is your **cash flow** that you are considering as your **savings** each year.

Since you are putting in $20,000 and taking out $20,000, you have not made any progress—youhaven't gained anything. This a very poor investment, since you actually lost the use of $20,000 for one year, despite the fact that it may be possible to sell the conveyor at the end of the year for approximately $15,000 and receive some return.

Investment Y

Investment Y requires the purchase of a $20,000 system, again with a life of 10 years. This alternate investment will produce a gross savings of $8,000 for several years, computed as follows:

1. Gross savings	$8,000
2. Less depreciation	2,000
3. Savings before taxes	6,000
4. Taxes @ 50%	3,000
5. Net savings	3,000
6. Add back depreciation	2,000
7. Cash flow	5,000
8. Payback period = four years	

The gross savings in investment Y of $8,000 is decreased to a cash flow of only $5,000. Therefore, it will take four years before you start making a profit on the capital you have invested.

Investment Z

In investment Z an expenditure of $20,000 is indicated, also with a ten-year life for the equipment. The equipment system will produce the following gross savings:

1st year	= $ 2,000
2nd year	= $ 6,000
3rd year	= $10,000
Each additional year	= $16,000

In evaluating the payback period, Table 20-1 shows the calculatkons over time.

Table 20-1. Investment Z Payback Period

	1st yr.	2nd yr.	3rd yr.	Every Additional Year
1. Gross savings	$2,000	$6,000	$10,000	$16,000
2. Less 10% depreciation	2,000	2,000	2,000	2,000
3. Savings before taxes	0	4,000	8,000	14,000
4. Taxes @ 50 percent	0	2,000	4,000	7,000
5. Net savings	0	2,000	4,000	7,000
6. Add back depreciation	2,000	2,000	2,000	2,000
7. Cash flow	2,000	4,000	6,000	9,000
8. Payback period = 4 years				

It appears that the $20,000 investment will be returned in four years. Comparing investments X, Y, and Z, we have the following:

	Payback Period	Cash Flow Each Additional Year
Investment X	1	$0
Investment Y	4	$5,000
Investment Z	4	$9,000

Each of the above investments requires an amount of $20,000; therefore, calculating the percentage return on each investment after the payback period, we obtain:

$$Annual\,Return\,on\,X = \frac{0}{20,000} = 0$$

$$Annual\,Return\,on\,Y = \frac{5,000}{20,000} = 25\%$$

$$Annual\,Return\,on\,Z = \frac{9,000}{20,000} = 45\%$$

The above calculation indicates that investment Z is the best selection.

One of the drawbacks with using only payback period calculations is that the length of the return is not factored in. For example, if the 25% return for investment Y was for the next five years, but the 45% return after payback of investment Z was only for one more year, then we would have to state that investment Y is the best selection—because the **total return** for investment Y is $45,000 computed in the following manner:

Cash flow of $5,000/year for 9 years = $45,000

The **total return** for investment Z is $30,000, figured thus:

cash flow in payback period = ($21,000)
+ ($9,000) in the fifth year = $30,000.

The **rate-of-return** method of evaluating investments corrects one of the problems of the payback period, by taking into consideration the length of return on the investment.

For example, a company requires replacement of a critical piece of equipment for its warehouse, and it has the choice of two alternate systems, each costing $20,000.

System A:	Cost	$20,000
	Return/year	$5,000
	Payback period =	4 years

Using the rate-of-return method, factoring in the length of the return, and assuming that each system has a life of 10 years, the return per year of system A is $5,000. Therefore, the total return will be $50,000, or $5,000 × 10-year life.

$$Rate\,of\,Return = \frac{Total\,return}{Original\,investment}$$

or,

$$\frac{\$50,000}{\$20,000} = 250\%$$

System A will return 250% over its 10-year life. The average yearly rate then for System A is:

$$\frac{250\%}{10\,years} = 25\%\,per\,year$$

System B also costs $20,000 but its yearly return is as follows:

1st year return	=	0
2nd year return	=	$1,000
3rd year return	=	$3,000
Each add'l year	=	$8,000

The payback period for system B is five years.

If you add the sum of the returns for 10 years of the system B's life, you will derive the following:

Year	$
1	0
2	1,000
3	3,000
4	8,000
5	8,000
6	8,000
7	8,000
8	8,000
9	8,000
10	8,000
Total Return	$60,000

Then,

$$Rate\ of\ Return = \frac{Total\ Return}{Original\ Investment} = \frac{\$60,000}{\$20,000} = 300\%$$

and the average yearly return for system B is equal to 30 percent:

$$300\% \div 10\ years$$

Summarizing the investments for the two systems, you obtain:

	System A	System B
Investment	$20,000	$20,000
Payback period	4 years	5 years
Total return (%)	250%	300%
Aver. return (%)	25%	30%

This verifies the decision to purchase system B. Obviously the advantage of the rate-of-return method lies in the fact that it takes into consideration the length of time over which a return can be expected. If you had used only the payback method, system A would have seemed the better investment of the two, since it showed a shorter payback period.

Present Value Concept

The examples above have assumed that the dollars used will remain at a fixed value from year to year. Unfortunately, dollars do not hold a constant value, and this is apparent if you have to choose between receiving $1,000 now or $1,000 one year from now: you would certainly choose the $1,000 now, because you could invest the $1,000 now and have more than $1,000 a year from now, if everything else remains the same.

Here is another example: Suppose you can invest $10,000 in one of two investments, X and Y. The investments are shown below:

	1st year	**Returns** **2nd year**	**3rd year**
X $10,000	$500	$300	$200
Y $10,000	$200	$300	$500

The total Return in each of the two investments is the same, however, investment X is the better choice because it has a larger first-year return of $500, which you can invest for a larger gain. This is better than having only $200 to invest, as in the case of investment Y.

The money you receive in the future is not worth as much as the money you receive now; therefore, in evaluating investment opportunities you should discount, by a certain amount, money to be received in the future.

Consider the possibility of investing one dollar for one year. At the year end that dollar placed in a bank at an interest rate of five percent would return to us $1.05. Or, reversing the procedure, you could invest $0.952 now and, at 5%, draw out $1.00 one year from now.

Thus, the **present value** of the dollar you will receive one year from now is $.952, if discounted at the rate of five percent.

To minimize the amount of calculations that must be made, use Table 20-2. The left column indicates the number of periods during which interest is compounded on the investment.

Table 20-2. Present value of $1.00.

n	6%	7%	8%	9%	10%	11%
1	0.9434	0.9346	0.9259	0.9174	0.9091	0.9009
2	0.8900	0.8734	0.8573	0.8417	0.8264	0.8116
3	0.8396	0.8163	0.7938	0.7722	0.7513	0.7312
4	0.7921	0.7629	0.7350	0.7084	0.6830	0.6587
5	0.7473	0.7130	0.6806	0.6499	0.6209	0.5935
6	0.7050	0.6663	0.6302	0.5963	0.5645	0.5346
7	0.6651	0.6227	0.5835	0.5470	0.5132	0.4817
8	0.6274	0.5820	0.5403	0.5019	0.4665	0.4339
9	0.5919	0.5439	0.5002	0.4604	0.4241	0.3909
10	0.5584	0.5083	0.4632	0.4224	0.3855	0.3522
11	0.5268	0.4751	0.4289	0.3875	0.3505	0.3173
12	0.4970	0.4440	0.3971	0.3555	0.3186	0.2858
13	0.4688	0.4150	0.3677	0.3262	0.2897	0.2575
14	0.4423	0.3878	0.3405	0.2992	0.2633	0.2320
15	0.4173	0.3624	0.3521	0.2745	0.2394	0.2090

continued

Table 20-2. Present value of $1.00. (continued)

16	0.3936	0.3387	0.2919	0.2519	0.2176	0.1883
17	0.3714	0.3166	0.2703	0.2311	0.1978	0.1696
18	0.3503	0.3959	0.2502	0.2120	0.1799	0.1528
19	0.3305	0.2765	0.2317	0.1945	0.1635	0.1377
20	0.3118	0.2584	0.2145	0.1784	0.1486	0.1240
21	0.2942	0.2415	0.1987	0.1637	0.1351	0.1117
22	0.2775	0.2257	0.1839	0.1502	0.1228	0.1007
23	0.2618	0.2109	0.1703	0.1378	0.1117	0.0907
24	0.2470	0.1971	0.1577	0.1264	0.1015	0.0817
25	0.2330	0.1842	0.1460	0.1160	0.0923	0.0736
26	0.2198	0.1722	0.1352	0.1064	0.0839	0.0663
27	0.2074	0.1609	0.1252	0.0976	0.0763	0.0597
28	0.1956	0.1504	0.1159	0.0895	0.0693	0.0538
29	0.1846	0.1406	0.1073	0.0822	0.0630	0.0485
30	0.1741	0.1314	0.0994	0.0754	0.0573	0.0437
35	0.1301	0.0937	0.0676	0.0490	0.0356	0.0259
40	0.0972	0.0668	0.0460	0.0318	0.0221	0.0154
45	0.0727	0.0476	0.0313	0.0207	0.0137	0.0091
50	0.0543	0.0339	0.0213	0.0134	0.0085	0.0054

From Table 20-2, you can determine the present value of one dollar for different investment periods and interest rates; for example:

- The amount you will receive in 6 years discounted at 7% = 0.6663
- The amount you will receive in 15 years discounted at 8% = 0.3152
- The amount you will receive in 20 years discounted at 9% = 0.1784
- The amount you will receive in 25 years discounted at 10% = 0.0923

To apply this knowledge to two investment projects requiring the same initial amount of capital, consider the following example:

- Investment X returns $300 in two years.
- Investment Y returns $400 in four years.

If you discount each investment at 8% using Table 20-2, for Investment X follow line 2 across to the 8% column, and for Investment Y follow line 4 across to the 8% column.

Investment X = 8% for 2 years = 0.8573
$300 × 0.8573 = $257.19

Investment Y = 8% for 4 years = 0.7350
$400 × 0.7350 = $294.00

Investment Y has the larger **present value;** therefore, it is the better of the two investments.

In another example, suppose your company must decide between two productivity improvement projects: In project A, you can invest $100,000 to purchase a gravity flow bin system. The company is very conservative and feels that this is a relatively safe investment that will return $30,000 the first year, $60,000 in the second year, and $60,000 in the third year. Because this is a relatively safe investment, the company decides to discount the investment at eleven percent, which is exactly the cost of acquiring the money to finance this productivity improvement program.

The calculation of the present value of the return on investment is as follows:

$30,000 for one year @ 11% discount = $30,000 × 0.9009 = $27,027

$60,000 for two years @ 11% discount = $60,000 × 0.8116 = 48,696

$60,000 for three years @ 11% discount = $60,000 × 0.7312 = <u>43,872</u>

Present value = $119,595

In project B the company can install a new packaging line that will increase a certain product's penetration of the market; but, since it is a fairly new product and not so well established, there is a high degree of risk involved for the investment in launching this product. You set the discount arbitrarily at 30%, or five times the cost of obtaining the money. In other words, the risk is high, but the gain could be high also. Calculating the returns, you obtain the following:

$40,000 for one year × 0.7692 = $ 30,768

$80,000 for two years × 0.5917 = 47,336

$140,000 for three years × 0.4552 = <u>63,738</u>

Present value = $141,832

Project A has a present value of $119,595, whereas project B has a present value of $141,832.

Taking another example, let us suppose that a company will invest in a project and receive the following returns:

Investment	Return 1st Year	Return 2nd Year	Return 3rd Year
$20,000	$6,000	$8,000	$10,000

Calculate the yield, or rate of return, on the above investment. First, you need to find the rate of discount that causes the sum of the present values to equal the investment. This is done on a trial-and-error basis; so, start by applying a discount rate of 6% to the returns and see what the sum of the present values turns out to be:

$ 6,000 × 0.0434 = $ 5,660

$ 8,000 × 0.8900 = $ 7,120

$10,000 × 0.8396 = <u>$ 8,396</u>

Present value = $21,176

The present value of $21,176 is more than the original investment of $20,351; therefore, the discount wasn't large enough. Now, try ten percent and see what happens:

$$\begin{aligned} \$\ 6.000 \times 0.9091 &= \$\ 5{,}455 \\ \$\ 8{,}000 \times 0.8264 &= \$\ 6{,}611 \\ \$10{,}000 \times 0.7513 &= \underline{\$\ 7{,}513} \\ \text{Present value} &= \$19{,}579 \end{aligned}$$

As you can see, the discounted rate of ten percent gave too low a figure, $19,579 versus the $20,351 of your investment. So, try eight percent, which gives the following:

$$\begin{aligned} \$\ 6{,}000 \times 0.9259 &= \$\ 5{,}555 \\ \$\ 8{,}000 \times 0.8264 &= \$\ 6{,}611 \\ \$10{,}000 \times 0.7513 &= \underline{\$\ 7{,}513} \\ \text{Present value} &= \$20{,}351 \end{aligned}$$

Therefore, these computations indicate, that the present values of the return at eight percent discount are equivalent to your original investment. This investment bears the same return that would have been achieved if the money had been deposited in a bank bearing an interest rate of eight percent. Small wonder then at the conservative stance of some companies in regard to capital investment.

NOTE: You do not have to be mathematically adept to justify equipment replacement or determine the quality of investments in order to arrive at a decision or a recommendation to the board. Having been informed of the rudiments of costing, you should be aware of the possibilities that exist in these areas:

1. There are many different ways to justify equipment replacement, depending on the dollar value of the equipment. A rule of thumb is that any method of justification is better than none at all.

2. The Least Total Cost Point (LTCP) method gives consistent results.

3. No equipment should be replaced unless there are consistent data to support the decision.

4. Justifying capital expenditure can be misleading when the wrong method is selected to make the decision.

5. Use the examples in the text as a guide for your capital investment decisions, and if you are unsure of your capability to judge the various methods, obtain professional accounting expertise to assist you.

21

Measuring the Productivity of Warehousing and Physical Distribution Operations

DATA, METHOD STUDIES, AND REPORTS THAT YOU CAN USE TO INCREASE PROFITABILITY

Planning, scheduling, and controlling production are functions that are necessary regardless of the size of the operation involved. The profitability of your enterprise may very well rest on how well you are is guided by the data available to you. In the first place, look at the reliability of decisions made by management in these particular areas of concern:

- the precision with which human work can be measured
- the timeliness of the reports that are available to management
- the methods used to study the work that is being performed
- the reporting methods.

Historical records or past experience, which is often used as a basis for predicting the work effort of the plant, is at best a very crude and often unreliable method for predicting the amount of work to be expected from an individual or the work force as a whole.

The need exists in most warehousing and physical distribution operations to have data that adequately represents what is actually occurring in the plant, and also to establish targets or goals that are achievable. Some of the data that have direct implications for the operation of a well-organized distribution center can be enumerated as follows:

- Line items or SKU's (storekeeping units) received per day, per week, per month, per year
- Number of line items or SKU's shipped per day, week, month, year
- Average line items or SKU'S per order
- Popularity of items in a listing from the fastest moving items to the slowest moving
- Dollar value per order

- Dollar value per customer
- Tonnage shipped per day, week, month, year

It is also of value to obtain the number of SKU'S picked per day, per week, month, year by employee.

CAUTION: When considering awards or bonuses based on production, remember that the workloads of various individuals may differ according to the areas of the warehouse in which they are working. Bin pickers should be grouped in one division, and break-bulk or bulk storage picking (which is normally done on a forklift truck) should be grouped separately in order to have a consistent measure of work effort among the employees.

If monetary awards for performance are not given in your plant, then some certificate or letter to the employee should recognize his or her work effort.

Using Methods Studies

For your plant to be well-organized and administered, you should have job descriptions for every functional area of the plant. Since the job description describes what you want each employee to do on the job, another question enters into the picture, and that is: How long will it take the employee to perform the task which has been assigned? The time element, therefore, is an important consideration in putting together the staffing tables of the plant and preparing the budgets for the year in which the number of employees to handle a given volume of production becomes a necessary element of the total package.

Relying on historical experience to determine the staffing for the facility is often not conducive to profitability. Therefore, to increase profits without being guilty of "speed-up" or any other abusive forms of unenlightened management, a method study for each of the tasks is necessary. Methods study attempts to improve the methods used to achieve a stated goal by eliminating, combining, or changing motions. The primary purpose, of course, is to eliminate all wasted motions and effort. After each job has been studied from the standpoint of the methods used, then it is time to establish a work measurement standard for the task.

Work Measurement

The term "work measurement" has the connotation of *time study using a stopwatch.* As a plant manager you should understand that there are quite a few different ways of setting work measurement standards for your employees. The stop-watch time study is only one of many methods that can be used. To give you a familiarity with the several measurement methods, we'll discuss them briefly, as follows:

Stopwatch Time Study

Stopwatch time studies have acquired a somewhat sleazy connotation, especially among labor unions, primarily because of the abuses of this type of activity in the past when, under the instigation of so-called scientific management, the results were equivalent to "speed-up." Since time study is a fundamental tool of the work measurement and a building block for many other work measurement systems, which do not have the same sinister associations, I would like to explain how a technician goes about developing a stopwatch time study.

The technician studies the job and then breaks the task down into its various measurable elements. Naturally, if the job content varies considerably during the course of a work shift, the results would be very unsatisfactory. Thus, in order to obtain reliable work measurement results, the task to be studied must be highly repetitive. For example, a bin order picker filling an order, or a person on a packaging line continuously filling boxes and packaging the contents. To illustrate, let's take a relatively simple task such as the person on a packaging line placing selected items into a corrugated container and taping the box and labeling it. A methods study sheet, illustrated in Figure 21-1, should contain a diagram of the work station arrangement together with a breakdown of the elements, a description of the complete task, and the equipment being used.

Date: ______________ Engineer: ______________ SKETCH

Location: ______________

____

Task: ______________

____

Equipment: ______________

____

____

____

____

Job Elements

1. ______________
2. ______________
3. ______________
4. ______________
5. ______________
6. ______________
7. ______________
8. ______________
9. ______________
10. ______________
11. ______________
12. ______________
13. ______________
14. ______________
15. ______________

Fig. 21-1: A typical methods study sheet, showing a diagram and a list of the task elements.

The diagram should illustrate in a very simplistic manner the general arrangement of the work place layout and the work station, which in this case would be the conveyor on the packaging line. The operator being studied would take items that have been selected and placed on conveyor A into the empty corrugated cartons, which would be conveyed along conveyor B, and then transfer the items from one conveyor to the empty corrugated boxes, which are taken from conveyor B. After the box has been filled, the operator slides the box onto the scale section of the conveyor and weighs it, places a label on it, and then pushes it down conveyor B, where it will be transported to the shipping department.

When Figure 21-1 is completely annotated and the job elements are described, it should give adequate detail concerning the work methods used.

NOTE: A time study should be based on the performance of a qualified, experienced operator. The reason being, that your observations should be based on the average effectiveness of an operator who is relatively skilled in the job performance, rather than someone who is relatively unskilled or is new to the task at hand, otherwise the study will be biased.

After the methods study has been completed, a stopwatch time study may be made. The observer begins by transferring the elements of the job to a time study sheet. The technician who is making the observations will record the starting and ending times of each element for a fairly large number of repetitions by the operator. The technician will use his or her best judgment in deciding when to end the number of repetitive observations in order to get a statistically reliable number of observations for each element.

In addition to the elemental time observations, the technician will rate the *effectiveness level* of the operator by means of a judgment factor of what he or she deems is "normal" work effort. In our example of the packaging line operator, if the observer feels that the operator is performing somewhat faster than can be expected, he/she might use a rating factor of as much as 125%. That would mean that the observer feels that the operator is working 25% harder than can normally be expected for the particular task. As you can see, there is a somewhat subjective factor which has been injected into these observations by denoting the relative effectiveness level.

The technician who is doing the rating will be rated periodically in order to develop and maintain the judgmental factor for the effectiveness level. As an example, technicians periodically will be asked to observe a person walking, and a good walker can maintain a three miles per hour walking speed. The observer is asked to rate the walking speed of the performer, and then the actual walking speed is determined. The technician will then be able to form a fairly close perception of what is normal for walking effort. It is a subjective factor, as we have indicated, and some technicians rate consistently high and some rate consistently lower than normal. So each technician has to bear this in mind when he is rating the effectiveness level of an employee that he/she is observing.

After reducing the elemental times to what is considered normal (for the 125% rating factor this means that it is necessary to deduct 25 percent from each of the elemental times), the technician introduces an added factor for what is known as *fatigue* allowances. Fatigue allowances are rest periods that are usually combined with any of the **delay** allowances that may be observed. Delays are contingency allowances, for example, in some instances the conveyor line might be stopped periodically for servicing or replenishing of selected items, and the like. For example, the conveyor lines may run out of selected items, or they may run out of the empty corrugated boxes: if these stoppages are usual events in this operation, they must be adjusted statistically in the work measurement study. In other words, stoppages that occur with a certain frequency must be statistically factored into the final results and allowances made for them.

When many different time studies have been performed in your plant, it will be possible to assemble a library of work measurement standards from a compilation of all of the time studies that have been performed. This library of standards, which forms the basis for a standard data file, makes it possible to compile a work standard by using the data file of these standard elements. After many observations have been made, there is a certain degree of reliability in the standard elements. When the standard data file is placed into a computerized system, then it is possible to assemble a work measurement standard simply by requesting all of the elements that are in the data file to make up the new standard, without even having to take any observations of worker performance.

Predetermined Time Standards

As the name suggests, predetermined time standards have been developed prior to their application in a work measurement form. These standards are primarily used by companies that do not want to give the appearance of using the stopwatch for work measurement standards compilation. The elemental times, which are contained in these predetermined time standard systems, have previously been developed by stopwatch timing; therefore, the fact that we have a predetermined time standard without using a stopwatch is a euphemistic deception, which does not deceive anyone who is familiar with work measurement principles.

Predetermined time standards, such as MTM (methods time measurement), or BMT (basic motion times) are extremely useful and relatively less expensive to compile than the ordinary stopwatch time standards. The underlying principle of both of these predetermined time standards is that all of the motions of the human body are capable of having assigned time values to them. As an example, to reach out at arm's length, to have a short reach, or to grasp the fingers, and so forth, it is possible, therefore, to combine all of the motions required to perform a specific task and, in this manner, develop a standard of work measurement. Allowances for fatigue and delays are also included in these standards so that, in essence, what you have is something that is very comparable to a stopwatch time study.

Work Sampling (Ratio-Delay)

Work sampling, or ratio-delay as it is sometimes called, is an excellent work measurement technique which is relatively innocuous as far as the observation of work effort is concerned. It was originally developed by a British technician, L.H.C. Tippett, who was also a statistician, during his work studies in English textile mills. In this observational methodology, workers are observed at random time intervals throughout a specific period of time. A chart of random numbers is used to produce a perfectly random set of time intervals, at which the observations of the workers are made.

The difference between ratio-delay and stopwatch time study is that the stopwatch technician must maintain his observations of a particular worker constantly during the work measurement process. With ratio-delay, since random periods are involved, several workers may be observed during the course of the ratio-delay study, simply by maintaining the randomness technique of the time intervals involved.

From a statistical standpoint, ratio-delay is a perfectly valid method for determining and measuring human work effort. The technician using this system during a random observation of the worker will either determine whether the operator is "working" or "not working." By taking a large sample of observations and by coding the elements of the worker's task, a valid work standard may be developed that is sufficient for all ordinary purposes. The author prefers to use this work measurement method rather than stopwatch time study, and in the past has used it to establish work standards for a number of occupations, including the following:

- frozen food packaging
- order picking
- forklift truck operations
- equipment maintenance operations
- manufacturing production operations

- receptionist's job
- typist
- insurance claims adjuster

HOW YOU CAN USE WORK MEASUREMENT DATA EFFECTIVELY

It is often necessary to collect data in order to provide the supportive backup for materials handling equipment or facilities expansion and the like. If your technical personnel are capable, they will be able to obtain the data necessary to justify self-leveling docks, for example, at your receiving and shipping areas. They will be able to provide supportive data for new or additional warehouse space, and so forth.

Suppose you know that the receiving department requires more dock space and powered dock plates rather than the manual type of plates that are being used at the present time. Your problem is that you are not convinced completely that you do need more dock space, nor that powered dock plates might be more effective in this operation. You do know, however, that some truckers have complained about not being unloaded on time and having to remain overnight with a truckload that could not be unloaded efficiently.

You assign your technician to give you the data required to justify both additional dock space and powered dock plates.

The technician enters into the project without any preconceived notions, and his task is simply to obtain sufficient data to assist management in making the decision(s). The technician's checklist looks something like this:

- Examine of the incoming truck registers to determine the arrival times of each truck at both the receiving and shipping docks.
- Determine how long it takes each trucker to get loaded or unloaded.
- Prepare a chart showing arrival times of all trucks and see what the peak hours are.
- Experiment with staggering your receiving and shipping department working hours in order to improve the situation. It may be advisable to start loading or unloading two hours earlier each day and extend the workday one or two hours in either department.
- Perform method studies in order to determine whether there are any disruptive operations being performed on the receiving or shipping docks that might be the cause of delays. The technician may find that examining documents and, in general, shuffling paper and other routine clerical tasks are being performed by the productive work force instead of by the clerical personnel.
- Conduct a relatively simple computer simulation study of the operation by using the existing work performance standards and projecting future work standards with a specific number of dock spaces and powered dock plates.

By examining the above data, sufficient indication should be obtained to indicate if a need exists for either additional dock space or for powered dock plates. Regardless of the results, the data obtained should help management make a decision, since an ROI may be prepared on the expansion and equipment purchase or lease.

Justify Additional Warehouse Space

Let us suppose that you are the plant manager of a pharmaceutical warehouse and are trying to prepare for a 25% increase in SKUs. This would translate into an approximately 25% increase in dollar volume, and thus one of the first things to decide is what are the types and sizes of the items that will be added to the inventory. We are primarily interested in the volumetric or total cubic volume which we must prepare for in this additional business increase.

You have also decided not to use the historical or past experience standards and will be using work sampling techniques in establishing work measurement standards. From the work standards you will obtain the approximate number of additional employees required in the order picking function which can be translated, also, into the number of additional order picking carts and other equipment required to equip each order picker.

Since we know from the above that we're going to have a 25% increase in SKUs, we can determine from this information and from forecasting experience what the quantity, type, and size of materials you are going to have to deal with. Therefore, you can estimate the number of additional bin shelves, storage racks, corrugated shipping boxes, and the like, that will be required in the expanded plant.

You can then make a layout showing the additional bin shelving plan and determine quite accurately the size of the plant expansion needed to house the additional inventory.

MANAGEMENT ACTION BASED ON OPERATING STATISTICS

Since the major concern of all plant managers is to assure the profitability of the company, when the data collection functions are operating smoothly in all areas, it is up to the plant manager to make sure that they are properly utilized. Another phrase for profitability is the least total cost of materials handling and documentation, which consists of all of the handling and clerical functions performed within the distribution center. Since profitability occurs when we reduce the total cost of the distribution operation, then we have to look at the entire system and view the enterprise from a systems standpoint.

Symptomatic with this systems viewpoint are the areas of concern which will make themselves known in the course of the proper utilization of the operating statistics and data that has been collected by all of the departments within the plant.

There are certain symptoms that can be gleaned from the operating statistics and that require corrective action on your part:

Declining Profits Due to Higher Distribution Costs

In this area the symptoms to watch for are higher indirect labor costs and all of the concomitant waste in distributive operations that have not been periodically scrutinized from the systems standpoint.

Inventory Control Problems

A symptom of inventory problems is having either too much or too little inventory of any one particular item. One of the ways to cure this problem is to review the data indicating the way in which items in inventory move or turn over. Every quarter, or at least semi-annually, the list should be purged of all of the slow movers. An attempt should be made to replace these items with ones that will be called for with a higher degree of frequency. The emphasis here is on inventory turnover, and if you can have your sales force or marketing arm turning over your inventory more than you have in the past you can assure yourself that you're on the right track. In some industries an inventory turnover of three or four is considered good, but in others, if you are not turning your inventory over ten or twelve times annually, you're not doing too well.

Improving Customer Service

Customer service is based on the length of the response time from the customer's order to the delivery of the product. When the response time is shortened, customer satisfaction invariably improves. One of the best ways to improve response time is to make sure that your inventory levels of all stocks are appropriate to the demand. In addition, the ability to get out the customer's order on time is the responsibility of all departments of the plant. The team has to work together to make this happen.

Maintenance Costs That Continue to Rise

Fully maintained, or overworked, materials handling equipment and other plant equipment will invariably increase maintenance costs. The weak points in your maintenance program can be determined by a comprehensive, preventive maintenance program and consistently good record-keeping. It is not sufficient to maintain good records, however, without the frequent analysis of these records and an action program which follows up the review and succeeds in reducing high maintenance costs.

Late Due-ins

When vendors do not respond appropriately, and deliveries of stock materials are late, this causes schedules to be missed, results in overtime, and creates customer problems, not to mention that the possibilities of buying against vendor contracts which sometimes becomes a costly process. The responsibility for decreasing vendor response time rests squarely upon the purchasing department and your follow-up.

Faulty Materials Flow

You may not be able to discern faulty materials flow; however, since it is not always obvious, it will show up, nevertheless, on the balance sheet in the form of reduced profits. A good way to analyze materials flow is to have your technicians perform a plant materials handling survey which will reveal the weak spots in the system.

Integrating Functions

In fine-tuning your plant in the total systems approach, you will see the need for integrating all related functions, such as materials handling, maintenance, equipment allocation, purchasing, receiving, shipping, order picking, and the like. In addition, the data which you will have your departments supplying you on a regular basis will enable you to make valid decisions in every facet of managing your plant.

Appendix A

EVALUATION OF THE
BELL-O-PAK "BOP SHEET"

The BELL-O-PAK "BOP Sheet" represents the first major breakthrough in palletization since the development of the "slipsheet." It is for this reason that I became interested in reviewing and analyzing its potential merits and possible disadvantages.*

In the field of materials handling there is almost no one system, or methodology, that is a panacea for the movement and handling of materials. The best we can do is arrive at a solution that gives us tradeoffs and cost benefits that permit us to determine what is the most acceptable and advantageous system or methodology, to be employed.

The obvious disadvantages of the slipsheet are that it requires a push-pull attachment for the forklift truck, which, in addition to representing a significant investment for each unit so equipped, requires identical equipment on the receiving end (otherwise the mechanical advantage of the slipsheet is lost and manual unloading must therefore be employed). Additionally, training time to reach proficiency with such equipment can be a lengthy and costly process. From the standpoint of getting the most weight and cube in a carrier, the slipsheet is second only to hand-stacking. With labor costs and time at a premium, we must look to another methodology in order to eliminate hand-stacking as well as all other manual handling, if possible.

The BELL-O-PAK BOP Sheet appears to have the potential for displacing the slipsheet and wooden pallets for use in certain materials handling operations. Obviously it will maximize cube utilization in storage and in transportation vehicles.

The BELL-O-PAK concept (the utilization of the expandable-collapsible feature of a bellows) was invented at the Beefeater Gin facility in London, and BELL-O-PAK USA is the exclusive licensee for the United States and Canada. Distribution of this fiberboard pallet is handled through a network of agents, dealers, and distributors throughout the U.S. and Canada, and supply of the product is therefore readily available.

The average weight of the BOP Sheet is only 7-3/4 pounds, and its most important (working) feature consists of two .080 solid fiberboard sleeves with .060 polyethylene lips affixed to the leading edge of each. The lips guide the chisel forks into the sleeves. It is at this point that the bellows effect comes into play, allowing the sleeves to expand to receive the forks (this expansion capability will accommodate blades up to 4-inches thick at the heel, though it should be noted that the average maximum thickness of most industrial lift truck blades at that point is no more than 2-inches).

---

*T. H. Allegri, P.E., author of the basic text, *Materials Handling Principles and Practice,* Van Nostrand Reinhold, July 1984.

Conversely, when the forks are withdrawn, the weight of the unitized load compresses the bellows of the sleeves so that the whole pallet is reduced to a thickness of only 5/8-inch; this compares to the 4-to-6-inches of a conventional wood warehouse or one-trip (expendable) pallet. In its collapsed state the configuration of the sleeves allows for a 3/8-inch opening to be retained through the entire length of the sleeve. It is this opening, coupled with the aforementioned plastic lips, virtually slipping or chiseling under the load in a manner not dissimilar from slipsheet operations. Compression tests conducted by the Pacific Testing Laboratories (L.R. No. 23810) indicated a total load of 14,700 pounds caused a deflection in initial width (sleeve opening) of only 1/16-inch.

In addition to this unique sleeve design (for which patents were allowed by the U.S. Patent and Trademark Office of the U.S. Department of Commerce on November 9, 1984; SC/Serial No. 06/442,196), the other (nonworking) part of the BOP Sheet is what is referred to as the "deck sheet." In essence, since the fiberboard sleeves may be attached to many other types of load bases, such as trays, boxes, bags, etc., the deck sheet technically serves only two somewhat minor purposes: (1) assuring that the sleeves are spaced and aligned properly, and (2) providing a target for manual pallet-loading to ensure that maximum load base parameters are not exceeded. Apparently due to the fact that the deck sheet plays no other critical role in the BOP Sheet's usability, the deck sheet of the current BOP Sheet configuration is made of 275-lb.-test, single-wall, double-faced corrugated kraft which appears to be adequate.

USING THE BOP SHEET

The effectiveness of the use of the BOP Sheet depends upon several factors:

- The inherent characteristics of the material to be handled
- The pallet pattern of the unit load
- The skill of the operator of the forklift truck
- The unitization of the load.

Demonstrations with cartoned and bagged materials indicated the following:

Bagged Materials

Using kraft, double-walled sacks filled with 100 pounds each of abrasive grit, it was possible to enter the pallet and lift a 3000-lb. load. No form of unitization, other than an interlocking stacking pattern, was utilized and it was noticed that there was some slight separation of the palletized sacks as the forklift driver entered the pallet. Some of this problem was determined to be due to the hesitation of the forklift driver.

It appears that, in approximately fifteen to thirty minutes, the average forklift driver can adapt to the small difference in handling methodology required to utilize the BOP Sheet effectively. Additionally, when the bagged material was locked in place with a high-sheer, low-tensile adhesive, such as Uni-Lock Type A or H, B. Fuller Co. Type No. 133 Dextrin, or F4764 Resin, there was no separation of the stacked material, and entry and exit of the forks were accomplished in a smooth and rapid fashion.

It was found that an application of a silicone lubricant to the forks of the lift truck at the beginning of each work shift increased the ease of entry of the forks into the BOP Sheet sleeves.

Cartons

Tests with corrugated boxes indicated that unitization and stability of the loaded containers can be increased by employing an interlocking pallet pattern when stacking the containers on the BOP Sheet. The amount of interlocking depends, of course, on the size and shape of the container. With a good interlocking pallet pattern no adhesive bonding, banding, or stretch-wrapping is required. Where increased stability of the unit load is desired, then any of the above methods of unitization may be employed.

Sea-containers, Trucks, Railroad Cars and Air Transport

There are many advantages in using BOP Sheets for sea, over-the-road, rail, and air transport. One of the main advantages is of course the tare weight of the fiberboard BOP Sheet pallet when compared with wood pallets. This savings in tare could amount to as much as 2500 pounds in extra product per 40-foot trailer or container. Another advantage is the space savings in carrier equipment in which there is an average savings of 205 cubic feet per 40-foot trailer or container.

A minor disadvantage of the BOP Sheet is that it is a one-entrance pallet. Wood pallets are usually two-way and some are four-way, in that a forklift operator may insert the forks from any side. It is customary, however, to use only one side for most handling operations. Straightening a skewed pallet is done with little or no damage to a wood pallet; however, the forks may shear through the bellows of a BOP Sheet sleeve, depending on the total weight of the load. Although this damage may occur to the BOP Sheet sleeve it is still a useable pallet and will continue to serve its purpose regardless of a sheared sleeve.

Continuity tests with the BOP Sheet have indicated 110 round trips as approaching the limit of the life of a BOP Sheet. This compares very favorably with the usual life of a wood pallet.

Sliding one pallet behind another, to the working face in the sea-container, railcar, or truck, cannot be done satisfactorily with the BOP Sheet. This disadvantage, however, has mitigating effects because when pallets are shoved by a forktruck one behind the other there may be damage to the floor and walls of the carrier, or to the product being handled. In this aspect of the BOP Sheet use, it has been observed that greater care is displayed by the forktruck operator when handling BOP Sheets, than when wooden pallets are used.

Cost Savings

The cost benefits will vary from one operation to another. Suffice to say that in terms of initial cost the BOP Sheet is less expensive than expendable, one-way wood pallets, and certainly less expensive than wood warehouse pallets. When using the BOP Sheet for storage purposes there are definite space and pallet cost savings. Also, while some distribution operations have recycled the BOP Sheet for several round trips, the inexpensive BOP Sheet is cost effective as a one-way shipping pallet.

Another large advantage of the BOP Sheet is that it causes less damage to product and personnel than the wood pallet. There have been, to date, no reported injuries from handling the BOP Sheet due to its light weight. Despite its light weight, it has been proved to be cost effective with loads up to 3000 pounds per pallet.

As a last advantage, it has no nails to work loose and no wood to split or splinter, resulting in virtual elimination of damage to product and injury to personnel from these causes, which are commonly associated with the use of wood pallets.

SUMMARY

Due to the BOP Sheet's advantages as indicated above, it is recommended that each operation experiment with the BOP Sheet to determine its advantages and/or disadvantages which may apply to that particular material flow system.

BOP Sheets have been used with barrels loaded with shot, with abrasives, etc., where four barrels are banded horizontally and set on the BOP Sheet. Apparently, the weight of the unit load aids in stabilizing the load and enabling the forklift operator to enter and exit the loaded BOP Sheet. Thus, it has been found that "heavier is better than lighter" in BOP Sheet methodology.

In addition to its use as a fiberboard pallet, the BELL-O-PAK concept has been applied to a number of other materials-handling operations. The bellows-type sleeves with their plastic entrance lips can be used alone under long loads, for example, by strapping the sleeves to the load through the bellows. Other applications are the use of the sleeves under tray-packs, under sling loads, and as hopper boxes.

The cost savings summary shown in Table A-1 indicates that the BOP Sheet affords the potential for large savings in any operation that is presently shipping or storing materials by means of wood pallets.

Table A-1. BOP Sheet Cost Savings Summary

	Wooden Pallet	**Slip Sheet**	**BOP Sheet**
Special Equip. Cost	0	$8M–$20M	0
Cost of Pallet*	$7.50	.65–$1.20	$3.95
Tare Weight	65 lbs.	3 lbs.	8 lbs.
Weight Savings per Truckload	0	2700 lbs.	2500 lbs.
Cubic Feet Savings per Truckload	0	242 c/f	242 c/f
Storage Requirements	0	–92%	–85%
Reusability Factor**	5	1	5
Cost per Trip***	1.50	.92	.79

*Based on latest available data (1983 volumes) from Association of Wooden Pallet Manufacturers.

**Actual industry usage averages 2 to 3 trips for wood pallet before repair or replacement is necessary. The slipsheet is, in some cases, capable of reuse but is rarely if ever returned. The BOP Sheet survived 110 complete cycles in actual tests.

***Cost Per Trip is based on above reusability factor notwithstanding cost of return which would be approximately $1.89 for the wood pallet compared to about 36 cents for the BOP Sheet, both on a per-return-trip basis (computed at an average transportation cost of $3 per cwt, 24,000-lb. minimum, at approximately 380 wood pallets per load vs. 2000 BOP Sheets per load).

Appendix B

MANUFACTURERS AND SUPPLIERS
OF MODELS AND LAYOUT/MATERIALS

Chartpak
Avery Products Corporation
One River Road
Leeds, MA 01053
(413) 584-5446

Creative Industries of Detroit
3080 E. Outer Drive
Detroit, MI 48234
(313) 366-3020

Design Engineering Company
600 Stokes Avenue
Trenton, NJ 08638
(609) 882-8800

Geographics, Inc.
P. O. Box R1
Blaine, WA 98230
(206) 332-6711

Industrial Pattern Works, Inc.
3170 Roosevelt Avenue
York, PA 17404
(717) 764-4920

Model Planning Company, Inc.
Box A264
Blairstown, NJ 07825
(201) 362-8112

Planprint Company, Inc.
68 King Road
Chalfont, PA 18914
(215) 249-3501

Appendix C

LEAD ACID BATTERY CONSTRUCTION

In a lead-acid industrial battery the plates are of cast lead in a grid supporting a framework around which certain chemical pastes are applied, as shown in Figure C-1.

Fig. C-1: A cast lead grid showing paste applied in the diamond-shaped spaces.

Since lead is a very soft metal, unless it is strengthened by some stiffening agent it would be inclined to warp or lose its shape; therefore, under very tight quality control, a certain amount of antimony is added to the lead to secure this additional strengthening feature. The resulting alloy of lead and antimony is heated in melting pots under very rigid temperature control and, upon melting, is poured into the grid molds. The reason for the temperature control is quite simple, because at its critical point, uncontrolled heating would cause the antimony to rise to the surface of the melting pot and become dissipated into the ambient air. Grid casting is fairly critical in that any premature or uneven cooling of the casting can cause porosity, which would severely reduce the useful life of the battery.

When the battery is in use, that is, being discharged, the chemical action taking place on the grids is more pronounced on the positive plates than on the negative plates of each cell because the gases formed during the charging are oxygen and hydrogen, the oxygen forming on the positive plate. It is for this reason that the grids to be used as the positive or anodes of each cell are of heavier construction than the negative grids (although they may appear to look the same).

When the grids have been cast and cooled, the chemical pastes are applied in what is commonly called the "pasting operation." The pastes are actually the active ingredients of the grid because the chemical paste used in a negative plate consists of a spongy lead material with an expander to maintain the spongy condition. The chemical pastes used in preparing the positive plates is composed of lead oxide, sulfuric acid, and water, and is known as the regenerative active material. The positive plate's regenerative active material grows and replenishes itself as it is used during the life of the plate. Each flake of the paste has a center of pure metallic lead surrounded by the oxide. In use, this center gradually, but continuously, oxidizes to form more oxide.

In the process of manufacturing the active materials, the manufacturer begins with reducing pure lead ingots into a molten mass that is poured into gang molds consisting of many rods about 18 inches long and about one-half inch in diameter. These rods are then cut into slugs and fed into a rotary mill. As the mill rotates, the slugs are constantly being rubbed against each other, causing friction and a subsequent oxidation takes place. Small, dust-like particles drop to the bottom of the mill where they are drawn off periodically.

This lead and other chemicals are mixed to a putty-like consistency that becomes the paste for use on the grids. This operation may be done either by hand or by machine, large grids are usually pasted by machine. When used in the mechanical operation, the active materials are automatically supplied to the grids and evenly distributed throughout the grid by a roller. This rolling operation results in a complete penetration of the paste into the grids. Small, thin grids are generally pasted by hand, and the paster places a predetermined amount of paste on the bare grid and works it into the interstices with a special pasting spatula.

Regardless of how they are pasted, after the pasting operation, the grids are known as unformed plates. These plates are then dried to remove any moisture from the active ingredients and to secure a solid bonding of the active ingredients with the grid structure itself.

From the baking ovens where the moisture has been removed, the plates are sent to the forming department, where they are placed in large vats containing low-specific-gravity electrolyte and given a slow forming charge.

After this process, they are now formed plates, either positive or negative as the case may be. When a battery is charged and discharged in the service cycle, small particles of the active material in the plates become dislodged and filter down to the bottom of the cell into a space which has been reserved for them, since they can no longer do any useful work in the cell.

There have been many methods attempted to devise a way to mechanically prevent this destructive sedimentation action from taking place. One of these methods is the use of fiberglass mats. Fiberglass matting is placed against both sides of the positive plates. This methodology increases the battery life substantially. The mats are placed on both sides of the positive plates and then a perforated plastic retainer is wrapped around both the positive plate and the mats as an additional measure of safety. This retainer serves two purposes: it tends to keep the mat in position, and it prevents the "treeing" of active material from the positive to the negative sides.

Other advances in manufacturing techniques since the use of these fiberglass mats has occurred include the finding that an even stronger mechanical retainer was required for exceptionally arduous applications, which led to the development of fiberglass tape. In some methods of battery construction, the fiberglass tape or ribbon is wrapped first vertically and then horizontally over the positive plate, the first wrapping completely covering the plate. The orientation of the fiberglass tape strands, unlike the fiberglass mats, can be controlled during their manufacture. In the tape, about 85% of the strands are oriented in one direction, and about 15% of the strands are laid on the bias to hold the strands together. This results in a very dense and uniform protective coating. Some manufacturers have employed a fiberglass mat called a sliver-type mat.

After the fiberglass tape has been applied, some manufacturers place a perforated plastic envelope over the top of all this, then a bottom shield is added to complete the positive plate. The positive and negative plates are assembled into groupings of positive and negative plates by burning all of the positive lead straps together and all of the negative straps together at the top or leg end of the battery. The groups are then meshed together with separators between each positive and negative plate. These separators are made of microporous rubber, resistant to both heat and acid. The separators are flat on one side and grooved on the other. This dielectric material serves as an insulator between the plates, but because they are sufficiently porous, they permit the free passage of the electrolyte. The grooved side of the separator is placed next to the positive plate to permit free circulation of a large volume of electrolyte to the positive plate. The flat side is placed next to the negative plate because the negative material tends to expand and would fill the grooves in the separator if they were present.

This assembly, now called an element, is placed in a hard rubber or plastic jar. A flat plastic splash plate is placed on top of the element. The splash plate has been designed to fit snugly under the terminals without the possibility of shifting during operation of the battery. This plate has several uses, for example:

- It prevents foreign matter, which might damage the plates, from entering from the top of the cell

- It prevents damage to plates or separators through the careless use of a hydrometer or a thermometer. If a hard rubber jar has been used as the container, then a hard rubber cover with lead inserts is placed into position on top. Posts are then melted (burned) onto the cover inserts. An asphaltic-base, heated and pliable compound is then applied to the edges of the cover where it meets the sides of the jar, totally encapsulating the battery.

The cell is now ready for the addition of the electrolyte; therefore, it is sent to the charging room where acid is added and it is given its initial charge and discharge cycle. After several cycles of being charged and discharged, the cell is now ready to enter service and it is inspected to ensure that the quality of the product has been maintained and its proper capacity has been established.

Appendix D

HOW TO GET THE MOST OUT
OF COMPUTER SIMULATION

A DEFINITION OF SIMULATION

This chapter will not make you, the Plant Manager, a computer expert. The purpose of this discussion, however, is to make you aware of some of the potential problem-solving capabilities that are within your grasp. Whether you do this yourself or hire a computer professional on a one-shot, part-time, or full-time basis, depends of course on the scope of the job that you want to get done.

Another approach that you should be aware of, also, is the possibility of using "canned" programs. This type of program, which will drive your computer with only minor changes, in some instances, can be adapted to the various specifics of your requirements.

When the technician speaks of stochastic simulation, system simulation, or, in everyday language, just simulation, the technician really is speaking about preparing a model of a real-life situation and then performing a series of sampling experiments upon the model, in order to test various parameters. The technician observes the behavior of the model while changing a number of different variables, usually in response to "what if?" types of questions. The behavior of the model through the various parameters then determines the basis for predicting the behavior in the real-life situation, which is useful in both understanding and controlling the real-life environment.

A *model,* therefore, is a representation of the real-life environment that we would have, for example, in a process or a system.

It is possible to classify models in several different ways, depending upon how closely they appear to represent the real situation. For the sake of understanding some technical jargon, the models that include all of the characteristics of the situation and possibly replace the real situation are called isomorphic, and models that group related variables are homorphic. In simplistic terms the isomorphic model is a real life situation which can become overwhelmingly cumbersome due to its complexity, that is the principal reason the homorphic modeling is used, because it describes the real situation with fewer details.

Structuring and observing the operation of a perfectly isomorphic model would enable us to make predictions accurately concerning the behavior of the real situation. However, when the subject of the model is very complex it is virtually impossible to structure an isomorphic model to represent the situation. Therefore, it is often necessary (and convenient) to use the homorphic model which groups related variables. The aim of this simulation is to reproduce the gross effects of interactions in the real environment rather than the detailed effects (which may be relatively insignificant) so that we can draw general conclusions. This is done in order to make the task of structuring the model and interpreting the results a lot less difficult. With any system simulation problem, it should be recognized that of primary importance is the establishment of the degree of homorphism that is necessary and adequate to achieve the objectives of the study. You have to inject enough realism into the model parameters by covering as many variables as possible, without making your algorithm (mathematical equations) so complex that you lose the overall task in a maze of complexity. Simulation models of the homorphic type, can also be classified by defining their characteristics in the following fashion:

- *Iconic Models.* Iconic models are used to describe static things or dynamic events at a point in time.

- *Analog Models.* In analog modeling one set of properties is substituted for another set of properties in accordance with certain specific rules. In the main, they are used to describe dynamic systems or processes; for example, this might include flow charts, schedules, plant layouts, and the like.

- *Symbolic Models.* Symbolic models use the interrelationships of various components of the subject under study, and these representations are in the form of symbols of both mathematical and logical context. This type of modeling represents the basic system simulation study.

In order to further delineate the particular homorphic symbolic model used in system simulation, one additional stratification is necessary. This stratification is termed the solution mode, as follows:

- *Solution by Analytic Methods.* This method requires the direct application of mathematical techniques to the solution of the model, with the result that an explicit answer is forthcoming that may be tested for acceptability.

- *Solution by Numerical Methods.* In this method the iterative procedure is used to test all the various possible states of a model in order to isolate the optimum state.

- *Solution by Monte Carlo Methods.* This method is also called *unrestricted random sampling* or *stochastic sampling.* In the main, it involves testing states of the model at various intervals by the use of random sampling applied to the various system elements By using these samples it is possible to determine if the model used is appropriate for the system and will adequately describe results.

HOW AND WHEN YOU CAN USE SYSTEM SIMULATION TO SOLVE PROBLEMS

In general, when solving symbolic model problems, an analytic method is desirable so that the precise answer can be derived. A numerical method of problem solving is acceptable when no analytic method exists, and a Monte Carlo solution is applied only if the other methodologies are either impossible or not very practical. This last condition is by no means an exceptional state. For example, let's look at a problem such as truck dispatching for order deliveries.

For the sake of simplicity we'll say that the warehouse or distribution center has five trucks. Assuming that all of the trucks have been loaded out during the last shift of the previous day and they are all ready to start at the same time every morning. Each truck has approximately the same number of orders to deliver and will be making approximately the same number of stops during the day. Since each order requires a varying amount of transportation time to its destination, it is apparent that different sequences will yield different route driving times. The scheduler's, or truck dispatcher's, problem is to assign a delivery sequence that yields a maximum amount of productive delivery time.

Since this is a relatively small problem, an exhaustive solution is hardly feasible, since the number of possible combinations is relatively vast. Nevertheless, since the potential for savings in this dispatching problem is relatively worthwhile, it requires a solution that is quite possible by applying system simulation. In this example the system simulation synthesizes, artificially, the operation of a real-time system, using homorphic symbolic models of the operation in which each element, in turn, executes a sequence of actions that depends upon and affects the interaction of the other elements concerned. For this reason it is especially suitable to the exploration of those systems having stochastic characteristics such that it will permit different variables to be inserted in the equations of the problem and different values for each of the variables, so that the different parameters may be tested and the results examined. In system simulation it is possible to use mathematical and logical models that are run rather than solved. The results of simulation usually give approximations to the truth, and in this regard a solution is not possible, because it has a finite meaning. For this reason, it is not a question of optimizing but rather a way of processing work elements through their logical sequences, and each simulation pass constitutes an observation of the performance of a single set of parameters configuring the system. By making successive passes with quantities that are varied ever so slightly, it is possible to determine the effect of varying each quantity.

There are several stages in applying the technique of system simulation to the investigation of real-life systems, as follows:

- Collecting the necessary data for the problem and reducing this data to a series of equations or another appropriate form.

- Structuring the model of the real-life system so that it is neither over-simplified nor trivialized to the point of worthlessness. If the model retains very many minor details of the real system, then the model becomes exceptionally cumbersome and difficult to handle.

- The data and the model are next combined in a sampling experiment which should be designed to discover how the real-life system tends to behave under a variety of conditions and restraints that are within the scope of the real-life situation.

It is of primary importance in any system simulation problem to establish the degree of homorphism (grouping of related variables) that is adequate in order to achieve the desired results of the simulation. For this reason, variations in the different systems being examined require specialized knowledge on the part of the modeler and the people he/she is working with. Therefore, a computer programmer who is setting up the model has to know almost as much about the real-life situation as the operator of the warehouse or the supervisor of the distribution center in order to be able to ask intelligent "what if" questions and to develop the model that is as realistic as it is possible to fashion.

In the course of the programmer's work it is advisable for you to review the type of "what if" questions the programmer has been asking. You can then assure yourself that the programmer is on the right track and the simulation has every possibility of producing the desired results.

INDEX